Changes in real earnings in the UK and London, 2002 to 2012

Author Name(s): **Sarah Levy, Office for National Statistics**

Abstract

Average earnings of employees in the UK have fallen in real terms since 2009. Average earnings in real terms are now at similar levels to those of 2002-03. There are some geographical differences. For instance, employees working in London earn more on average than UK employees and their average real earnings fell less rapidly than the UK average from 2010 to 2012. There are also differences between full-time and part-time employees in the private and public sectors. The decline in real wages has short-term implications for the economy and economic indicators. It is possible that it also marks a permanent change in long-term wage growth trends, but it is too early to be sure about this.

1. Introduction

Average earnings of employees in the UK have fallen in real terms since 2009. This represents a change from the strong growth in real wages over the previous three decades. Although it is too early to be sure whether there has been a permanent change in the long-term trend, the decline in real wages has now been sustained for three consecutive years. Average earnings in real terms are now at similar levels to those of 2002-03. Therefore it is worth looking carefully at the evidence and its implications for the economy and economic indicators.

In this article, average earnings are presented in both 'nominal' and 'real' terms. By contrast with nominal earnings, which are expressed in the prices prevailing at the time ('current prices'), real earnings adjust the nominal values for past years to remove the effect of inflation. For most of this article we use data for 2002 to 2012 from the Annual Survey of Hours and Earnings (ASHE) and present real earnings in '2012 constant prices', or 2012 money (see **Background notes**).

The ASHE analysis looks at employees' gross hourly earnings excluding overtime[1]. Hourly earnings are analysed in preference to weekly earnings because this makes it easier to compare full-time and part-time workers. The median is used as a measure of the average (see **Background notes**). This article does not explore distributions of earnings around the average, but readers can download some information on distributions from our website (see **References**: ASHE tables).

It should be noted that this article looks only at changes in hourly earnings. These are just one aspect of labour market analysis in the context of the recent period of recession and slow growth.

A full analysis would take into account a variety of factors including changes in working patterns, hours worked and involuntary underemployment. These may affect estimates of earnings in ways which are difficult to capture. For instance, involuntary underemployment in the form of temporary lay-offs or reduced hours affect a person's total earnings over a period of time even if their hourly pay rate is not affected. Although this is not the subject of the current article, Appendix 1 presents some data from ASHE on changes in hours worked over the 2002-12 period. Other changes have been documented in recent Office for National Statistics (ONS) articles and Statistical Bulletins (see for example **References**: Patterson, 2012; ONS, 2012c; and ONS, 2013b).

At the same time, the gross measure of pay used here does not capture the full impact of austerity measures introduced in recent years. Many of these affect net (rather than gross) pay via changes in taxation, National Insurance contributions and, for public sector workers, increases in employee pension contributions from April 2012. Thus, this article should not be interpreted as providing a full picture of the impact of the recession and economic slowdown on people's take-home pay.

The remainder of this article is organised as follows:

- Part 2 provides an overview of changes in nominal and real earnings of employees in the UK and its regions, using data from ASHE.
- Parts 3 and 4 take a more detailed look at the ASHE data on changes in real earnings of employees in the private and public sectors, focusing on the UK and London.
- Part 5 looks briefly at the self-employed, using information from the Family Resources Survey of the Department for Work and Pensions (DWP).
- Part 6 discusses the implications of falling real wages for the economy and for economic indicators produced by ONS.
- Part 7 concludes.

Notes

1. Gross pay means pay **before** tax or other deductions, and excludes payments in kind; net pay or 'take-home' pay is pay **after** such deductions. The measure of gross hourly earnings from ASHE used in this article excludes overtime but includes incentive payments (see **Background notes**) as well as premium payments for shift work and night or weekend work not treated as overtime.

2. Changes in earnings of employees in the UK and its regions, 2002-12

Figure 1 shows average (median) hourly earnings excluding overtime for employees in the UK and in London, from 2002 to 2012. By downloading the data associated with Figure 1, users can obtain information for all English regions and for Scotland, Wales and Northern Ireland.

In the seven years to 2009, UK employees' median hourly earnings grew by 3.7% a year on average in nominal (current price) terms. With relatively low inflation, median real earnings (in 2012 constant prices) grew by 1.6% a year on average. This continued a trend of positive growth in real earnings every year since the late 1970s, with the exception of periods of slightly negative growth lasting less than one year during the recessions of the early 1980s and 1990s[1].

Since 2009 average nominal earnings of UK employees have remained quite flat. With Consumer Prices Index (CPI) inflation averaging 3.7% in the 12 months to April 2010, 2011 and 2012, there was a sharp fall in median earnings in real terms from their peak of £12.25 per hour (2012 prices) in 2009 to £11.21 per hour in 2012 – roughly the same as their real value in 2003. This may be because of pay freezes for people who remain in the same job or it may reflect changes in the composition of jobs that people do, with some high-paid jobs being cut as the economy adjusts following the shock of 2008-09 and more low-paid jobs being created. The 'average' earnings outcome for UK employees as a whole is probably the result of a combination of both pay freezes and economic restructuring.

The Average Weekly Earnings (AWE) indicator, which is the ONS's lead measure of changes in wages and salaries (see **Background notes**), supports this analysis. Although earnings levels recorded by the AWE and ASHE are not directly comparable, a comparison of changes in UK employees' total pay from the AWE with CPI inflation shows similar trends to the deflated ASHE data presented here: negative real wage growth in most months since mid-2008 (see Appendix 2).

Figure 1: Median hourly earnings excluding overtime of all employees, UK and London

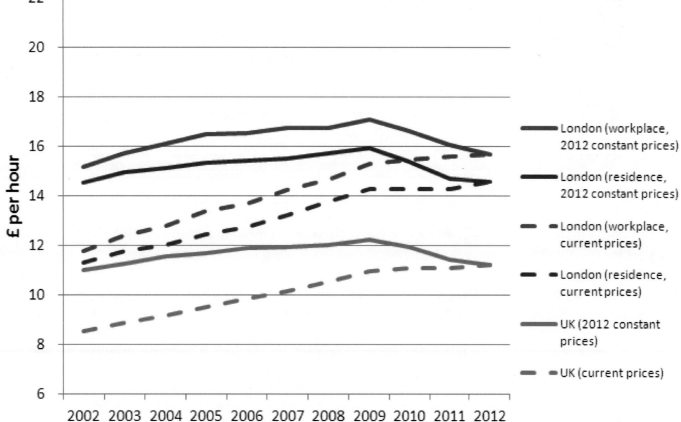

Source: Annual Survey of Hours and Earnings (ASHE) - Office for National Statistics

Notes:
1. Results are for employees on adult rates of pay, whose pay for the survey pay period was not affected by absence.
2. London is shown on a residence basis (for employees resident in London) and on a workplace basis (for employees working in London, including people commuting from outside London).

3. Real earnings (in 2012 constant prices) are calculated using the UK Consumer Prices Index (CPI) for the 12 months to April (see Background notes).
4. A change in the weighting of ASHE onto a SOC2010 basis in 2011 explains some of the decrease in real wages since 2009. ONS analysts estimate that without the change to SOC2010, the annual average contraction in real earnings in 2010-12 would have been reduced from 2.9% to 2.7% for the UK and from 3.0% to 2.9% for London (residence basis).
5. There are two additional discontinuities in the series, in 2004 and 2006, due to improvements to the survey. In both cases, these slightly reduced the estimates of median earnings (in current prices) with respect to the methodology used previously, at a time when both nominal and real earnings were rising.

Readers should note that between 2010 and 2011 ASHE was reweighted in line with the Standard Occupational Classification (SOC) 2010, having previously been on a SOC 2000 basis. This accounts for a small proportion of the decrease in real earnings in these years (see Figure 1, note 4), but does not materially alter the trends described above.

Figure 1 also shows median hourly earnings excluding overtime for employees living in London. Although London-resident employees earn more on average than UK employees, their median real earnings fell slightly faster than the UK average from 2010 to 2012. In 2012, their median earnings were estimated at £14.56 per hour, similar to their real value in 2002. By contrast, employees working in London (including those commuting from outside London) experienced a less rapid decline in median real earnings in 2010-12 than was the case for employees in the UK as a whole. In 2012, their median earnings were estimated at £15.70 per hour, similar to their real value in 2003.

Although regional trends are similar on both residence and workplace bases (see the data behind Figure 1), for London average earnings are higher when presented on a workplace basis than when presented on a residence basis, while for the East and South East they are lower, reflecting the large numbers of people who commute to work into London from these regions. On the other hand, average earnings are higher on a residence basis than on a workplace basis for the East Midlands and, to a lesser extent, for the West Midlands.

The next two sections show trends for employees in the private and public sectors. It should be noted that the analysis is about changes in real earnings over time, not about differences between earnings levels in the two sectors. Although there is a pay gap between the private and public sectors, most of the gap can be explained by factors such as the type of jobs that people do and the differing proportions of men and women in the two sectors (see **References**: ONS, 2012b).

Notes

1. This is based on a time series of median gross weekly earnings of full-time employees going back to 1968, when the New Earnings Survey (NES) was introduced (see **Background notes**). Before 1989, wages are deflated using a modelled CPI series (see **References**: ONS, 2012e).

3. Real earnings of employees in the private sector, UK and London

Figure 2 shows median real earnings (in 2012 constant prices) of full-time employees working in the private sector. For London, private sector full-time median earnings are generally higher on a workplace basis than on a residence basis, particularly for men. However, while at UK level full-time male employees in the private sector saw positive real wage growth until 2009 (except in 2007), in London male private sector employees experienced declining average wages in real terms in 2009 as well as in 2010, 2011 and 2012. As a result:

- Male full-time employees resident in London earned £15.54 per hour on average in 2012, compared with £16.14 in real terms in 2002 – a drop of 4%.
- On a workplace basis, male full-time employees in London earned £17.33 per hour on average in 2012, compared with £17.81 in real terms in 2002 – a drop of 3%.

Male full-time employees working in the private sector in London and in the UK as a whole have experienced a bigger fall in real wages over the past decade than 'all employees' including female full-time employees, part-time private sector employees and public sector workers (Figure 1).

For female private sector full-time employees in London, real wages also fell on both residence and workplace bases in 2009, 2010, 2011 and 2012. However, as was the case at UK level, the decline was less than for men. At UK level and in London on a workplace basis, female private sector full-time employees ended up with slightly higher real earnings in 2012 than in 2002.

Figure 2: Median hourly earnings excluding overtime of full-time employees in the private sector, UK and London (2012 constant prices)

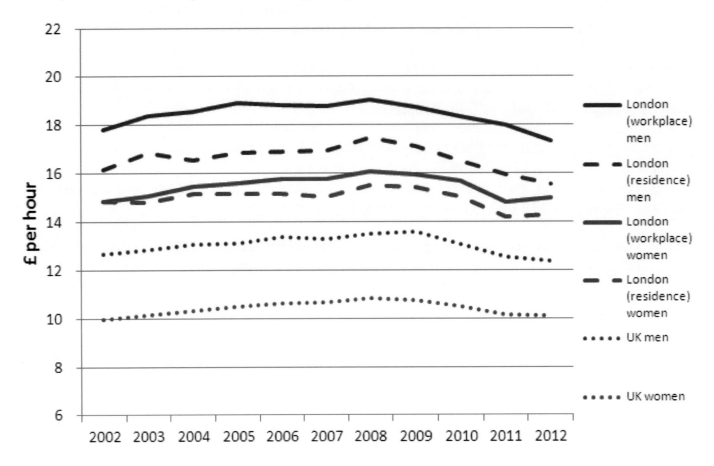

Source: Annual Survey of Hours and Earnings (ASHE) - Office for National Statistics

Notes:

1. Results are for employees on adult rates of pay, whose pay for the survey pay period was not affected by absence.
2. London is shown on a residence basis (for employees resident in London) and on a workplace basis (for employees working in London, including people commuting from outside London).
3. Real earnings (in 2012 constant prices) are calculated using the UK Consumer Prices Index (CPI) for the 12 months to April (see Background notes).
4. A change in the weighting of ASHE onto a SOC2010 basis in 2011 explains some of the decrease in real wages since 2009.
5. There are two additional discontinuities in the series, in 2004 and 2006, due to improvements to the survey. In both cases, these slightly reduced the estimates of median earnings (in current prices) with respect to the methodology used previously, at a time when nominal and real earnings were rising.
6. ASHE breakdowns by public and private sector are produced according to the legal status of the employers. Between 2008 and 2009 Lloyds Banking Group, the Royal Bank of Scotland Group and HBOS PLC were reclassified from the private sector to the public sector.

Figure 3 shows median real earnings (in 2012 constant prices) of part-time employees working in the private sector. Such workers have lower median hourly earnings than their full-time counterparts, and the male-female pay gap is narrower. In London, part-time women employees in the private sector have slightly higher median earnings than part-time men.

Part-time private sector employees' experience of median real earnings growth in recent years has been different from that of full-time employees in the private sector. At UK level, median real earnings fell in 2008 before recovering in 2009 and falling again in 2010-12. At London level, there was a similar 'double dip' pattern – with the first 'dip' starting in 2007 in some cases – for male and female part-time employees on a workplace basis and for male part-time employees on a residence basis. For female part-time employees on a London residence basis, real wage growth has been relatively weak since 2005. Nevertheless, for all the part-time employee groups shown in Figure 3 except resident women, median real earnings were higher in 2012 than in 2002.

Figure 3: Median hourly earnings excluding overtime of part-time employees in the private sector, UK and London (2012 constant prices)

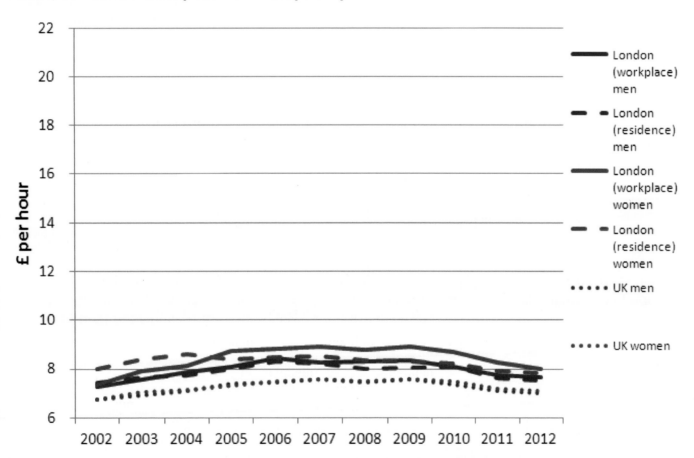

Source: Annual Survey of Hours and Earnings (ASHE) - Office for National Statistics

Notes:
1. Results are for employees on adult rates of pay, whose pay for the survey pay period was not affected by absence.
2. London is shown on a residence basis (for employees resident in London) and on a workplace basis (for employees working in London, including people commuting from outside London).

3. Real earnings (in 2012 constant prices) are calculated using the UK Consumer Prices Index (CPI) for the 12 months to April (see Background notes).
4. A change in the weighting of ASHE onto a SOC2010 basis in 2011 explains some of the decrease in real wages since 2009.
5. There are two additional discontinuities in the series, in 2004 and 2006, due to improvements to the survey. In both cases, these slightly reduced the estimates of median earnings (in current prices) with respect to the methodology used previously, at a time when nominal and real earnings were rising.
6. ASHE breakdowns by public and private sector are produced according to the legal status of the employers. Between 2008 and 2009 Lloyds Banking Group, the Royal Bank of Scotland Group and HBOS PLC were reclassified from the private sector to the public sector.

4. Real earnings of employees in the public sector, UK and London

The government's June 2010 Budget announced a two-year pay freeze for public sector employees starting in 2011/12, but full-time public sector workers' average earnings had already begun to decline in real terms before the pay freeze began.

Figure 4 shows median real earnings (in 2012 constant prices) of full-time employees working in the public sector. The trends are similar to those affecting their counterparts in the private sector, although the increase in 2002-09 is stronger and the fall in median real earnings is less marked than in the private sector: for instance, in 2010 to 2012 the decline in median real earnings averaged 2.1% per year for full-time male public sector workers in the UK compared with 3.1% per year for their private sector counterparts.

For full-time public sector workers, the fall in median real wages was delayed for longer after the start of the 2008-09 recession than in the case of full-time private sector workers. For men at UK level and for all of the groups analysed in London, real earnings of public sector full-time employees continued to rise until 2009; for UK women they continued to rise until 2010. By contrast, for private sector full-time employees the decline began in 2009 for most of the groups analysed (see Figure 2).

Figure 4: Median hourly earnings excluding overtime of full-time employees in the public sector, UK and London (2012 constant prices)

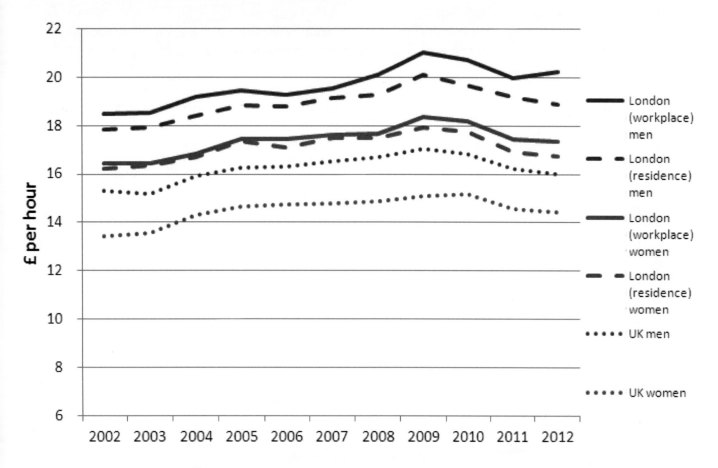

Source: Annual Survey of Hours and Earnings (ASHE) - Office for National Statistics

Notes:

1. Results are for employees on adult rates of pay, whose pay for the survey pay period was not affected by absence.
2. London is shown on a residence basis (for employees resident in London) and on a workplace basis (for employees working in London, including people commuting from outside London).
3. Real earnings (in 2012 constant prices) are calculated using the UK Consumer Prices Index (CPI) for the 12 months to April (see Background notes).
4. A change in the weighting of ASHE onto a SOC2010 basis in 2011 explains some of the decrease in real wages since 2009.
5. There are two additional discontinuities in the series, in 2004 and 2006, due to improvements to the survey. In both cases, these slightly reduced the estimates of median earnings (in current prices) with respect to the methodology used previously, at a time when nominal and real earnings were rising.
6. ASHE breakdowns by public and private sector are produced according to the legal status of the employers. Between 2008 and 2009 Lloyds Banking Group, the Royal Bank of Scotland Group and HBOS PLC were reclassified from the private sector to the public sector.

As a result of the combination of relatively strong increases in real wages in 2002-09 and the delayed impact of the 2008-09 recession on public sector pay, full-time employees in the public sector in the UK and in London had higher median real earnings in 2012 than in 2002. However, these figures show changes in gross earnings only; as explained above, they do not show take-home pay, which, in the public sector, was affected by increases in pension contributions from April 2012.

Figure 5: Median hourly earnings excluding overtime of part-time employees in the public sector, UK (2012 constant prices)

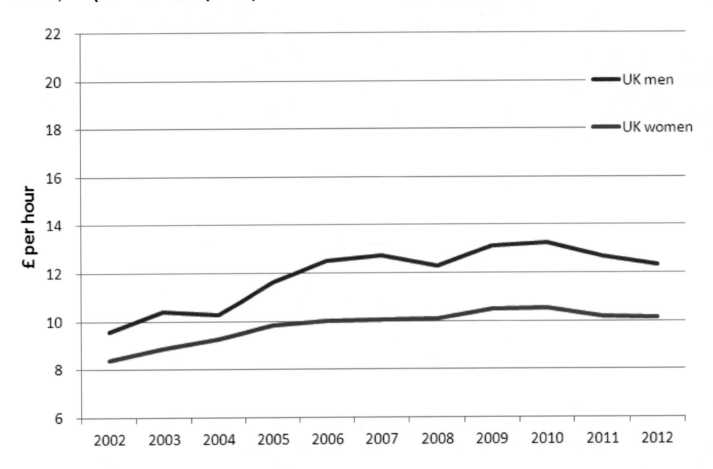

Source: Annual Survey of Hours and Earnings (ASHE) - Office for National Statistics

Notes:
1. Results are for employees on adult rates of pay, whose pay for the survey pay period was not affected by absence.
2. Real earnings (in 2012 constant prices) are calculated using the UK Consumer Prices Index (CPI) for the 12 months to April (see Background notes).
3. A change in the weighting of ASHE onto a SOC2010 basis in 2011 explains some of the decrease in real wages since 2009.
4. There are two additional discontinuities in the series, in 2004 and 2006, due to improvements to the survey. In both cases, these slightly reduced the estimates of median earnings (in current prices) with respect to the methodology used previously, at a time when nominal and real earnings were rising.
5. ASHE breakdowns by public and private sector are produced according to the legal status of the employers. Between 2008 and 2009 Lloyds Banking Group, the Royal Bank of Scotland Group and HBOS PLC were reclassified from the private sector to the public sector.

Figure 5 shows results for part-time public sector employees. It shows the UK only because some of the results at London are unreliable for this type of analysis, where we are interested in detecting small changes over time. As in the private sector, part-time workers in the public sector have lower median hourly earnings than their full-time counterparts. However, in the public sector there is a large gap between median earnings of part-time male and female employees. This may reflect the type of job done by male and female part-time workers in the public sector.

In the UK public sector, part-time male workers' median real earnings growth was negative in 2008; but it recovered strongly in 2009-10 before continuing to decline in 2011-12. Part-time female workers experienced positive changes in median real earnings every year from 2002 until 2010, and only saw decreases in 2011-12.

Over the decade to 2012, male part-time employees' median real earnings rose by 29%, while those of their female counterparts rose by 21%. This contrasts with the experience of private sector part-time employees, where, for the UK, increases in median real earnings were 4% and 5% respectively over this period (Figure 3).

5. Real incomes of the self-employed, UK and London

In April-June 2012, self-employed people comprised 14% of people in employment in the UK and 18% of people in employment in London, according to ONS's Labour Force Survey (see **References**: ONS, 2013c). ASHE does not collect information on the self-employed. However, data on incomes of self-employed people is collected by DWP in its Family Resources Survey.

Figure 6: Median income from self-employment of people living in the UK and London

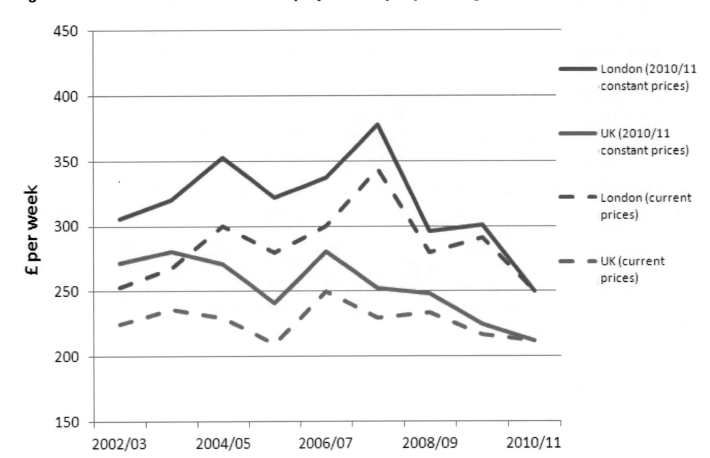

Source: Family Resources Survey - Work and Pensions

Notes:
1. Location is defined on a residence basis.
2. Income is gross income of adults. Income from self-employment is only for those whose main employment status is 'self-employed'; it does not include amounts earned from self-employment by others e.g. employees.
3. Real earnings (in 2010/11 constant prices) are calculated using the UK CPI for April-March (see Background notes).

Figure 6 shows a time series from 2002/03 to 2010/11 (the latest year available) of median real income per week from self-employment. Income from self-employment is quite variable, making it hard to interpret the trends. However, the pattern suggests that the effects of the recession began to be felt in the UK in 2007/08 and in London in 2008/09. Between 2007/08 and 2010/11 median real income from self-employment (in 2010/11 constant prices) fell by 16% for the UK as a whole and by one-third (from a higher starting point) for people living in London. This may reflect underlying changes following the recession, such as increases in the numbers of self-employed people which have not been matched by increases in the amount of work available, resulting in rising underemployment rates among the self-employed (see **References**: ONS, 2013c).

6. Implications of falling real wages

In the short term, businesses are the main beneficiary of falling real wages. Lower labour costs may help them to survive an economic downturn and to avoid job cuts. In the longer term, they may influence firms' investment decisions, for instance by encouraging them to use more labour and less machinery. If this kind of 'factor substitution' is sustained, it could contribute to a reduction in productivity, with the risk that firms may become less competitive. In the private sector, falling real wages may also be a reflection of a change in the composition of jobs on offer, reflecting a shift in the structure of the economy towards less productive jobs for other reasons.

For people and households, falling real wages implies falling purchasing power (unless they can work longer hours to compensate or borrow to finance their spending). Many families will have to reduce expenditure and may change their spending habits, looking for cheaper goods and services. This, in turn, will have an impact on demand for what businesses produce. UK businesses may have to look for alternative markets either at home or – in the face of weak domestic demand – abroad. As well as reducing demand for basic items such as food and clothing, falling real wages are likely to have an impact on markets for major assets such as property. Thus housing demand and house price growth tend to remain subdued when real wages are falling.

As a major employer, the government saves money if nominal wages are frozen, as is currently the case in the public sector. In addition, the government is a major provider of welfare benefits. In the context of austerity, the government has argued the case for saving money by capping increases in working-age welfare benefits to reflect the falling real earnings of employees in the private sector. The size of the government's pension liability would also be reduced if it used negative (or lower) projections of real wage growth, reflecting recent years' data.

Finally, falling real wages may have implications for the calculation of economic indicators produced by ONS. An example of this is productivity. The ONS Productivity Handbook notes that according to the economist Paul Krugman, productivity is one of the most important economic indicators because "A country's ability to improve its standard of living over time depends almost entirely on its ability to raise output per worker" (see **References**: Camus, 2007, Chapter 1).

However, analysis by ONS (see **References**: Grice, 2012 and Patterson, 2012) points to evidence of a 'productivity conundrum' (or puzzle) in recent years: labour productivity in the UK fell during the 2008-09 recession and, by contrast with the previous two recessions of the early 1980s and early 1990s, it has not recovered since then. Real wage trends may help to resolve this puzzle, not just because a sustained fall in real wages may lead to factor substitution, as described above, but because it may affect the calculation of real GVA and GDP (see **Box 1: Real wages and productivity**).

Box 1: Real wages and productivity

ONS publishes labour productivity statistics every quarter. These include output per worker and output per hour worked (see **References**: 2013a). The output side of the equation is based on Gross Value Added (GVA). GVA plus taxes (less subsidies) on products is equivalent to Gross Domestic Product (GDP). Around two-thirds of GDP consists of 'compensation of employees', which is predominantly workers' earnings.

ONS's productivity statistics use the chained volume measure of GVA. This removes price effects so that output is expressed in real terms. In the National Accounts, changes in real wage trends may affect the deflators used to calculate the various elements of the chained volume measure of GVA. ONS is investigating the methods used to deflate GVA as part of its research into the productivity conundrum and its GDP continuous improvement programme.

7. Conclusion

Median real wages in the UK have fallen since 2009 and are now at similar levels to what they were a decade ago. There are some geographical differences. For instance, employees working in London earn more on average than UK employees and their median real earnings fell less rapidly than the UK average from 2010 to 2012.

There are also differences between the private and public sectors, and between full- and part-time employees. Full-time male employees in the private sector have seen the greatest reductions in real earnings since the 2008-09 recession. In 2012 their median earnings were worth less in real terms than in 2002. On the other hand, at UK level and in London on a workplace basis, full-time female private sector employees ended up with slightly higher real earnings in 2012 than in 2002.

Full-time public sector employees have also experienced declining real wages since the 2008-09 recession. However, the decline started later and followed strong growth in earlier years. Therefore, their median real earnings remained higher in 2012 than a decade earlier.

For part-time employees, there was less of a decrease in real earnings following the recession and, for most of the groups analysed, there was an increase in the decade to 2012. This was particularly evident in the public sector, where male part-time employees' median real earnings rose by 29% between 2002 and 2012, while those of their female counterparts rose by 21%.

The available evidence suggests that for the self-employed, on the other hand, there was a sharp decline in median real income between 2007/08 and 2010/11 (the latest year available). This was particularly so in London, where median real income from self-employment fell by one-third over this period.

The weakness of real earnings explored in this article may be a short-term phenomenon or a change in trend. In either case, it will have important implications for people and households, businesses, government spending and the economy as a whole. It may also have implications for some of ONS's economic indicators, such as the measure of productivity.

Background notes

1. The Annual Survey of Hours and Earnings (ASHE) is an ONS survey based on a 1% sample of employee jobs taken from HM Revenue and Customs PAYE records. Information on earnings and hours is obtained from employers and treated confidentially. ASHE does not cover the self-employed nor does it cover employees not paid during the reference period. The reference period for the survey is in April of each year. In ASHE, full-time employees are defined as those who work more than 30 paid hours per week or those in teaching professions working 25 paid hours or more per week.

2. A time series of weekly earnings of full-time employees from the New Earnings Survey (NES) and ASHE, starting in 1968, is available from the 'ASHE request 848' (see **References**). Before 1997, the data is on a GB-only basis. Information for the UK is available from 1997 when ASHE was introduced.

3. ONS also collects information on earnings from the Monthly Wages and Salaries Survey, which is used to construct the Average Weekly Earnings (AWE) indicator. This survey asks 9,000 employers to provide information about total pay and numbers of employees, and is ONS's lead measure of changes in the level of earnings. However, it does not permit the kinds of breakdowns that are possible using ASHE.

4. The Family Resources Survey (FRS) is a Department for Work and Pensions (DWP) survey designed to provide information about living conditions and resources. In the period 2002/03 to 2010/11 it covers the UK, with an achieved sample of around 24,000 households a year. Data is collected throughout the year, starting in April and ending in March.

5. The analysis presented here is based on the median rather than the mean. The median is the value below which 50% of employees/self-employed people fall. It is ONS's preferred measure of average earnings as it is less affected than the mean by the relatively small number of very high earners and the skewed distribution of earnings. It therefore gives a better indication of typical pay than the mean.

6. This analysis uses a deflator based on the UK Consumer Prices Index (CPI) to calculate real earnings over time. The Figures show past years' median earnings expressed in 'constant prices' of the latest period for which data is available: 2012 for ASHE and 2010/11 for the FRS. In the case of ASHE, the calculations use the annual percentage change in the CPI to April each year (the month when ASHE data is collected); in the case of the FRS, the calculations use the average annual percentage change in the CPI over the survey months (April to March) of each year, for instance 2010/11 uses April 2010 to March 2011 data.

7. The ASHE analysis excludes results where pay was affected by absence in the relevant pay period. This is standard practice for such analysis, but readers should note that it may lead to overestimates of hourly pay when there is involuntary underemployment, as has been the case during the recent economic downturn (see **References**: ONS 2012c). This is because

employers may use enforced absences or reduced hours to cut costs and prevent job losses. In such cases, average hourly earnings over a period of time would be affected even if hourly pay is not affected while the person is working.

8. The measure of gross hourly earnings from ASHE used in this article includes incentive payments, which are defined as profit sharing, productivity, performance and other bonus or incentive pay, piecework and commission. However, in ASHE such payments only relate to work carried out in the relevant pay period. A time series and further analysis for bonus payments can be found in the AWE (see **References**: Anyaegbu, 2012).

9. In the National Accounts, Gross Value Added (GVA) is the total value of output of goods and services produced less the goods and services used up to produce the output.

10. Details of the policy governing the release of new data are available by visiting www.statisticsauthority.gov.uk/assessment/code-of-practice/index.html or from the Media Relations Office email: media.relations@ons.gsi.gov.uk

These National Statistics are produced to high professional standards and released according to the arrangements approved by the UK Statistics Authority.

Copyright

References

1. Anyaegbu (2012):

   Average Weekly Earning: Bonus payments in Great Britain 2011-2012, ONS, 19 September 2012, available at: www.ons.gov.uk/ons/rel/awe/average-weekly-earnings/bonus-payments-in-great-britain/index.html

2. ASHE tables

   Annual Survey of Hours and Earnings (ASHE) published tables are available at: www.ons.gov.uk/ons/rel/ashe/annual-survey-of-hours-and-earnings/index.html

3. ASHE Nomis data

Time series data from ASHE can be downloaded via the Nomis website: www.nomisweb.co.uk

4. ASHE request 848

    An 'ad hoc data and analysis' table entitled 'Historical median and percentile gross weekly earnings time-series, GB and UK 1968 to 2012' was published in December 2012 as Request No. 000848 at www.ons.gov.uk/ons/about-ons/what-we-do/publication-scheme/published-ad-hoc-data/labour-market/december-2012/index.html

5. Camus (2007)

    The ONS Productivity Handbook: A Statistical Overview and Guide, Dawn Camus (ed), ONS 2007. Available at: www.ons.gov.uk/ons/guide-method/method-quality/specific/economy/productivity-measures/productivity-handbook/index.html

6. DWP – FRS

    Information about the DWP's Family Resources Survey (FRS) can be found at http://research.dwp.gov.uk/asd/frs/

7. Grice (2012):

    'The Productivity Conundrum, Interpreting the Recent Behaviour of the Economy', Joe Grice, ONS, 24 August 2012. Available at: www.ons.gov.uk/ons/rel/elmr/the-productivity-conundrum/interpreting-the-recent-behaviour-of-the-economy/art-interpreting-the-recent-behaviour-of-the-economy.html

8. ONS (2012a):

    'Real wages up 62% on average over the past 25 years', ONS, 7 November 2012. Available at: www.ons.gov.uk/ons/rel/lmac/earnings-in-the-uk-over-the-past-25-years/2012/index.html

9. ONS (2012b):

    'Estimating differences in public and private sector pay at the national and regional level', ONS, 22 November 2012. Available at: www.ons.gov.uk/ons/rel/lmac/public-and-private-sector-earnings/november-2012.html

10. ONS (2012c):

    'People in Work Wanting More Hours Increases by 1 million since 2008', ONS, 28 November 2012. Available at: www.ons.gov.uk/ons/rel/lmac/underemployed-workers-in-the-uk/2012/index.html

11. ONS (2012d):

Index of Labour Costs per Hour (ILCH) Q3 2012 (experimental). ONS Statistical Bulletin, 13 December 2012. Available at: www.ons.gov.uk/ons/rel/ilch/index-of-labour-costs-per-hour--experimental-/q3-2012/index.html

12. ONS (2012e):

'Modelling a Back Series for the Consumer Price Index', Robert O'Neill and Jeff Ralph, ONS, 18 December 2012. Available at: www.ons.gov.uk/ons/rel/cpi/modelling-a-back-series-for-the-consumer-price-index/1950---2011/index.html

13. ONS (2013a):

Labour Productivity, 3 January 2013. ONS Statistical Bulletin. Available at: www.ons.gov.uk/ons/rel/productivity/labour-productivity/q3-2012/index.html

14. ONS (2013b):

Labour Market Statistics, 23 January 2013. ONS Statistical Bulletin. Available at: www.ons.gov.uk/ons/taxonomy/index.html?nscl=Labour+Market

15. ONS (2013c):

'Self-employed up 367,000 in four years, mostly since 2011', ONS, 6 February 2013. Available at: www.ons.gov.uk/ons/rel/lmac/self-employed-workers-in-the-uk/february-2013/index.html

16. Patterson (2012):

'The Productivity Conundrum, Explanations and Preliminary Analysis', Peter Patterson, ONS, 16 October 2012. Available at: www.ons.gov.uk/ons/rel/elmr/the-productivity-conundrum/explanations-and-preliminary-analysis/index.html

17. Pike (2012):

'Patterns of Pay: Results of the Annual Survey of Hours and Earnings', 1997 to 2011. Ryan Pike, ONS, 24 February 2012. Available at: www.ons.gov.uk/ons/rel/ashe/patterns-of-pay/1997---2011-ashe-results/index.html

Appendix 1: Hours and employee jobs

Figure A1: Hours worked and number of employee jobs, 2002-12 (UK)

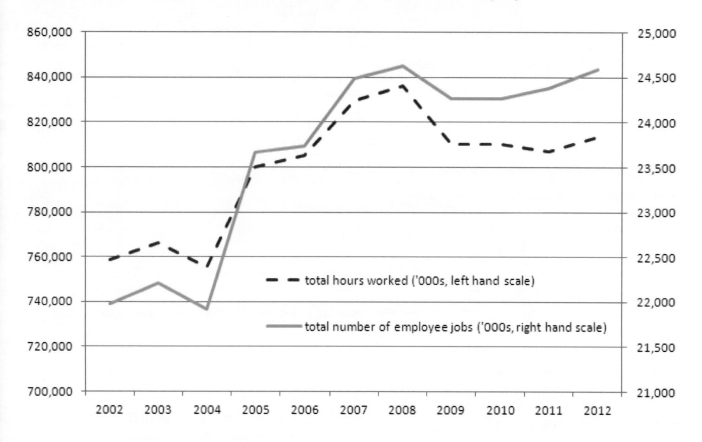

Source: Annual Survey of Hours and Earnings (ASHE) - Office for National Statistics

Notes:
1. Results are for employees on adult rates of pay, whose pay for the survey pay period was not affected by absence.
2. There are three discontinuities in the series: in 2004 and 2006, due to improvements to the survey, and in 2011 due to a change in the weighting of ASHE from a SOC2000 onto a SOC2010 basis.

Figure A2: Hours worked and number of employee jobs, 2002-12 (London)

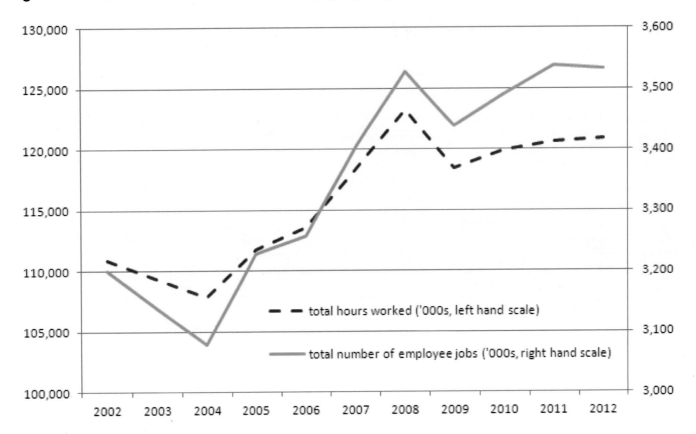

Source: Annual Survey of Hours and Earnings (ASHE) - Office for National Statistics

Notes:
1. Results are for employees on adult rates of pay, whose pay for the survey pay period was not affected by absence.
2. London is defined on a workplace basis.
3. There are three discontinuities in the series: in 2004 and 2006, due to improvements to the survey, and in 2011 due to a change in the weighting of ASHE from a SOC2000 onto a SOC2010 basis.

Figure A3: Hours per employee job, 2002-12 (UK and London)

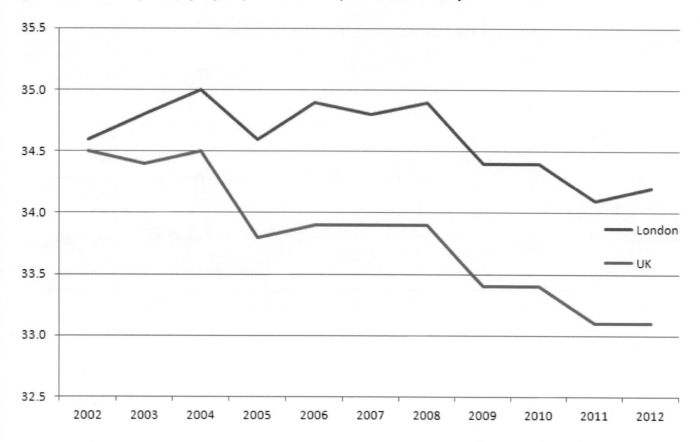

Source: Annual Survey of Hours and Earnings (ASHE) - Office for National Statistics

Notes:
1. Results are for employees on adult rates of pay, whose pay for the survey pay period was not affected by absence.
2. London is defined on a workplace basis.
3. There are three discontinuities in the series: in 2004 and 2006, due to improvements to the survey, and in 2011 due to a change in the weighting of ASHE from a SOC2000 onto a SOC2010 basis.

Appendix 2: Average weekly earnings and inflation

Figure A4: Change in Average Weekly Earnings and CPI inflation

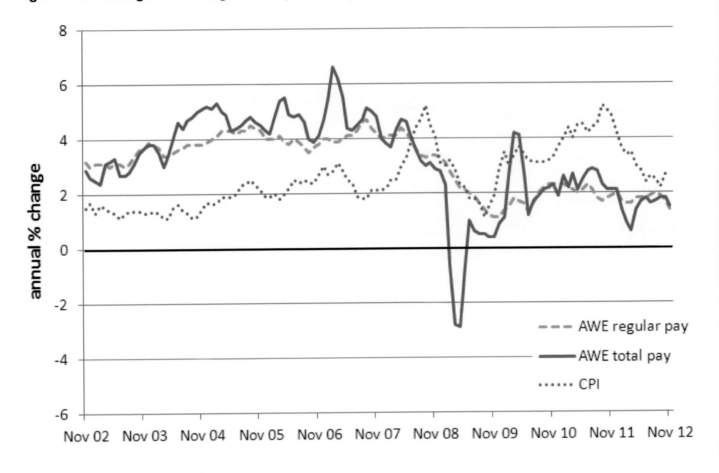

Source: Office for National Statistics

Notes:
1. The Consumer Prices Index (CPI) series is for the UK and is compiled from prices data based on a large and representative selection of individual goods and services. The Average Weekly Earnings (AWE) series are for GB and are sourced from the Monthly Wages and Salaries Survey.
2. Estimates of regular pay in the AWE series exclude bonuses and arrears of pay. Estimates of total pay in the AWE series include bonuses but exclude arrears of pay.
3. The AWE figures are based on three month averages: they show the changes in the average seasonally adjusted values for the three months ending with the relevant month compared the same period a year earlier. The CPI figures are single-month figures, not seasonally adjusted.
4. The AWE estimate for November 2012 is provisional.

The link between under 18 conceptions and unemployment, England and Wales, 2008–10

Abstract

This short story examines the link between under 18 conceptions and unemployment in England and Wales. It forms part of a wider release containing an analytical toolkit looking at teenage conceptions and measures of deprivation and an article analysing teenage conceptions in relation to measures of deprivation.

Key points

• An analytical toolkit looking at teenage conceptions and measures of deprivation has been developed by ONS and is freely available online for the first time.

• An article analysing under 18 conceptions in relation to measures of deprivation has been published.

• With the exception of London, there was an east-west split in the link between under 18 conception rates and unemployment rates for England and Wales, 2008 to 2010.

• Of the English regions Yorkshire and The Humber had the strongest link between under 18 conception rates and unemployment rates for 2008 to 2010, while London had the weakest link for any of the English regions.

Under 18 conceptions and unemployment

From statistical analysis it was calculated that the unemployment rate accounted for 65% of the variation in the under 18 conception rate[1] at local authority level across England and Wales[2]. This means that, broadly, the higher the unemployment rate, the higher the under 18 conception rate.

Map 1 shows the picture for the link between the under 18 conception rate and unemployment rate for 2008 to 10.

Map 1 - Under 18 conception rate and unemployment rate correlation values by region/country, England and Wales, 2008–10

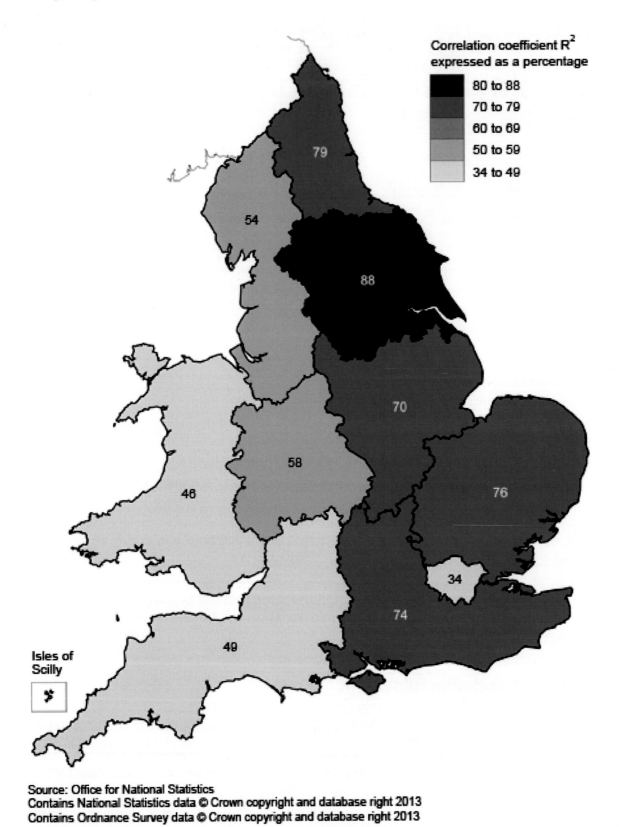

Correlation coefficient R^2 expressed as a percentage

- 80 to 88
- 70 to 79
- 60 to 69
- 50 to 59
- 34 to 49

Isles of Scilly

Source: Office for National Statistics
Contains National Statistics data © Crown copyright and database right 2013
Contains Ordnance Survey data © Crown copyright and database right 2013

Source: Office for National Statistics

Map 1 shows that there was an east-west split across England and Wales in how strongly correlated under 18 conception rates were with unemployment rates, with regions in the east generally showing a stronger link than in the west. There was also a north-south aspect as the north generally had a stronger link than the south. The only exception to the east-west split was London, which had a correlation value more in line with the west.

Yorkshire and The Humber had the strongest correlation at 88%, which means that the unemployment rates in the region accounted for 88% of the variation in the under 18 conception rates in the region for 2008 to 2010. This was nine percentage points more than the North East, which had the second strongest link between under 18 conception rates and unemployment rates at 79%. London had the lowest correlation value at 34%, twelve percentage points less than Wales which had the second lowest correlation value in England and Wales.

Notes

1. The under 18 conception rate is the number of conceptions to women aged under 18 per 1,000 women aged 15 to 17 in the area concerned.

2. Regional correlation values have been calculated by plotting the relevant local authority rates for under 18 conceptions against unemployment and applying a trend line of best fit. The goodness of fit of the values against the line determines the correlation value. The closer the value is to 1 the more strongly correlated under 18 conceptions are with unemployment.

Background notes

1. Details of the policy governing the release of new data are available by visiting www.statisticsauthority.gov.uk/assessment/code-of-practice/index.html or from the Media Relations Office email: media.relations@ons.gsi.gov.uk

Copyright

An Analysis of Under 18 Conceptions and their Links to Measures of Deprivation, England and Wales, 2008-10

Author Name(s): **Phil Humby, Area Based Analysis**

Abstract

This article explores the most recent annual under 18 conception data using three year aggregates and averages. It highlights patterns in the data and explores possible reasons for these patterns. Under 18 conceptions are considered in context, with comparisons drawn to under 16 conceptions as well as selected population and urban aspects. Under 18 conceptions and their links to measures of deprivation at the national and regional level are made using the new Office for National Statistics (ONS) Conceptions-Deprivation Analysis Toolkit. The measures of deprivation chosen for this article are the English Indices of Multiple Deprivation, the percentage of children living in poverty and the unemployment rate.

Acknowledgements

1. The author would like to thank colleagues from the Office for National Statistics, the Department of Health, the Department for Education and the Welsh Government for their input into this article during peer review. Particular thanks go to Tom Mahoney for his work on the interactive Conceptions-Deprivation Analysis Toolkit.

Definitions

Conception statistics bring together records of birth registrations collected under the Births and Deaths Registration Act (1953) and of abortion notifications received under the Abortion Act (1967), amended by the Human Fertilisation and Embryology Act (2008). They include all pregnancies of women usually resident in England and Wales which lead to one of the following outcomes:

• a maternity at which one or more live births or stillbirths occur, which is/are registered in England and Wales;

• a termination of a pregnancy by abortion under the 1967 Act, which takes place in England and Wales.

Conception statistics do not include miscarriages or illegal abortions[1].

Under 18 conceptions are conceptions to women aged 17 or under. Under 18 conception rates are under 18 conceptions per 1,000 women aged 15 to 17.

Notes

1. For more information about conceptions issues, processing and terminology see the conceptions metadata document.

Key points

• An analytical toolkit looking at teenage conceptions and measures of deprivation has been developed by ONS and is freely available online for the first time.

• Under 18 conception rates were generally high in local authorities containing seaside towns, the Welsh Valleys, major urban centres and in bands in the north of England.

• Under 18 conception rates were strongly linked to under 16 conception rates.

• Under 18 conception rate rankings were correlated with rankings for English Indices of Multiple Deprivation at local authority level; under 18 conception rates were correlated with unemployment rates and the percentage of children in poverty.

• London was not as strongly correlated as other regions when looking at the link between under 18 conceptions and measures of deprivation.

• Under 18 conception rates were found not to be strongly correlated to the urban-rural classification of local authorities or to their population density.

Introduction

The purpose of this article is to conduct analysis into under 18 conceptions to identify patterns in the data and to demonstrate some of the analytical techniques that could be undertaken in further research. The relationship between under 18 conceptions and measures of deprivation are also examined. The measures assessed in this article are the English Indices of Multiple Deprivation, child poverty and unemployment, although it is recognised that these measures of deprivation may themselves be correlated with one another.

As part of this analysis a Conceptions-Deprivation Analysis Toolkit was developed, allowing comparisons between regions and local authorities on various datasets to be made. The toolkit contains more datasets than are explored in this article[1].

This article and the Conceptions-Deprivation Analysis Toolkit are not the only way to analyse conceptions and their link to deprivation, but simply one way of analysing the data available on some datasets of interest; other deprivation measures are available. Techniques used in this article include the Pearson product-moment correlation coefficient, a measure of the strength of relationship between two variables, and quintile analysis.

This article begins by looking at the importance of teenage conceptions data and outlines some of their users and uses, including looking at the policy context of conception statistics. Analysis of under 18 conception statistics is split into seven sections:

1. Under 18 conceptions over time.

2. Regional and sub-regional analysis of under 18 conceptions.

3. Under 18 conception comparisons with under 16 conceptions.

4. Under 18 conceptions and urban aspects (looking at links with population density and the Urban-Rural Classification).

5. Under 18 conceptions and the English Indices of Multiple Deprivation.

6. Under 18 conceptions and child poverty.

7. Under 18 conceptions and unemployment.

Within the analysis, some possible explanations for differences in the correlations between the English regions and Wales are put forward along with suggestions for further analysis in the summary section.

Notes

1. The datasets available in the under 18 conceptions-deprivation analysis toolkit can be found in Annex 1.

The importance of the issue of teenage conceptions

It is widely understood that teenage conception and early motherhood can be associated with poor educational achievement, poor physical and mental health (for both mother and child), social isolation and poverty. There is also recognition that socio-economic disadvantage can be both a cause and a consequence of teenage motherhood (Swann et al, 2003)[1]. This led the Labour Government (1997 to 2010) to set a target to halve the under 18 conception rate in England by 2010, when compared with 1998. Local authorities set 10 year strategies in place, aiming to reduce the local rate between 40% and 60%. These local targets aimed to help underpin the national 50% reduction target. The Department for Education was charged with monitoring the overall situation and many local authorities appointed teenage pregnancy co-ordinators to focus specifically on reducing teenage conceptions in their area.

These targets were discontinued under the Coalition Government, which came to power in 2010; however, teenage pregnancy has remained an area of policy interest. The under 18 conception rate is one of the three sexual health indicators in the Public Health Outcomes Framework (2013–2016) covering English measures of progress on child poverty, continuing the focus on preventing teenage conceptions as well as the social impact on teenage mothers. In Wales teenage conceptions are used as an indicator in the Sexual Health and Well-being Action Plan for Wales, 2010–15.

It should be noted that teenage conceptions can be the result of planning within established relationships and as such are not always cause for concern.

Notes

1. A list of the risk factors associated with teenage conception can be found in Annex 2 and Annex 3 so that some of the causes of under 18 conception and the impact it has on the child can be better understood by people using the statistics.

Users and uses of conception statistics

The Department for Education (DfE) is a key user of conception statistics. DfE monitors the number and rate of under 18 conceptions and provide these data to local authorities to assist them in their wider work to reduce child poverty and narrow inequalities.

The Department of Health (DH) is also a key user of conception statistics. DH monitors the rate of under 18 conceptions under the Public Health Outcomes Framework (2013–2016) as part of the measures of health improvement.

In Wales, teenage conception rates are used widely as outcome indicators in the sexual health context. For example they are used in the Sexual Health and Well-being Action Plan for Wales, 2010–15, as well as being a general indicator of health and health inequality, such as in Our Healthy Future. The under 18 conception rate is the most commonly used and, along with the underage rate (under 16 years), forms a key health indicator for children and young people. See, for example, the Child Poverty targets.

English local authorities use the conceptions data, particularly the number and rate of under 18 conceptions to feed into their Joint Strategic Needs Assessments and to inform their commissioning decisions. They also use the statistics to make comparisons with other local areas and with the county, region and national level.

Sexual health charities that provide the public with information, advice and support services use the statistics to promote services that contribute to the reduction in conceptions.

Academics use the data to examine the success of policy at the national and local level as well as to inform research on various demographic topics.

The article and toolkit will be of particular interest to those in local authorities looking at under 18 conceptions and/or deprivation measures, those working with young mothers and those involved with family planning initiatives targeted at young women. It will also be of interest to those looking to measure the success of local policies. The toolkit allows users to look at their statistical neighbours[1] and draw comparisons, as well as looking at geographical ones.

The analyses and data may also be of interest to people who need to comprehend and evaluate conceptions statistics and feed into under 18 conception or child poverty strategies.

Notes

1. Statistical neighbours are local authorities which are deemed to be most statistically similar across a range of socio-economic and demographic factors.

1. Under 18 conceptions over time

Key points:

• In both England and Wales under 18 conception rates fell between 1998 and 2010.

• Under 18 conception rates fell in all English regions between 1998 and 2010.

• The under 18 conception rate fell the most in Wales (31.5%) and the least in the North West (19.1%) over this period.

• The difference between the under 18 conception rates in 1998 and 2010 was highest in Wales (17.3 conceptions per thousand women aged 15 to 17) and lowest in the East of England (a rate difference of 8.1).

Prior to 1969, the first year for which abortions data are available, conception figures would have simply referred to the number of maternities[1].

Figure 1 shows the under 18 conception rates[2] for England, Wales, and England and Wales back to 1998[3].

Figure 1 - Under 18 conception rates, England and Wales, 1998–2010

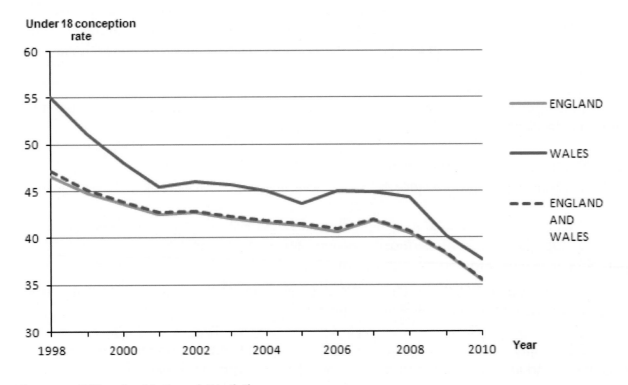

Source: Office for National Statistics

Figure 1 shows that the under 18 conception rate for Wales was higher than that for England and for England and Wales throughout the period; the rate for England and Wales almost exactly matched the rate for England due to the vast majority of under 18 conceptions in England and Wales taking place in England.

It can be seen that the rate for under 18 conceptions has been generally falling and that the under 18 conception rate for Wales has fallen more than for England or for England and Wales. Between 1998 and 2010, the under 18 conception rate for Wales fell by 17.3 conceptions per 1,000 women aged 15 to 17 (from 55.0 to 37.7), while the rate for England and Wales fell by 11.6 (from 47.1 to 35.5) and the rate for England fell by 11.2 (from 46.6 to 35.4).

While the reduction in the under 18 conception rate for England over the period 1998 to 2010 was considerable (24%), it did not meet the target level of reduction (50%). The responsibility for meeting the target was taken by local authorities who themselves had individual targets. The regional variation of under 18 conception rates can be seen in Figure 2.

Figure 2 - Under 18 conception rates, by region, 1998–2010

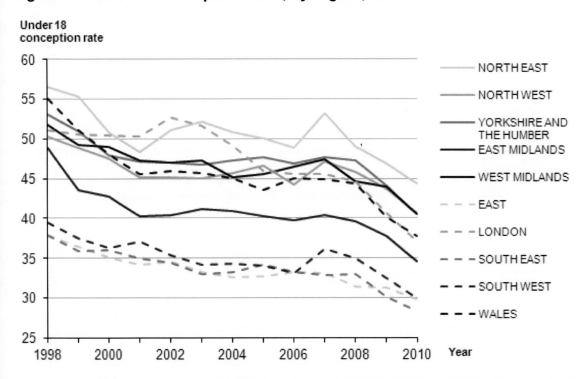

Source: Office for National Statistics

Figure 2 shows that all of the English regions and Wales experienced considerable declines in under 18 conception rates. The regional trends in the data are not as smooth as at the national level, seen in Figure 1, because smaller geographic areas are more prone to yearly fluctuations. The under 18 conception rates for all regions except London fell considerably between 1998 and 2001 and then rose in a number of regions in 2002. A larger increase in under 18 conception rates can be seen between 2006 and 2007, most notably in the North East and South West.

The East of England, the South East and South West all had relatively low rates of under 18 conception throughout the period, while the East Midlands had the fourth lowest under 18 conception rate each year. The North East generally had the highest under 18 conception rate, although for a brief period it had the second highest rate in the early 00s, when London became the region with the highest under 18 conception rate.

Table 1 - Under 18 conception rates by region/country, England and Wales, 1998–2010

Region/country (number of local authorities)[1]	Under 18 rate 1998	Under 18 conception rate 2010	Difference between under 18 conception rates for 1998 and 2010	Percentage change in under 18 conception rates between 1998 and 2010
North East (12)	56.5	44.3	12.2	-21.6
North West (39)	50.3	40.7	9.6	-19.1
Yorkshire and The Humber (21)	53.1	40.5	12.6	-23.7
East Midlands (40)	48.8	34.5	14.3	-29.3
West Midlands (30)	51.7	40.5	11.2	-21.7
East (47)	37.9	29.8	8.1	-21.4
London (32)	51.1	37.1	14.0	-27.4
South East (67)	37.8	28.3	9.5	-25.1
South West (36)	39.4	29.9	9.5	-24.1
Wales (22)	55.0	37.7	17.3	-31.5

Table source: Office for National Statistics

Table notes:

1. City of London has been combined with Hackney and the Isles of Scilly have been combined with Cornwall throughout this article. As such, separate statistics are not available for these local authorities, meaning that there are 346 local authorities in the table but 348 local authorities exist for England and Wales.

Table 1 shows that there was a great deal of variation in the regional reduction in under 18 conception rates between 1998 and 2010. It can be seen that under 18 conception rates fell the most in Wales, by 17.3 conceptions per 1,000 women aged 15 to 17, while they fell the least in the East of England, by 8.1 conceptions per 1,000 women aged 15 to 17 in the region. In percentage terms, under 18 conception rates in Wales fell the most (by 31.5%), while they fell the least in the North West (19.1%). The discrepancy between the East of England having the smallest fall in under 18 conception rates and the North West having the smallest fall in percentage terms can be explained by the East of England having a much lower under 18 conception rate in 1998 than the North West (37.9 compared with 50.3). This means that the same decrease in the under 18 conception rate will have a bigger percentage decrease in the East of England than in the North West.

Having looked at the correlation between under 18 and under 16 conceptions it is natural to consider whether under 18 conceptions were simply a reflection of the general level of fertility. Figure 3 shows the under 18 conception rate and the total conception rate over time.

Figure 3 - Under 18 and total conception rates, England and Wales, 1998–2010

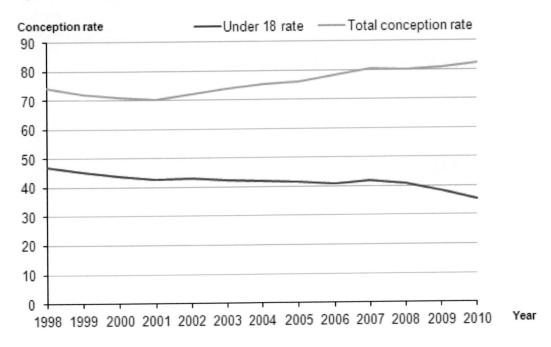

Source: Office for National Statistics

Figure 3 shows that there is a large gap between the conception rates for under 18s and all women. Interestingly, the trend in the under 18 conception rate mirrors the trend in the total conception rate[4] from 1998 to 2001. There are a number of factors which could explain the recent reduction in teenage conceptions, including the following:

• The programs invested in by successive governments (for example sex and relationships education, improved access to contraceptives and contraceptive publicity).

• A shift in aspirations of young women towards education (Broecke and Hamed, 2008).

• The increased media awareness of young people and the perception of stigma associated with being a teenage mother (McDermott et al, 2004).

Notes

1. At that point there was a lack of specific interest in the under 18 age group, with conceptions to women aged under 16 or under 20 taking more prominence, although figures for individual year of age at the national level were reported.

2. The under 18 conception rate is the number of conceptions to women aged under 18 per thousand women aged 15 to 17. It should be noted that population figures are subject to revision and are normally revised after a Census for inter-census years; as a result conception rates are subject to change.

3. Data are available back to 1975 for England and Wales, however they are not directly comparable as ONS changed the methodology for estimating age at conception in 1999 and applied to 1997 conception statistics. Whilst a time series was created back to 1986, these data are for England and Wales only. The data are available in the statistical bulletin for conceptions 2010.

4. The total conception rate is all conceptions per thousand members of the female population aged 15 to 44 in the relevant area.

2. Regional and sub-regional analysis of under 18 conceptions

Key points:

• The North East had the highest under 18 conception rate and the smallest range of any English region or Wales.

• High rates of under 18 conception were generally found in local authorities containing cities or seaside towns, in the Welsh Valleys and in two belts in the North of England.

• Low rates of under 18 conception were generally found in the London commuter belt, mid Wales, local authorities not containing cities or seaside towns south of Yorkshire and The Humber and the North West, and in a band between the two belts of high under 18 conception rates in the North of England.

• More than half of the local authorities in the North East had under 18 conception rates in the highest 20% of local authority under 18 conception rates, but none in the lowest 40%.

When looking at under 18 conception data three year aggregates are often used due to the smoothing effect it has on the annual data by reducing the effect of anomalous years on the overall trend in conception rates. In any year anomalies can occur and these can distort the data, so by taking a three year aggregate any anomalies have a lesser impact on the statistics. This smoothing effect means that we can be more confident that any rise or fall in the three year aggregate is likely to be genuine as it is evened out by two other years. Furthermore, conception statistics are routinely subjected to disclosure control, by adopting three year aggregates disclosure control needs to be applied less frequently so more data are available for people to use, this is particularly true for under 16 conceptions where county district data might otherwise be unavailable.

Table 2 shows under 18 conception rates for the English regions and Wales, along with the local authorities with the highest and lowest under 18 conception rates in region, using three year aggregated data for 2008 to 2010.

Table 2 - Under 18 conception rates by region/country, England and Wales, 2008–10

Region/ Country	Rate	Lowest under 18 conception rate in region		Highest under 18 conception rate in region		Range (highest to lowest)
		Local authority	Rate	Local authority	Rate	
North East (12)	46.8	Northumberland	34.4	Hartlepool	59.7	25.3
North West (39)	43.5	Ribble Valley	21.5	Manchester	64.9	43.4
Yorkshire and The Humber (21)	44.1	Harrogate	17.8	Kingston upon Hull, city of	62.8	45.0
East Midlands (40)	37.3	Rutland	11.1	Nottingham	59.4	48.3
West Midlands (30)	43.1	Malvern Hills	20.3	Stoke-on-Trent	59.0	38.7
East (47)	30.8	Brentwood	15.7	Great Yarmouth	55.1	39.4
London (32)	40.9	Richmond upon Thames	20.2	Lambeth	63.0	42.8
South East (67)	30.5	Windsor and Maidenhead	14.5	Thanet	53.8	39.3
South West (36)	32.4	East Dorset	16.8	Torbay	55.7	38.9
Wales (22)	40.8	Monmouthshire	23.8	Merthyr Tydfil	59.8	36.0

Table source: Office for National Statistics

Table 2 shows that the North East had the highest overall under 18 conception rate. However, it also had the smallest range in under 18 conception rates from 34.4 per 1,000 in Northumberland to 59.7 in Hartlepool, giving an overall range between the local authorities with the highest and lowest under 18 conception rates in the region of 25.3. The local authority in the North East with the lowest under 18 conception rate was higher than the local authority with the lowest under 18 conception rate in any other English region or Wales.

The South East had the lowest under 18 conception rate at 30.5 conceptions per 1,000 women aged 15 to 17. The local authority in the South East with the highest rate of under 18 conception (Thanet with a rate of 53.8) was lower than the highest under 18 conception rate in any other English region or Wales.

The East Midlands had the greatest range with a difference between the highest and lowest under 18 conception rates in region of 48.3 conceptions per 1,000 women aged 15 to 17. This ranged from Rutland (11.1) to Nottingham (59.4). However, Rutland has a relatively small population of teenage women and as such should be treated with some caution. Rushcliffe was the local authority with the next lowest under 18 conception rate in the East Midlands at 17.3. Were this used instead, then the East Midlands would have had a range of 42.1 and consequently had the fourth largest range, with Yorkshire and the Humber then having the largest.

Of the ten local authorities with the highest under 18 conception rate in region/country, four contained seaside towns (Hartlepool, Great Yarmouth, Thanet and Torbay) and five were cities (Manchester, Kingston upon Hull, Nottingham, Stoke-on-Trent and Lambeth). The remaining local authority (Merthyr Tydfil) was in the Welsh Valleys.

The overall five highest and lowest local authority under 18 conception rates in England and Wales can be seen in Table 3.

Table 3 - Under 18 conception rates by local authority, England and Wales, 2008–10

Local authorities with the lowest under 18 conception rates		Local authorities with the highest under 18 conception rates	
Local authority (Region)	Rate	Local authority (Region)	Rate
1. Rutland (East Midlands)	11.1	1. Manchester (North West)	64.9
2. Windsor and Maidenhead (South East)	14.5	2. Lambeth (London)	63.0
3. Waverley (South East)	14.6	3. Kingston upon Hull, City of (Yorkshire and The Humber)	62.8
4. Tandridge (South East)	15.1	4. Southwark (London)	61.5
5. Brentwood (East)	15.7	5. Greenwich (London)	61.3

Table source: Office for National Statistics

It is apparent that the local authorities with the highest under 18 conception rates are all city based (with Lambeth, Southwark and Greenwich all being in London). The local authorities with the lowest under 18 conception rates are more rurally located, with only Rutland not being located in the Home Counties. This suggests that there may be a link between under 18 conceptions and population size or density, these relationships will be explored later in the article.

By mapping the data it can be determined whether there were any patterns in under 18 conception rates which might hold true for England and Wales as a whole. This can be seen in Map 1.

Map 1 - Under 18 conceptions by local authority, England and Wales, 2008–10

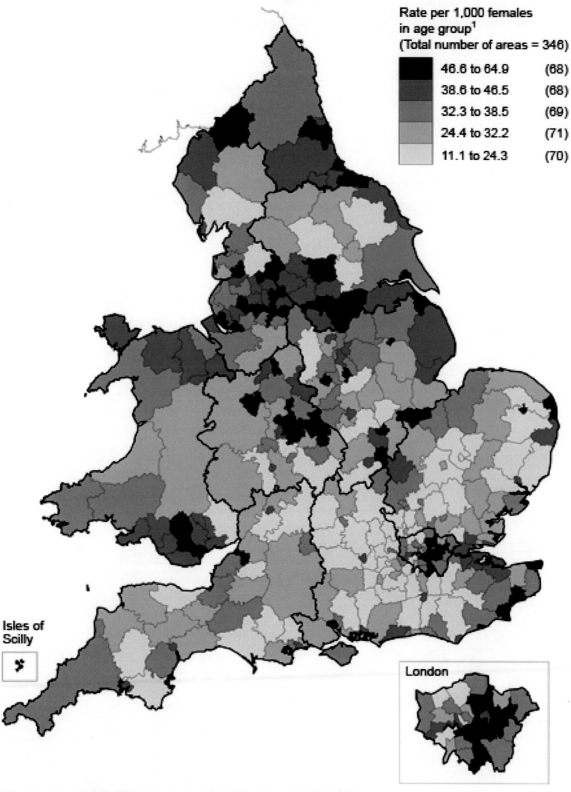

Rate per 1,000 females
in age group[1]
(Total number of areas = 346)

■	46.6 to 64.9	(68)
	38.6 to 46.5	(68)
	32.3 to 38.5	(69)
	24.4 to 32.2	(71)
	11.1 to 24.3	(70)

Isles of
Scilly

London

1 To preserve confidentiality, counts for City of London and Isles of Scilly
  have been combined with those for Hackney and Cornwall respectively.
Source: Office for National Statistics
Contains National Statistics data © Crown copyright and database right 2013
Contains Ordnance Survey data © Crown copyright and database right 2013

Source: Office for National Statistics

Map 1 shows that there were distinct areas of high and low rates of under 18 conception in England and Wales. Areas where there were high rates of under 18 conception tend to include:

• Local authorities containing seaside towns.

• Two belts across the North of England, one at the top of the Midlands and another across the very North of England.

• The Welsh Valleys.

• Cities.

Areas where there were low rates of under 18 conceptions tend to include:

• Mid Wales.

• Local authorities which do not contain cities or seaside towns below the North West and Yorkshire and The Humber.

• A band of local authorities between the two belts across the North of England.

• London commuter belt.

Another way to assess the distribution of under 18 conception rates is to look at the quintile distribution of each English region and Wales. This will help to highlight regional disparities. The distribution of under 18 conception rates by region/country can be seen in Table 4, which details the percentage of local authorities in each English region and Wales within each quintile[1].

Table 4 - Quintile distribution of under 18 conception rate by region/country, England and Wales, 2008–10

Region/ Country	Percentage of Local Authorities in Quintile[1]					Low[2]	High[3]
	Quintile 1	Quintile 2	Quintile 3	Quintile 4	Quintile 5		
North East (12)	0.0	0.0	8.3	33.3	58.3	0.0	91.7
North West (39)	5.1	10.3	20.5	28.2	35.9	15.4	64.1
Yorkshire and The Humber (21)	14.3	19.0	4.8	33.3	28.6	33.3	61.9
East Midlands (40)	12.5	30.0	25.0	17.5	15.0	42.5	32.5
West Midlands (30)	10.0	23.3	16.7	13.3	36.7	33.3	50.0
East (47)	34.0	27.7	17.0	14.9	6.4	61.7	21.3
London (32)	12.5	9.4	31.3	12.5	34.4	21.9	46.9
South East (67)	37.3	19.4	22.4	13.4	7.5	56.7	20.9
South West (36)	27.8	30.6	22.2	11.1	8.3	58.3	19.4
Wales (22)	4.5	9.1	18.2	54.5	13.6	13.6	68.2

Table source: Office for National Statistics

Table notes:

1. Quintile 1 contains those local authorities with the lowest under 18 conception rates, whereas Quintile 5 contains those local authorities with the highest under 18 conception rates. The quintile the local authority is placed in is based on the ordering of conception rate in England and Wales.
2. Low denotes the percentage of local authorities within region/country contained within quintiles 1 and 2.
3. High denotes the percentage of local authorities within region/country contained within quintiles 4 and 5.

Table 4 shows that in five English regions and Wales at least half of the local authorities had high rates of under 18 conceptions, compared with three regions where at least half of the local authorities within the region had low rates of under 18 conceptions.

The North East had no local authorities with low under 18 conception rates. It also had the highest percentage of local authorities with high under 18 conception rates at 91.7%; 58.3% of local authorities in the North East were in Quintile 5. This is unsurprising given the narrow range in under 18 conception rates for the North East. Wales had the highest percentage of local authorities in Quintile 4 at 54.5%.

The East of England had the highest percentage of local authorities with low rates of under 18 conception at 61.7%. The South West had the lowest percentage of local authorities with high rates of under 18 conception at 19.4%. The South East had the highest percentage of local authorities in Quintile 1 at 37.3%, whilst the South West had the highest percentage of local authorities in Quintile 2 at 30.6%.

So, overall the North East had high quintile distribution, meaning that high under 18 conception rates were prominent in the region, while the East, South East and South West had low quintile distribution, meaning that low rates of under 18 conception rates were prominent in the regions.

Notes

1. Quintiles are derived by ordering the local authorities in England and Wales by under 18 conception rate and splitting them up into five groupings of similar size based on the ordering. There are 348 local authorities in England and Wales, of which 346 are recorded in under 18 conceptions: City of London and Isles of Scilly are combined with Hackney and Cornwall respectively. Due to the number of local authorities not being divisible by five and the fact that rates are taken to one decimal place, meaning that there may be several local authorities with the same rate on a quintile boundary, boundary groupings may differ in size.

3. Under 18 conception comparisons with under 16 conceptions

Key points:
• When mapped using quintiles, under 16 conception rates in England and Wales looked similar to under 18 conception rates.

• Three of the local authorities with the five highest under 18 conception rates also appeared in the local authorities with the five highest under 16 conception rates.

• Under 18 conception rates are very strongly correlated with under 16 conception rates, with the English regions and Wales being more strongly correlated than England and Wales as a whole.

• The rankings for under 18 conception rate rankings were more strongly correlated with under 16 conception rate rankings than under 18 conception rates were with under 16 conception rates at the England and Wales level.

One area which has not been greatly examined has been the strength of the links between under 18 conceptions and under 16 conceptions. Under 16 conceptions are an area of interest due to the legal age of consent being 16; a firm downward trend in conception rates was also part of the Labour Government's teenage conceptions target. Figure 4 shows the under 18 and under 16 conception rates[1] over time.

Figure 4 - Under 18 and under 16 conception rates, England and Wales, 1998–2010

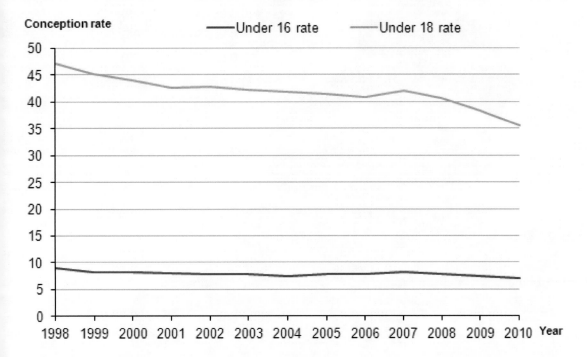

Source: Office for National Statistics

Figure 4 shows that there is a large difference between the rates for under 18 and under 16 conceptions and both have fallen since 1998. The low under 16 rate is reflective of the small number of under 16 conceptions included within under 18 conceptions, as the base populations used to calculate the rates are broadly similar.

To help determine whether under 16 conceptions are a strong predictor of under 18 conceptions the distribution of under 16 conception rates can be seen in Map 2.

Map 2 - Under 16 conceptions by local authority, England and Wales, 2008–10

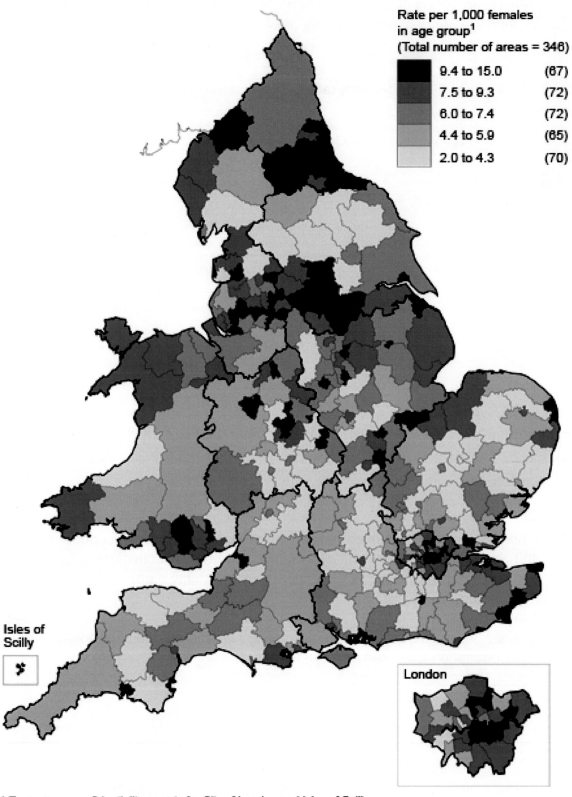

Rate per 1,000 females
in age group[1]
(Total number of areas = 346)

■	9.4 to 15.0	(67)
■	7.5 to 9.3	(72)
■	6.0 to 7.4	(72)
■	4.4 to 5.9	(65)
■	2.0 to 4.3	(70)

Isles of
Scilly

London

1 To preserve confidentiality, counts for City of London and Isles of Scilly
 have been combined with those for Hackney and Cornwall respectively.
Source: Office for National Statistics
Contains National Statistics data © Crown copyright and database right 2013
Contains Ordnance Survey data © Crown copyright and database right 2013

Comparing Map 2 with Map 1, we can see that the distribution of conceptions across England and Wales did not differ greatly, with local authorities which had high rates of under 18 conceptions having high rates of under 16 conceptions and those local authorities with low rates generally having low rates for under 18 conceptions.

The local authorities with the highest and lowest rates of under 16 conceptions can be seen in Table 5.

Table 5 - Under 16 conception rates by local authority, England and Wales, 2008–10

Local authorities with the lowest under 16 conception rates		Local authorities with the highest under 16 conception rates	
Local authority (Region/Country)	**Rate**	**Local authority (Region/Country)**	**Rate**
1. St Albans (East)	2.0	1. Middlesbrough (North East)	15.0
2. Uttlesford (East)	2.1	2. Southwark (London)	14.9
3. Elmbridge (South East)	2.3	3. Halton (North West)	14.7
4. Rutland (East Midlands)	2.5	4. Merthyr Tydfil (Wales)	13.7
5. Wokingham (South East)	2.5	5= Manchester (North West)	13.6
6. Harrogate (Yorkshire and The Humber)	2.5	5= Greenwich (London)	13.6
		5= Tameside (North West)	13.6

Table source: Office for National Statistics

Table 5 reveals that three of the local authorities with the five highest under 18 conception rates also appeared in the local authorities with the five highest under 16 conception rates (Southwark, Manchester and Greenwich). Furthermore four of the seven local authorities were cities, the remaining three comprised of large towns (Halton, which contains Runcorn and Widnes; Tameside, which is part of Greater Manchester; and Merthyr Tydfil).

Rutland appeared in the local authorities with the five lowest conception rates at both the under 16 and under 18 levels. Of the local authorities with the lowest under 16 conception rates in Table 5, only Rutland (East Midlands) and Harrogate (Yorkshire and The Humber) were outside of the Home Counties.

Table 6 shows the level of correlation between under 16 conceptions and under 18 conceptions in terms of numbers, rates and the rate ranking for the local authority for 2008 to 2010.

Table 6 - Correlation of under 18 conceptions with under 16 conceptions, England and Wales, 2008–10

Region/Country (number of local authorities)[1]	Rates R^2	Regional Rank R^2
England and Wales (346)	0.8735	0.8739
North East (12)	0.6832	0.5343
North West (39)	0.8279	0.8702
Yorkshire and The Humber (21)	0.9331	0.9757
East Midlands (40)	0.9064	0.8331
West Midlands (30)	0.8021	0.7947
East (47)	0.8323	0.8219
London (32)	0.8881	0.8914
South East (67)	0.8698	0.8702
South West (36)	0.8001	0.7392
Wales (22)	0.8450	0.6728

Table source: Office for National Statistics

Table notes:

1. When looking at correlation statistics, such as the coefficient R^2, the number of data points (in this case local authorities) helps determine how robust the statistic is. As such statistics for the English regions and Wales with fewer local authorities are not as robust as English regions with more local authorities.

Table 6 shows that under 16 conception rates accounted for 87.4%[2] of the variation in under 18 conception rates across England and Wales and for at least 68.3% of variation in each of the English regions or Wales.

Rankings of rates were marginally better correlated than rates at the England and Wales level, with under 16 conception rate rankings again accounting for 87.4% of the variation in under 18 conception rate rankings (a difference between rates and ranks of 0.04%). However, the majority of the English regions and Wales were more strongly correlated when looking at rates rather than ranks.

Rates were least strongly correlated in the North East (0.6832), which was also the region with the lowest correlation for ranks (0.5343). Yorkshire and The Humber was the region with the strongest correlation for both rates (0.9331) and regional ranks (0.9757).

Notes

1. The under 18 conception rate is the number of under 18 conceptions per 1,000 women aged 15 to 17. The under 16 conception rate is the number of under 16 conceptions per 1,000 women aged 13 to 15.

2. This is the R^2 value multiplied by 100.

4. Under 18 conceptions and urban aspects

Key points:

• There was weak correlation between under 18 conception rates and population density.

• There was also weak correlation between under 18 conception rates and the Urban-Rural Classification.

It has previously been put forward that under 18 conceptions are more likely to take place in urban than rural areas. Under 18 conception rates for local authorities can be plotted against their population density values to see how linked they were. This can be seen in figure 5.

Figure 5 - Under 18 conception rates and population densities, England and Wales, 2008–10

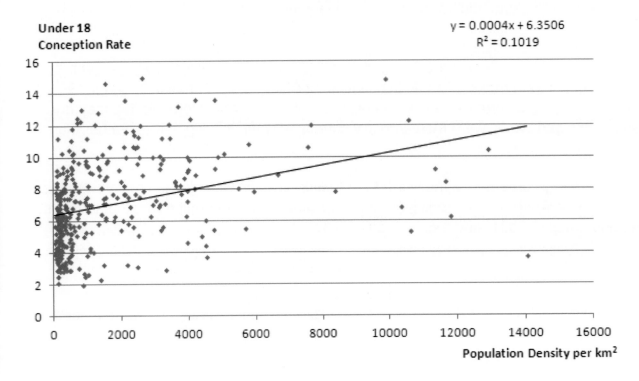

Source: Office for National Statistics

Figure 5 shows that for 2008 to 2010 population density accounted for 10.2% of the variation in under 18 conception rates[1,2]. As such, population density did not provide a good explanation of variation in under 18 conception rates, particularly with the clustering of data points close to the Under 18 conception rate axis.

Urban-Rural Classification[3] for England as updated in 2009 also did not provide a good explanation of under 18 conception rates for 2008 to 2010, yielding an R2 value of 0.2364. This means that less than a quarter of the variation in local authority under 18 conception rates is explained by the classification.

Given the weak correlation values for under 18 conception rates with population density and with the Urban-Rural Classification, further analysis for the English regions and Wales was not undertaken. This weak correlation is surprising given that cities appeared to have higher rates of under 18 conception than rural areas.

Notes

1. Correlation, denoted by the R^2 value, is a measure of how well one variable describes a change in another over a dataset. The more closely associated the two variables are the closer the value will be to one. If the two variables have an R^2 value of one, then if we plot the two variables against one another on a scatter plot they will all fall on the trend line for the data. The further away the R^2 value is from one the more spread out the data will appear on the scatter plot.

2. This is the R2 value multiplied by 100.

3. The data used are for England only as data for Wales are not produced on a consistent basis. There is an alternative Welsh dataset but this has a different number of categories so is not directly comparable. There are consistent datasets available for a lower level of geography but conceptions data are not available at this level. Given that Wales comprises 22 local authorities out of 348 for England and Wales, it is not likely to have a significant impact upon the overall correlation given that conceptions data for Wales are not extreme.

5. Under 18 conceptions and the English Indices of Multiple Deprivation

Key points:

• There was strong correlation between under 18 conception rates in England and the English Indices of Multiple Deprivation. This correlation was stronger for the English Indices of Multiple Deprivation with under 18 conception rate rankings than with under 18 conception rates.

• London and the South West did not have strong correlation between the English Indices of Multiple Deprivation and under 18 conceptions.

• Just over two-thirds of the most deprived local authorities had high incidents of under 18 conception in England, while just under two-thirds of the least deprived local authorities had low incidents of under 18 conception in England.

• The North West had the highest number of local authorities in quintile 5 for IMD rankings, under 18 conception rate rankings and both in conjunction with one another. London had the second highest in all three categories.

• Half of the local authorities in quintile 1 for the IMD rankings were in the South East, while just over a third of the local authorities in quintile 1 for under 18 conception rate rankings were in the same region.

The English Indices of Multiple Deprivation[1] (IMD) were chosen for analysis as under 18 conception are often associated with deprived areas.

When comparing under 18 conceptions with IMD it is important to note that ideal data for comparison are not available[2]. Furthermore, the IMD data are for one in every three years, rather than a three year aggregate measure. As such we are using the latest IMD rankings data available (that for 2010) in combination with the latest under 18 annual conception data (2008 to 2010).

The picture for England can be seen in Figure 6. Due to IMD giving the most deprived area a rank of one and the least deprived area with the highest value, as such the under 18 conception rate rankings have been inverted for consistency so that the local authority with the highest under 18 conception rate has a rank of one.

Figure 6 - Inverted under 18 conception rate ranking 2008–10 and IMD 2010, England

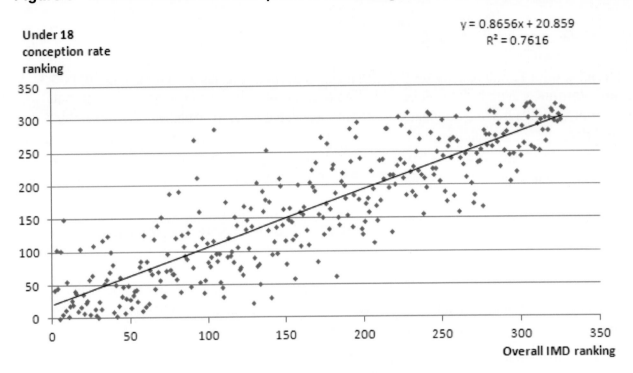

Source: Office for National Statistics, Communities and Local Government

Figure 6 shows that the IMD rank accounted for 76.2%[3] of the variation in local authority rankings of under 18 conception rates in England. Rankings have been used rather than rates as IMD is provided in ranks and this provides the most consistent comparison. Were we to switch to using local authority under 18 conception rates (rather than their ranks) then the R2 value would fall to 0.7409 which, reduces the explanation in variation of under 18 conceptions (by 2.1 percentage points).

Having identified that the IMD rank and the under 18 conception rate rank were strongly correlated, the regional picture can now be looked at to see how much variation there was in the English regions. This can be seen in Table 7.

Table 7 - Regional under 18 conception rate ranking and IMD, England, 2008–10

Region (number of local authorities)[1]	Local authority under 18 conception rate rankings within region and Regional IMD rankings (R^2)	Local authority under 18 conception rates within region and Regional IMD rankings (R^2)
North East (12)	0.7641	0.7604
North West (39)	0.6448	0.6299
Yorkshire and The Humber (21)	0.7316	0.8068
East Midlands (40)	0.7908	0.7512
West Midlands (30)	0.6855	0.6892
East (47)	0.7265	0.7296
London (32)	0.4676	0.4325
South East (67)	0.7468	0.7444
South West (36)	0.4248	0.4695

Table source: Office for National Statistics

Table notes:

1. When looking at correlation statistics, such as the coefficient R2, the number of data points (in this case local authorities) helps determine how robust the statistic is; as such statistics for the English regions and Wales with fewer local authorities are not as robust as English regions with more local authorities.

Table 7 shows that there was large variation, regionally, in the correlation that IMD rankings had with under 18 conception rates and with under 18 conception rate rankings. Four of the English regions were more strongly correlated with under 18 conception rates than with the rankings of those rates, while the other five regions were more strongly correlated with the rate rankings. This is consistent with the 2.1 percentage point difference between the R^2 values for IMD ranks with under 18 conception rates and with under 18 conception rate rankings.

Yorkshire and The Humber had the highest R^2 value for correlation between regional IMD rankings and local authority under 18 conception rates within region (80.7%). The East Midlands had the highest R^2 value for correlation between regional IMD rankings and local authority under 18 conception rate rankings within region (79.1%). The South West had the lowest R^2 value for correlation between regional IMD rankings and both local authority under 18 conception rates within region (42.5%). London had the lowest R^2 value for correlation between regional IMD rankings and local authority under 18 conception rate rankings within region (43.3%).

Looking at the rankings data, London tended to have relatively low rankings for IMD but tended to have relatively high levels of under 18 conceptions. Conversely, the South West tended to have relatively high rankings for IMD but had relatively low levels of under 18 conception.

London is characterised as a region for high income (in part due to well paying industries and the prevalence of the London Weighting Allowance), a young, mobile, highly-educated population (due to a regular influx of graduates), a generally buoyant housing market with access to transport and other services. As such, it is likely to score well in the income, barriers to housing and services, health deprivation and disability, and education, skills and training domains[4]. Given this, it can be seen as unsurprising that London did not have a strong correlation between under 18 conceptions and the local authority rankings for the IMD in region.

The South West is characterised by more rural attributes, with relatively few cities or large towns, meaning that it is likely to have a large proportion of local authorities with barriers to housing and services (such as nearby post offices and food shops). It is a region with a relatively old population (and associated health issues), with 26.2% of its population in 2008 to 2010 being 60 or older, 2.6% or more than any other region, meaning that it is more likely to have health related deprivation and disability than London (which also has the lowest proportion of people aged 60 or over of any region at 15.7%). With the older population and rural community aspects of the South West it is not particularly surprising that the region did not have a strong correlation between under 18 conceptions and the local authority rankings for IMD in region.

The number of local authorities which appeared in the highest and lowest quintiles for IMD rankings, under 18 conception rate rankings and both in conjunction with one another can be seen in Table 8. This shows the degree of connectedness and levels of disparity in the English regions.

Table 8 - Quintile distribution of IMD and under 18 conceptions by region/country, England, 2008–10

Region/ Country[1] (number of local authorities)	Number of Local Authorities					
	Quintile 1 IMD	Quintile 5 IMD	Quintile 1 U18CRR[2]	Quintile 5 U18CRR[2]	Quintile 1 Both	Quintile 5 Both
England (324)	65	65	65	65	41	47
North East (12)	0	8	0	7	0	7
North West (39)	1	19	2	14	1	13
Yorkshire and The Humber (21)	3	7	3	6	1	5
East Midlands (40)	7	7	5	5	4	3
West Midlands (30)	2	6	2	11	1	6
East (47)	15	1	16	3	11	1
London (32)	1	14	4	11	1	9
South East (67)	32	2	23	5	20	2
South West (36)	4	1	10	3	2	1

Table source: Office for National Statistics

Table notes:
1. Quintile 1 represents those local authorities with the lowest deprivation scores for IMD and the lowest under 18 conception rate rankings. Conversely, Quintile 5 represents those local authorities with the highest deprivation scores for IMD and highest under 18 conception rate rankings.
2. U18CRR is Under 18 conception rate ranking.

From Table 8 it can be seen that just over two-thirds of the most deprived local authorities had high incidents of under 18 conception in England. Just under two-thirds of the least deprived local authorities had low incidents of under 18 conception in England.

The North West had the highest number of local authorities in quintile 5 for IMD rankings, under 18 conception rate rankings and both in conjunction with one another. London had the second highest in all three categories. When combined, London and the North West had just over half of all local authorities in quintile 5 for the IMD rankings and just under half of all local authorities appearing in quintile 5 for both IMD rankings and under 18 conception rate rankings.

Half of the local authorities in quintile 1 for the IMD rankings were in the South East, while just over a third of the local authorities in quintile 1 for under 18 conception rate rankings were in the same region. Half of the local authorities in quintile one for the IMD rankings in conjunction with quintile one for the under 18 conception rate rankings were in the South East. All of the local authorities which appeared in quintile 5 for IMD ranking in the West Midlands appeared in quintile 5 for under 18 conception rate rankings.

The local authority in the North West (Ribble Valley) and the local authority in London (Richmond upon Thames) which appeared in quintile 1 in the IMD rankings also appeared in quintile 1 in the under 18 conception rate rankings. The North East had no local authorities in quintile 1 for either IMD rankings or under 18 conception rate rankings.

Overall, under 18 conceptions and IMD were reasonably well correlated in England, with large variation at regional level. This means that there were likely to be higher rates of under 18 pregnancy in areas of high deprivation. Two regions, London and the South West, had very different correlation values from the other regions but this could be explained by looking at the IMD domains and characteristics of those regions. As the IMD is skewed, due to regional characteristics of the component domains, the correlation with under 18 conceptions is also skewed resulting in a lower R^2 value. As such, IMD is not always a good predictor of under 18 conceptions due to regionally specific characteristics.

Notes

1.   IMD is measure of relative deprivation. It uses several domains to produce a series of rankings, informing which local authorities are more deprived than others. The rankings do not reveal the extent to which one area may be more or less deprived than another. The domains used for IMD are:

• Income

• Employment

• Health deprivation and disability

• Education, skills and training

• Barriers to housing and services

• Crime

- Living environment

2. Directly comparable data for England and Wales are not available (the composition of the English IMD and the Welsh IMD are different), as such the measure for England has been used for the national picture. Data for Wales are available at LSOA level for 2008 and 2011 and at local authority level for 2011.

3. This is the R2 value multiplied by 100.

4. That said London still has large pockets of deprivation with areas of low income. London also has a high crime rate so will score poorly in the crime domain. However, this is unlikely to offset the scores from the other domains.

6. Under 18 conceptions and child poverty

Key points:
• Under 18 conception rates in England were well correlated with the percentage of children living in poverty.

• London was not as strongly correlated as other English regions for under 18 conceptions with the percentage of children living in poverty.

Child poverty[1] was chosen for analysis as living in poverty is another factor that is often associated with under 18 conceptions. When comparing under 18 conceptions with child poverty data it is important to note that ideal data for comparison are not available[2]. Child poverty percentages have been averaged over three years.

Figure 7 - Under 18 conception rate and percentage of children living in poverty, England, 2008–10

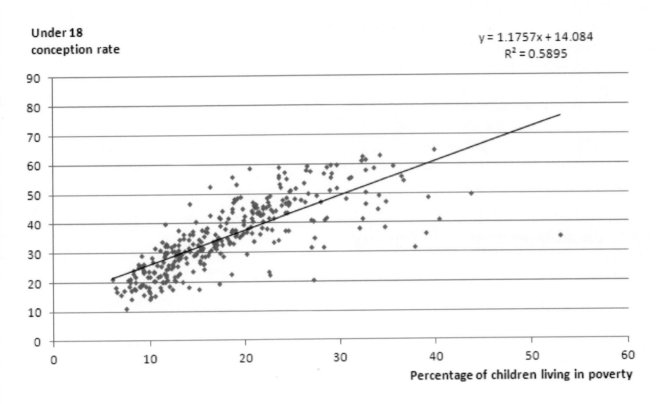

Source: Office for National Statistics, HM Revenue and Customs

As can be seen in Figure 7, the percentage of children living in poverty explained 59.0% of the variation in under 18 conception rates between 2008 and 2010. There appears to be a stronger correlation than is indicated by the R^2 value in Figure 8 as there are a few outliers to the right of the graph, which are influencing the trend line. This could imply that the relationship between under 18 conception rates and the percentage of children living in poverty is non-linear, which would mean that additional factors need to be examined as part of a regression model and an appropriate correlation method adopted.

Having identified that the percentage of children living in poverty and the under 18 conception rate had a moderate correlation, the regional picture can now be looked at to see how much variation there was sub-nationally. This can be seen in Table 9.

Table 9 - Under 18 conception rate and percentage of children living in poverty, by region, England, 2008–10

Region (number of local authorities)	Local authority under 18 conception rates and percentage of children living in poverty, by region (R^2)
North East (12)	0.7431
North West (37)	0.6043
Yorkshire and The Humber (21)	0.8524
East Midlands (40)	0.7301
West Midlands (30)	0.6654
East (45)	0.7885
London (32)	0.2210
South East (67)	0.7970
South West (36)	0.6102

Table source: Office for National Statistics

Table 9 shows that there was large variation, regionally, in the correlation of the percentage of children living in poverty with under 18 conception rates. Under 18 conceptions for London were again not as strongly correlated as the other English regions with the percentage of children living in poverty. London had the lowest R^2 value at 0.2210 while Yorkshire and the Humber had the highest at 0.8524. Interestingly, the other four eastern regions (the North East, the East Midlands, the East of England and the South East) had similar R^2 values, all falling between 0.7301 and 0.7970, meaning that there were strong correlations between under 18 conception rates and the percentage of children living in poverty in those regions. The North West (0.6043), the West Midlands (0.6654) and the South West (0.6102) had more moderate correlation values.

In order to establish the patterns in the data for child poverty and under 18 conceptions, they have been plotted in figures 8 and 9, with local authorities in London highlighted to show their position relative to other local authorities in England.

Figure 8 - Ranked local authority percentages of children living in poverty, England, 2008–10

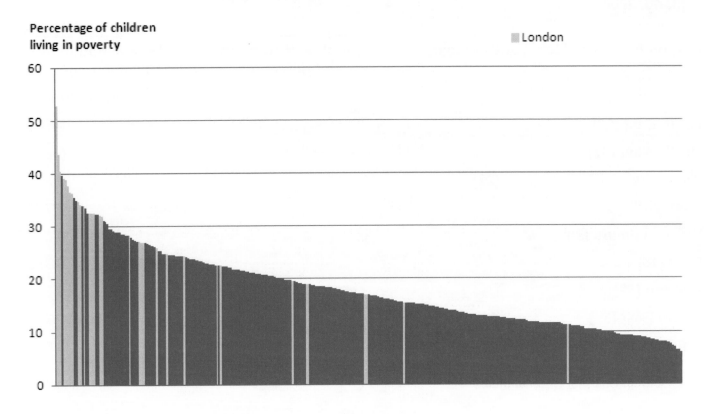

Source: HM Revenue and Customs

From Figure 8 it can be seen that London had some high rates of child poverty. The cluster of light blue on the left side of the chart reveals that it was experiencing the majority of the worst local authority percentages of children in poverty (more than 30%). Figure 8 can be compared with the under 18 conception rate pattern for England as seen in Figure 9.

Figure 9 - Ranked local authority under 18 conception rates, England, 2008–10

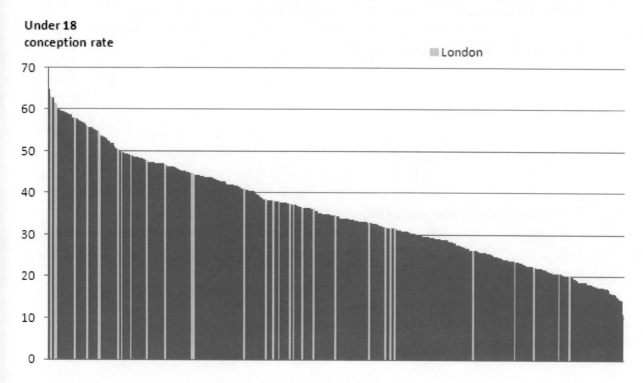

Source: Office for National Statistics

Notes:

1. This chart has been produced without those unitary authorities comprising the former counties of Bedfordshire and Cheshire for consistency.

Figure 9 shows that under 18 conception rates for local authorities in London were more evenly distributed, with many more appearing on the right side of Figure 9 than on Figure 8. The worst under 18 conception rates, those above 50, contain a far lower concentration of London local authorities than those local authorities with the worst child poverty levels.

London had under 18 conception rates that were generally lower than might be expected given the levels of child poverty. One possible explanation for the low level of correlation in London is the difference in culture within the London region. London tends to attract a lot of international migrants and migrants have higher levels of fertility, (Tromans et al 2009). This means that if migrant families are deemed to be living in poverty then this is likely to affect a larger number of children and increasing the percentage of children living in poverty.

Overall, under 18 conceptions and child poverty were reasonably well correlated in England, with large variation at regional level. This means that in areas of high child poverty there are likely to be high under 18 conception rates. London had a very different correlation value from the other regions; this is believed to be due to the fertility of London's migrant population.

Notes

1. Child poverty is deemed to occur when children are living in families in receipt of out of work benefits or tax credits where their reported income is less than 60% median income.

2. Child poverty data for Wales are unavailable for 2008; as such they have not been included in this comparison. Child poverty values for those unitary authorities which comprise the former counties of Cheshire and Bedfordshire are also unavailable and as such have been excluded from this analysis. This means that the North West and East of England have two local authorities each which are not accounted for.

7. Under 18 conceptions and unemployment

Key points:

• Under 18 conception rates were well correlated with unemployment rates.

• There was an east-west divide in how well the rates were correlated with one another, with rates in the east (except London) being strongly correlated, with rates in the west (and London) being moderately correlated.

Unemployment has been chosen for analysis as it can be seen as an indicator for deprivation and poverty. Employment is a domain in the English Indices of Multiple Deprivation and is naturally linked to income. Children growing up in areas with high unemployment were likely to experience deprivation and these areas were likely to have high under 18 conception rates.

Figure 10 - Under 18 conception rate and unemployment rate, England and Wales, 2008–10

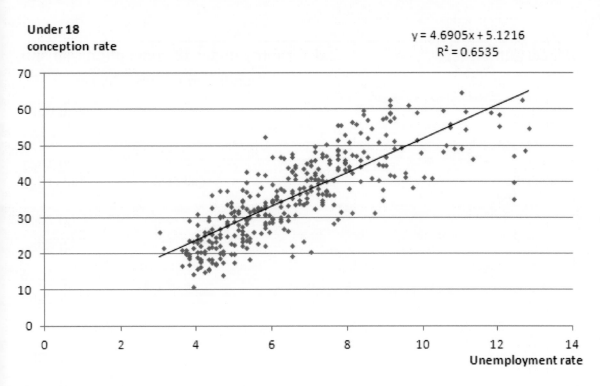

Source: Office for National Statistics

Figure 10 shows that the unemployment rate was well correlated with the under 18 conception rate across England and Wales. The unemployment rate accounted for 65.4% of the variation in the under 18 conception rate[1]. Table 10 shows the regional R^2 values for correlation between under 18 conception rates and unemployment rates for local authorities.

Table 10 - Under 18 conception rate and unemployment rate, by region/country, England and Wales, 2008–10

Region (number of local authorities)	Local authority under 18 conception rate and unemployment rate, by region, R^2
England and Wales (346)	0.6535
North East (12)	0.7885
North West (39)	0.5441
Yorkshire and The Humber (21)	0.8807
East Midlands (40)	0.7016
West Midlands (30)	0.5844
East (47)	0.7646
London (32)	0.3433
South East (67)	0.7352
South West (36)	0.4880
Wales (22)	0.4648

Table source: Office for National Statistics

Table 10 shows wide variation in regional correlation for under 18 conception rates and unemployment rates, with R^2 values ranging from 0.8807 in Yorkshire and the Humber to 0.3433 in London. Alongside London, the South West and Wales had R^2 values below 0.5, whilst the North West and the West Midlands had R^2 values between 0.5 and 0.6.

Surprisingly, the disparate R^2 values reveal an east-west divide: the eastern coastal regions were strongly correlated, while other English regions and Wales had moderate correlations. This can be seen in Map 3.

Map 3 - Under 18 conception rate and unemployment rate correlation values by region/ country, England and Wales, 2008–10

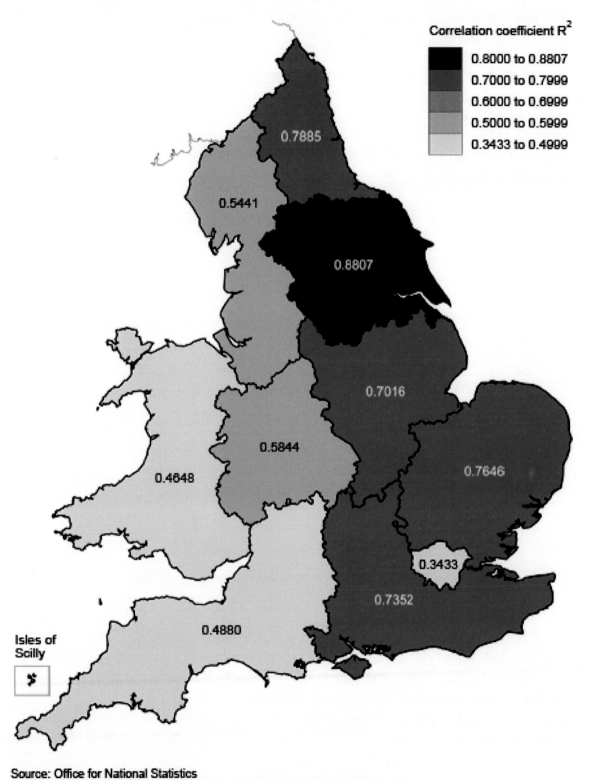

Correlation coefficient R^2

- 0.8000 to 0.8807
- 0.7000 to 0.7999
- 0.6000 to 0.6999
- 0.5000 to 0.5999
- 0.3433 to 0.4999

0.7885

0.5441

0.8807

0.7016

0.5844

0.4648

0.7646

0.3433

0.7352

0.4880

Isles of Scilly

Source: Office for National Statistics
Contains National Statistics data © Crown copyright and database right 2013
Contains Ordnance Survey data © Crown copyright and database right 2013

Source: Office for National Statistics

To help assess what might have been contributing to the particularly low correlations for the under 18 conception rate and the unemployment rate, the correlation chart was adapted to reflect the different regions. This means that it could be seen whether the areas of poor correlation had higher under 18 conception rates than would be expected given the correlation coefficient for England and Wales or lower under 18 conception rates.

Figure 11 shows the correlation for the unemployment rate with the under 18 conception rate for 2008 to 2010, for England and Wales, highlighting London boroughs and South West local authorities in the national picture.

Figure 11 - Under 18 conception rate and unemployment rate, London, South West, Wales and England and Wales, 2008–10

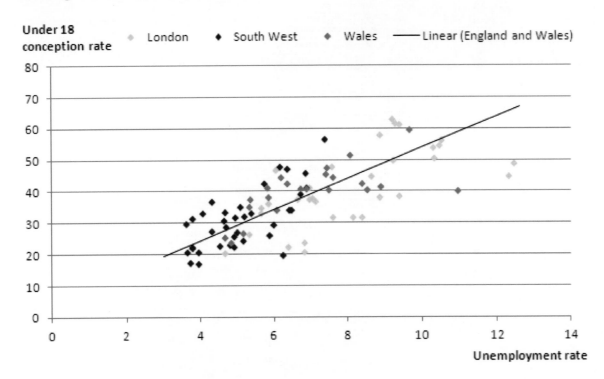

Source: Office for National Statistics

Figure 11 shows that London had more points below the trend line than above it, meaning that for the level of unemployment the under 18 conception rates were lower than expected. This may be a reflection of redundancies during the recession of white collar workers which are highly concentrated in London. This is supported by the rising unemployment rates across the London boroughs between 2008 and 2010. The weak correlation for London could also be a reflection of the ease of access to out of area family planning, which may mean that family planning services are more likely to be used, or the cultural differences in London due to greater ethnic diversity from first, second and third generation migrants.

Figure 11 shows that the South West had more points above the trend line than below it, meaning that the under 18 conception rates were higher than would have been expected for the levels of employment. Looking at the full-time and part-time employment splits, it is apparent that in 2010 the South West had the highest proportion of part-time workers across the English regions. This means that just because someone was employed they were not necessarily as employed as much as they wanted to be, so they could still have faced poverty despite being employed. It is important to note that seasonal working is an important factor for the South West, with agriculture and seasonal tourism comprising a large part of the economy.

Wales had the majority of its data points above the England and Wales trend line, meaning that under 18 conception rates were higher than would have been expected given the rates of unemployment. That said, one local authority, Blaenau Gwent, had a particularly high unemployment rate without a particularly high under 18 conception rate. Looking at the full-time and part-time employment splits for 2010, Wales had the same proportion of full-time and part-time workers as the South West and would expect to have a similar pattern in under 18 conceptions to the South West. That said, the Welsh data points are closer to the trend line than those of the South West, suggesting that employment in Wales is, perhaps, less seasonal due to economic composition.

Overall, under 18 conception rates and unemployment rates were well correlated, meaning that areas with high levels of unemployment were likely to have high under 18 conception rates. There is tremendous variation in the regional correlation coefficients with an almost east-west split for 2008 to 2010. The English regions with the worst correlation and Wales have been looked at more closely to identify reasons for their differences. The natural extension of this is to look at workless households, economic inactivity rates and economic composition for the regions/country.

Notes

1. Adding this to the 60.6% of the variation in under 18 conception rates shows there must be overlap. The strength of the correlation of the percentage of children living in poverty and the unemployment rate could be examined and built into a model for under 18 conception rate analysis.

Summary

An analytical toolkit looking at under 18 conceptions and measures of deprivation has been developed by ONS and is freely available online for the first time.

In this article under 18 conceptions have been analysed in order to identify to what extent under 18 conceptions may be correlated with other datasets which could be built into a forecasting model in further research. This may be of benefit to those working with young mothers or those involved with family planning initiatives targeted at young women. There may be more recent data available for some of the data series used in the article and/or toolkit, but these are not for the same time period as available conceptions data so have not been used.

Looking at conception data for 2008 to 2010, it has been determined that under 18 conceptions are strongly correlated with under 16 conceptions and the English Indices of Multiple Deprivation.

There was moderate correlation between under 18 conceptions and the percentage of children living in poverty in England and the unemployment rate for England and Wales for 2008 to 2010. There is variation in the strength of the relationship between these datasets at regional level and the reasons for this variation have been analysed. In England, London had much lower levels of correlation than other regions. The North West, the West Midlands and the South West also had more moderate R^2 values when compared with the eastern regions, suggesting that there is something different in the social make up of eastern and western regions within England.

It has been determined that under 18 conceptions were not reflective of population density or the urban-rural classification due to weak correlations.

Ideas for further work looking at under 18 conceptions and measures of deprivation include, but are not limited to:

• Looking at other datasets associated with deprivation.

• Undertaking multivariate analysis: looking at the interconnectedness of relationships of deprivation factors and under 18 conceptions through statistical modelling.

• Establish why the east-west divide exists.

• Establishing why London is not as strongly correlated as other regions when looking at under 18 conceptions and the percentage of children living in poverty or unemployment rates, to see if lessons can be learnt both for London and other regions.

• Examine how workless households, economic inactivity and economy composition impact on under 18 conception rates.

• Undertaking local authority analysis using sub-local authority data.

Annex 1

Annex 1 - Measures of deprivation included in the Conceptions-Deprivation Analysis Toolkit

Dataset	Time Period	Geography	Source
Under 18 conceptions	1998-2010 single year data, 2008-10 three year aggregated data	Country (England and Wales), Region, Local Authority, County District	ONS
Under 16 conceptions	2008-2010 three year aggregated data	Country (England and Wales), Region, Local Authority, County District	ONS
Urban-Rural Classification	Based on Census 2001 population estimates	Country (England), Region, Local Authority, County District	ONS
Population density	2008-2010 single year data, 2008-10 three year averaged data	Country (England and Wales), Region, Local Authority, County District	ONS
Indices of Multiple Deprivation (Overall)	2010	Local Authority, County District	ONS
Indices of Multiple Deprivation (Income)	2010	Local Authority, County District	ONS
Indices of Multiple Deprivation (Employment)	2010	Local Authority, County District	ONS
Percentage of children living in poverty	2008-2010 single year data, 2008-10 three year averaged data	Country (England), Region, Local Authority, County District, new unitary authorities	HM Revenue & Customs (HMRC)
GCSE results	2007/2008, 2008/2009, 2009/2010 single year data , 2007/2008-2009/2010 averaged data	Country (England), Region, Local Authority, County District, new unitary authorities	Department for Education
GCSE results for free school meal pupils	2007/2008, 2008/2009, 2009/2010 single year,	Country (England), Region, Local Authority,	Department for Education

Dataset	Time Period	Geography	Source
	2007/2008-2009/2010 averaged data	County District, new unitary authorities	
Unemployment	2008-2010 single year data, 2008-10 three year averaged data	Country (England and Wales), Region, Local Authority, County District	ONS
Economic Inactivity	2008-2010 single year data, 2008-10 three year averaged data	Country (England and Wales), Region, Local Authority, County District	ONS
Housing all tax bands	2008-2010 single year data, 2008-10 three year aggregated data	Country (England and Wales), Region, Local Authority, County District, new unitary authorities	Valuation Office Agency, HMRC
Housing tax band A	2008-2010 single year data, 2008-10 three year aggregated data	Country (England and Wales), Region, Local Authority, County District, new unitary authorities	Valuation Office Agency, HMRC
Percentage of dwellings in tax band A	2008-2010 three year aggregated data	Country (England and Wales), Region, Local Authority, County District, new unitary authorities	ONS calculations on data from Valuation Office Agency, HMRC
Social rented housing	2008/2009, 2009/2010, 2010/2011 single year data and 2008/2009-2010/2011 aggregated data	Country (England), Region, Local Authority, County District, new unitary authorities	Department for Communities and Local Government
Lone parent benefits	November 2008, November 2009, November 2010 single year data, 2008-2010 three year averaged data	Country (England and Wales), Region, Local Authority, County District, new unitary authorities	Department for Work and Pensions
Crime (total and by category)	2008-2010 single year data, 2008-10 three year aggregated data	Local Authority, County District, new unitary authorities	Home Office

Dataset	Time Period	Geography	Source
Population	Mid year estimates for 2008, 2009, 2010, 2008-2010 three year aggregated data	Country (England and Wales), Region, Local Authority, County District	ONS
Statistical neighbours		Country (England and Wales), Region, Local Authority, County District	ONS

Annex 2

Risk factors associated with becoming a teenage parent[1]

The following is a list of potential risk factors, these indicate an increased risk of becoming a teenage parent, they do not mean that you will necessarily become a teenage parent if you experience one or more of these factors. These include:

• Being a child of a teenage parent.

• Being a teenage parent already.

• Being a young women who accesses termination services.

• Living in poverty/areas of high deprivation.

• Having low educational attainment and/or disengagement from school.

• Being in or leaving care.

• Having a history of running away from home.

• Being exposed to inappropriate sexual activities.

• Being sexually abused or exploited.

• Having low self-esteem, poor emotional health and/or self harm.

• Having low aspirations and expectations.

• Having inadequate family support including domestic abuse.

• Misusing alcohol and/or drugs.

• Having multiple sexual partners.

• Having early onset of sexual activity (under 16 years old).

• Being involved in youth offending.

- Engaging in risky sexual behaviour.

- Being sexually active but not accessing contraception.

- Being vulnerable to sexual exploitation.

- Demonstrating inappropriate sexual behaviour.

- Being the victim of a sexual assault.

- Having child-protection concerns and multi agency involvement with the young person/family.

Young people with multiple risk factors and/or chaotic lifestyles are those deemed to be most at risk.

Notes

1.   Source: Wigan Teenage Pregnancy Strategy Implementation Plan 2009/10.

Annex 3

Risk factors for those born to teenage mothers[1]

The following are a list of possible outcomes. Being born to a teenage mother does not necessarily mean that any of these outcomes will be experienced. These include:

- Having a low birth weight.

- Having congenital anomalies.

- Having low life expectancy.

- Having low life expectations.

- Having lower educational achievement.

- Growing up in poverty.

- Having an increased likelihood of infant mortality.

- Having an increased likelihood of behavioural problems.

- Not having their father involved in their life due to relationship breakdown.

Notes

1.   Sourced from:

1. Department for Education and Skills, 2006, 'Teenage Pregnancy Next Steps: Guidance for Local Authorities and Primary Care Trusts on Effective Delivery of Local Strategies'

2. Swann C, Bowe K, McCormick G and Kosmin M, 2003, 'Teenage pregnancy and parenthood: a review of reviews', Health Development Agency

3. Botting B, Rosato M and Wood R, 1998, 'Teenage mothers and the health of their children', Population Trends 93, pp 19 –28

4. Hofferth SL and Reid L Early, 2002, 'Childbearing and Children's Achievement and Behaviour over Time', Perspectives on Sexual and Reproductive Health 34, No1, pp 41–9

Background notes

2. Details of the policy governing the release of new data are available by visiting www.statisticsauthority.gov.uk/assessment/code-of-practice/index.html or from the Media Relations Office email: media.relations@ons.gsi.gov.uk

Copyright

Size of Firms in London, 2001 to 2012

Author Name(s): **Sarah Levy and James Harris, Office for National Statistics (ONS)**

Abstract

This article presents analysis of numbers of workplaces and employees in London and its 33 local authorities, broken down by enterprise size band and SIC 2007 industry sector, for the period 2001 to 2012. The figures are calculated using data from the Inter-Departmental Business Register (IDBR). Although workplaces and employees are counted at local level, the methodology uses enterprise size bands that are based on numbers of employees working for the enterprise in the UK as a whole. Thus it is possible answer questions like 'How many employees work for large retailers in Tower Hamlets?' and 'How has this changed over the past decade?'

Introduction

Local planners and policy makers need information about businesses. The kinds of questions they ask are: How many businesses are there in my area? What sector of the economy do they belong to? Are they large or small? How many people do they provide employment for? How has the picture changed over time?

The first part of this article (**Part 1: Methodology**) explains how we have developed a way to address these questions, and the challenges involved. The second part (**Part 2: Results**) presents key results for London and each of its 33 local authorities over the period 2001-12, accompanied by a series of charts and maps. In the third part (**Part 3: Next steps**) we outline further analysis that will be published shortly and future work.

Part 1: Methodology

Background

In 2008, Greater London Authority (GLA) Economics published a working paper entitled Employment in London by firm size (Prothero, 2008) which proposed a new method for analysing official statistics on the size structure of firms in London and other parts of the UK. The paper pointed out that official sources such as the Small- and Medium-Sized Enterprise (SME) statistics of the Department for Business Innovation and Skills (BIS) and the business statistics publications of the Office for National Statistics (ONS) present different figures on this topic, but none of them meet the policy and planning requirements of organisations like the GLA.

The 2008 GLA Economics paper proposed a new approach based on the ONS's Inter-Departmental Business Register (IDBR). The IDBR is a statistical register based on administrative sources and surveys which contains information on businesses in all parts of the economy. It covers nearly all of UK economic activity including that of public sector bodies (which are not – strictly speaking – businesses). An organisation will be on the IDBR if it is registered for Value Added Tax (VAT), and/ or pays employees through a Pay As You Earn (PAYE) scheme and/or is an incorporated business registered at Companies House[1]. Some very small businesses, self-employed people and non-profit-making organisations are not on the IDBR as they are not registered in any of these ways.

BIS has developed a methodology for estimating 'unregistered' businesses using self-employment data from ONS's Labour Force Survey[2]. Such information can be added to the IDBR data if an analysis of total employment is required. However, the approach presented in this article focuses on numbers of employees (rather than total employment) and workplaces of registered businesses.

The information about employees on the IDBR is drawn mainly from the Business Register and Employment Survey (BRES). Estimates from other ONS surveys are also included. For the smallest businesses, either PAYE jobs or figures imputed from VAT turnover are used.

The IDBR database is organised on two levels: one dataset contains enterprise-level information while the other has information about 'local units' (the physical locations or workplaces which make up the enterprise). In the case of a small business, the enterprise and the local unit may be the same thing, but large enterprises may have many local units. For instance, a supermarket chain would appear in the enterprise-level dataset as employing several thousand people, and the entire workforce would be recorded at the address where the enterprise is registered. By contrast, in the 'local unit' dataset, the supermarket chain's workforce will be recorded where people actually work, both at the head office and in the local branches. Adding up numbers of employees in all of the locations of the business recorded on the local unit database gives the employee figure on the enterprise-level database.

From the point of view of local planners and policy makers, a combination of enterprise-level and local unit level information from the IDBR is needed. This is because workers need to be counted in the location where they work (their workplaces) but they would normally be thought of as working for a 'large firm' if their branch were part of an enterprise that employs many people nationally, even if their own workplace was a small one.

The methodology developed for the 2008 paper by GLA Economics combined enterprise-level and local unit level information from the IDBR. First it created 'enterprise size bands' based on numbers of employees working for the enterprise in the UK as a whole. Then it produced analysis of numbers of people employed by local units in London within these enterprise size bands.

This analysis was further split by industry sector (the part of the economy that the business belongs to). The results showed, for example, how many employees work for SMEs in the retail sector in London. Industry sector could be defined either on the basis of the enterprise (reflecting the predominant activity of the whole firm), or at local level (reflecting the activity of the workplace). For the analysis presented in this article, we have chosen the latter approach (see **Definitions**). If the figures for employees working in local retailing units of all sizes in London are added up, they give the total number of employees in the retail sector in London.

It should be noted, however, that the IDBR does not provide official estimates of numbers of employees in the UK. These are published in ONS's monthly Labour Market Statistics series (see **References**). ONS also recommends using the BRES for detailed industry sector and geographical breakdowns of official employee statistics.

Recent developments

In 2013, at the request of the GLA, ONS's London Region Office undertook to develop the methodology proposed by the 2008 GLA Economics paper with a view to creating a standardised approach that could be used in future, and could be replicated for other parts of the UK. A particular emphasis of this work has been to produce figures for local authorities and smaller areas within London and to provide a time series as far back as possible. The earliest year for which IDBR datasets are available is 2001.

The need for results for small geographical areas has proved challenging because of the requirement to protect the confidentiality of the IDBR data. This means making sure that it is impossible for users to identify a particular business from the published results, in practice by suppressing results where there are too few local units or one 'dominant' local unit. This is more likely to happen when analysing results in small geographical areas than when looking at London or the UK as a whole (see below: **Protecting confidentiality**).

It is possible to present information for local authorities in London broken down by industry sector with relatively low levels of suppression. It is also possible to present results for the small areas known as 'Middle-layer Super Output Areas' (MSOAs) which nest within local authorities[3], but when the analysis team tried producing breakdowns for MSOAs by industry sector most of the results had to be suppressed. Therefore, MSOA-level information, which will be published shortly (see **Part 3: Next steps**), will not contain industry sector breakdowns.

Definitions

The following definitions have been adopted for the purpose of this work:

Enterprise size bands. Local units are placed in size bands according to the number of employees working for the business/organisation in the UK as a whole (the 'enterprise'). These are referred to as enterprise size bands. The standard definition of a SME (used by the UK government and the EU[4]) is an enterprise with fewer than 250 employees. For the purpose of this project, the full set of enterprise size bands are as follows, with enterprises in the first four bands being SMEs:

1. zero employees (the business has one or more owners/proprietors but no employees)
2. 1-9 employees
3. 10-49 employees
4. 50-249 employees
5. 250-499 employees
6. 500 to 2,499 employees
7. 2,500+ employees

The full set of enterprise size bands can be analysed at London level, but for lower geographies it is necessary to combine size bands. The simplest breakdown is two categories: (i) SMEs made up of size bands 1-4 and (ii) large enterprises made up of bands 5-7. SMEs with fewer than 10 employees (size bands 1-2) are known as 'micro' enterprises; these include enterprises which do not have any employees.

Industry sectors. The industry sectors used for this analysis are:

- Primary and utilities
- Manufacturing
- Construction
- Wholesale and motor trades
- Retail
- Transportation and storage
- Accommodation and food service activities
- Information and communication
- Financial and insurance activities
- Real estate activities
- Professional, scientific and technical
- Administrative and support service activities
- Public administration and defence; compulsory social security
- Education
- Human health and social work activities
- Arts, entertainment and recreation
- Other service activities

These sectors are based on ONS's Standard Industrial Classification 2007 (SIC07) sections (also known as '1-digit' classifications). However, some sections have been combined and one has been split in response to GLA requirements[5].

We have chosen to define industry sector based on the economic activity of the local unit (reflecting the activity of the workplace) rather than that of the enterprise (reflecting the predominant activity of the whole firm). This is because the activity of the local unit is of most interest to local planners and policy makers. Users should note, however, that there may be substantial differences between the two approaches if enterprises have workplaces that carry out different economic activities. In addition, under SIC07 head office activities are identified separately at local unit level and appear in the professional, scientific and technical sector. For instance, in this analysis employees working at the head office of a manufacturing company would be appear in the professional, scientific and technical sector rather than in the manufacturing sector.

For years before 2009, it has been necessary to convert the IDBR data from the bases on which it was collected (SIC92 and SIC03) onto a SIC07 basis to allow comparability over the whole time series. Caution should be exercised in interpreting the pre-2009 industry sector breakdowns because the conversion process relies on modelling, which is based on assumptions (see **Appendix 1**). Also, we believe that the conversion process does not fully account for changes in the treatment of head office activities before the introduction of SIC07. This means that particular caution is advised when looking at pre-2009 results for places where head office activity is important (see

Appendix 1). For both of these reasons, the pre-2009 industry sector breakdowns on a SIC07 basis that are presented in this article and the accompanying data tables should be treated as experimental statistics, even though the underlying data (collected on SIC92 and SIC03 bases) is a National Statistic.

Geography. Geographical location is defined at local unit (workplace) level. For instance, when reporting on the number of employees working in Havering, the numbers refer only to people who work at locations in Havering. If a firm has its headquarters in Havering but half of its employees are based at a workplace in Redbridge, the employees working in Redbridge are not included in the Havering results but are included in the Redbridge results.

Empty premises. For the purposes of the IDBR analysis presented in this paper and accompanying tables, local units with no employment have been removed on the grounds that these units are 'empty premises', not workplaces. In 2012, this reduced the total number of local units in London by 0.6% compared with the standard IDBR tables available on the ONS website (see **References**).

Protecting confidentiality

As already mentioned, the ONS is required to protect the confidentiality of the IDBR data. In areas where there are few firms or a 'dominant' firm, if results were to be published it might be possible for users to infer how many people were employed by a particular business. Although numbers of people employed is not generally seen as commercially sensitive, it is a legal requirement for ONS to protect this information because it has been provided in confidence by the businesses concerned.

For this analysis, four steps have been taken to ensure that confidentiality is protected. Results are suppressed if:

1. There are fewer than 5 local units in any cell of a table (primary suppression).
2. One local unit is dominant in any cell and it might therefore be possible for a reader to work out which that local unit was (primary suppression).
3. Results in other parts of a table or set of tables allow readers to work out the results that have been removed during primary suppression. This involves removing information that does not need to be suppressed in its own right but could be used to deduce suppressed results (secondary suppression).

In addition, as a fourth step, results for numbers of local units are rounded to the nearest 5 and results for numbers of employees are rounded to the nearest 100. This also helps to protect confidentiality.

Comparisons with other data sources

Most of the publications that are currently available on this topic – such as the BIS SME statistics and ONS's business statistics – do not use the definition of enterprise size adopted here. Therefore our results (see **Part 2: Results**) are not comparable with them. However, employment data from ONS's BRES will soon be available on NOMIS on a similar basis as our analysis, with enterprise size band defined at the level of the UK as a whole.

ONS generally recommends BRES as the definitive source of official employee statistics for detailed analysis by industry sector and small geographical areas. However, for this analysis we have chosen to use the IDBR because it is possible construct a time series from 2001 to 2012, whereas BRES data is only available for 2009, 2010 and 2011. Also, for the BRES data published on NOMIS, enterprise size bands are expected to be based on the total number of people employed (including owner/proprietors). By contrast, the standard UK Government and EU definition of an SME is based on employee numbers (see above: **Definitions**).

Nevertheless, readers should be aware that BRES data will shortly be available on a similar basis, and that there are some differences between the results based on the IDBR and those based on BRES. Apart from the difference between the use of employee-based and employment-based size bands, these differences are mainly attributable to the following factors:

- The BRES is a survey, so it provides an up-to-date snapshot at a point in time (September each year). The IDBR is a register of businesses. The IDBR extracts used for this analysis are taken in March, but the employment information on them is drawn from the BRES of the previous September and from other ONS surveys. The IDBR is not updated in full every year because only a sample of enterprises is surveyed each year. Therefore the employment information on the IDBR relates to a variety of time periods.
- In the IDBR, much of the information on micro enterprises comes from PAYE records or is imputed from VAT turnover. It is for such enterprises that the differences between the IDBR and BRES estimates are greatest.

Notes

1. For further information, see www.ons.gov.uk/ons/about-ons/who-we-are/services/unpublished-data/business-data/idbr/index.html

2. See in **References**.

3. There are 983 MSOAs in London. For a description of this geography, see www.ons.gov.uk/ons/guide-method/geography/beginner-s-guide/census/super-output-areas--soas-/index.html

4. The EU legal definition, available at http://ec.europa.eu/enterprise/policies/sme/facts-figures-analysis/sme-definition/ also incorporates the turnover or balance sheet total of the business.

5. 'Primary and utilities' comprises four SIC07 sections:

    A: Agriculture, forestry and fishing;

    B: Mining and quarrying;

    D: Electricity, gas, steam and air conditioning supply;

    E: Water supply, sewerage, waste management and remediation activities.

    SIC07 section G: 'Wholesale and retail trade; repair of motor vehicles and motorcycles' has been split so that the retail sector is shown separately from wholesale and motor trades. Further information on SIC07 is available at www.ons.gov.uk/ons/guide-method/classifications/current-standard-classifications/standard-industrial-classification/index.html

Part 2: Results

The information presented in this section is based on analysis of 'local units', or workplaces. Workplaces may belong to private sector businesses or to public sector or not-for-profit organisations. Workplaces are allocated to enterprise size bands according to the number of employees working for the business/organisation in the UK as a whole (see above: **Definitions**).

The analysis looks at numbers of workplaces and numbers of employees in London and its 33 local authorities. These two variables are classified according to enterprise size bands and which industry sector (or part of the economy) they belong to.

Size of firms in London

Chart 1 shows that the number of workplaces in London rose from 366,290 in 2001 to 414,375 in 2012. There were decreases in the early 2000s and in 2010-11. The number rose in 2012, but the magnitude of the increase is overstated in the figures, as improvements to HM Revenue and Customs computer systems lead to the inclusion in 2012 of businesses that had not previously been recorded on the register. The pattern was similar in the UK as a whole, where the number of workplaces rose from 2.4 million to 2.6 million over this period.

The growth in the number of workplaces was accompanied by growth in numbers of employees between 2001 and 2012. According to the IDBR, the number of employees rose from 3.6 million to 4.2 million in London and from 23.9 million to 26.8 million in the UK, with slower growth or downturns in the early 2000s and in 2010-11. It should be noted that the IDBR figures are not official estimates of numbers of employees in London and the UK. These are published in ONS's monthly Labour Market Statistics series (see **References**).

Chart 1: Number of workplaces and employees in London, 2001-12

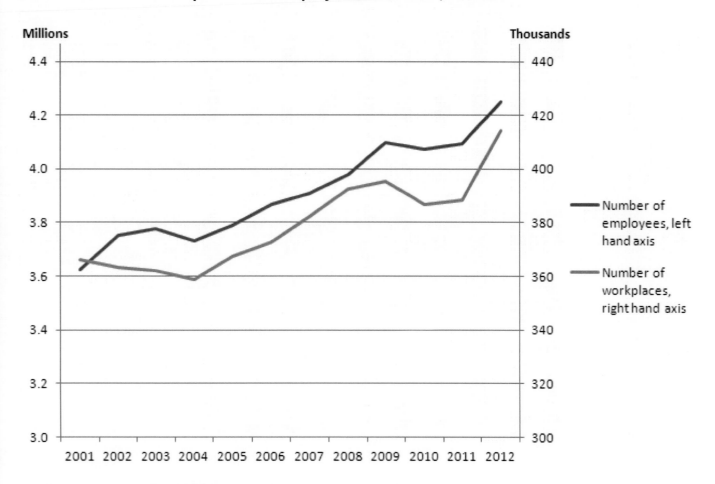

Source: Office for National Statistics

Notes:

1. Local units with zero employment and enterprises with zero employment have been excluded from this analysis.
2. The large increase in numbers of workplaces between 2011 and 2012 should be treated with caution. At UK level, nearly half of the increase (31,000 of 68,000 enterprises) was attributable to improvements to HM Revenue & Customs computer systems leading to previously excluded businesses being added to the IDBR.

Chart 2 shows that the proportion of SME workplaces in London has remained steady since 2001 at 88-89% of all workplaces. The proportion of SME workplaces is slightly lower in the UK as a whole than in London: it was around 85-86% over this period.

Workplaces belonging to large firms (with 250 or more employees) comprised 11-12% of workplaces in London between 2001 and 2012. Most of these were associated with enterprises with 2,500 or more employees.

Chart 2: Proportion of workplaces in London by enterprise size band, 2001-12

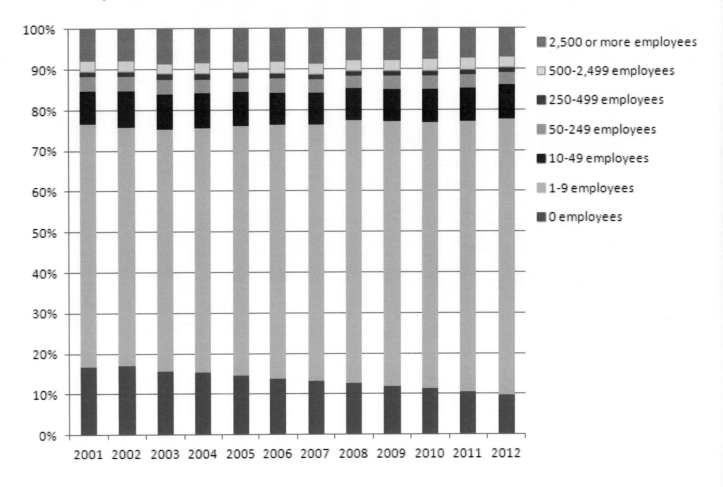

Source: Office for National Statistics

Notes:
1.   Local units with zero employment and enterprises with zero employment have been excluded from this analysis.

Most SME workplaces belong to micro enterprises (those with fewer than 10 employees): in 2012, 87% of SME workplaces in London were associated with micro enterprises. Within this category, the proportion with zero employees fell over this period, while the proportion with 1-9 employees rose. This is understood to be because of the increasing propensity for sole traders to register as limited companies because of the legal and commercial advantages available and because registration has become easier over the past decade. When a sole trader sets up as a limited company, they are recorded as an employee of that company rather than as an owner/proprietor.

Chart 3 shows the proportion of employees in London working for different sizes of enterprise. Although SME workplaces comprise nearly 90% of workplaces in London, only two-fifths of employees work for an SME. Over three-quarters of London's workplaces belong to micro enterprises, but micro enterprises provided work for only 15% of its employees in 2012. Most employees work for large enterprises, and almost four out of ten employees in London work for a firm employing 2,500 or more employees. The proportions are similar for the UK as a whole.

Chart 3: Proportion of employees in London by enterprise size band, 2001-12

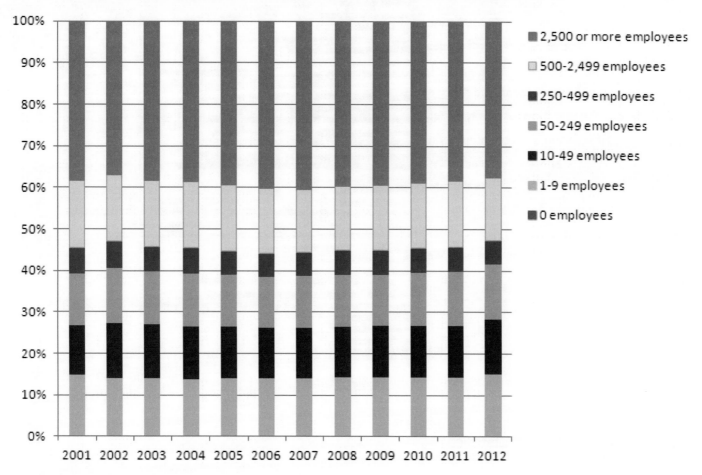

Source: Office for National Statistics

Notes:

1. Local units with zero employment and enterprises with zero employment have been excluded from this analysis.

Chart 4: Number of employees in London, by industry sector: 2002, 2007 and 2012

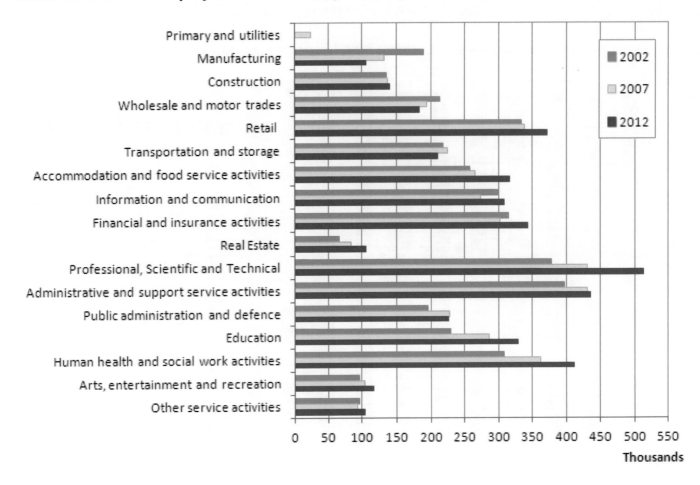

Source: Office for National Statistics

Notes:

1. Results which appear to be zeros in the above chart may be values which have been suppressed for disclosure control. Please refer to the data table.
2. Local units with zero employment and enterprises with zero employment have been excluded from this analysis.
3. The industrial sectors presented are based upon the UK Standard Industrial Classification (SIC) 2007, with two changes: sectors A, B, D and E have been combined to create new classification 'Primary and utilities'; and sector G has been split, where divisions 45 and 46 combine to form 'Wholesale and motor trades' while division 47 forms 'Retail'. Further information on SIC 2007 can be found at www.ons.gov.uk/ons/guide-method/classifications/current-standard-classifications/standard-industrial-classification/index.html
4. Data prior to 2009 has been converted from SIC 1992 and SIC 2003 onto SIC 2007 to provide a consistent time series. See Appendix 1 for more details.

Chart 4 shows that in 2012, the top five industry sectors in London in terms of where employees worked were the professional, scientific and technical sector, the administrative and support services sector, the human health and social work sector, the retail sector, and financial and insurance activities. Nearly half of all employees in London worked in one of these sectors. The biggest increases in numbers of employees over the decade to 2012 were in real estate activities, education, and health and social work activities. Numbers also appear to have risen in the professional, scientific and technical sector, but much of this is likely to be due to improved classification of head office activities over this period. It has not been possible to capture this classification change fully in our time series (see **Chart 6** below and **Appendix 1**).

Chart 5 shows that most industry sectors saw little change in the proportion of employees working for SMEs over the decade to 2012. The main exception was the education sector, which saw a sharp increase. It should be noted that an increase in the proportion of employees working for SMEs does not necessarily imply that there are more SMEs or that SMEs are expanding; it may be because large businesses have been broken up or closed down. In the case of the education sector, it may also reflect changes in government policy.

Overall, the industry sector with the highest proportion of employees in SMEs in 2012 was 'other service activities' (74%), while the sector with the lowest proportion (2%) was public administration and defence.

Chart 5: Proportion of London's employees working in SMEs, by industry sector: 2002, 2007 and 2012

Source: Office for National Statistics

Notes:

1. Results which appear to be zeros in the above chart may be values which have been suppressed for disclosure control. Please refer to the data table.

2. Local units with zero employment and enterprises with zero employment have been excluded from this analysis.

3. The industrial sectors presented are based upon the UK Standard Industrial Classification (SIC) 2007, with two changes: sectors A, B, D and E have been combined to create new classification 'Primary and utilities'; and sector G has been split, where divisions 45 and 46 combine to form 'Wholesale and motor trades' while division 47 forms 'Retail'. Further information on SIC 2007 can be found at www.ons.gov.uk/ons/guide-method/classifications/current-standard-classifications/standard-industrial-classification/index.html

4. Data prior to 2009 has been converted from SIC 1992 and SIC 2003 onto SIC 2007 to provide a consistent time series. See Appendix 1 for more details.

Size of firms in London's local authorities

ONS is publishing detailed tables for London's local authorities alongside this article (see below: **Data available with this publication**). This section provides examples of the analysis that can be produced using these tables by looking at a selection of industry sectors and local authorities.

Chart 6 shows the ten local authorities in London with the largest number of employees in the professional, scientific and technical sector in 2012. In terms of where employees work, this was the largest industry sector in London in 2012, with 513,700 employees. It should be noted that there are also many self-employed people working in this sector, but they are not covered by this analysis.

The professional, scientific and technical sector includes legal and accounting firms, management consultancies, architectural and engineering firms, scientific research bodies and advertising/market research firms. It also includes head offices of firms whose main activity may be in other industry sectors. In some London local authorities, employees working at head offices accounted for a large proportion of those working in the professional, scientific and technical sector in 2012 (for instance 19% in Westminster and 43% in Hillingdon, see **Appendix 1**).

Chart 6 does not show figures for earlier years. This is because comparisons over time may be misleading for the professional, scientific and technical sector in some local authorities because the process of converting the IDBR data from SIC92 and SIC03 onto a SIC07 basis (see **Definitions**) does not fully capture changes in the treatment of head office activities before the introduction of SIC07. Therefore, employees of head offices may be recorded in other sectors before 2009, and numbers of employees in the professional, scientific and technical sector are likely to be underestimated.

The proportion of employees in the professional, scientific and technical sector working for SMEs varies considerably between local authorities. For instance, in 2012 it was 60% in Westminster but only 36% in the City of London.

Chart 6: Top ten London local authorities by number of employees in the professional, scientific and technical sector, 2012

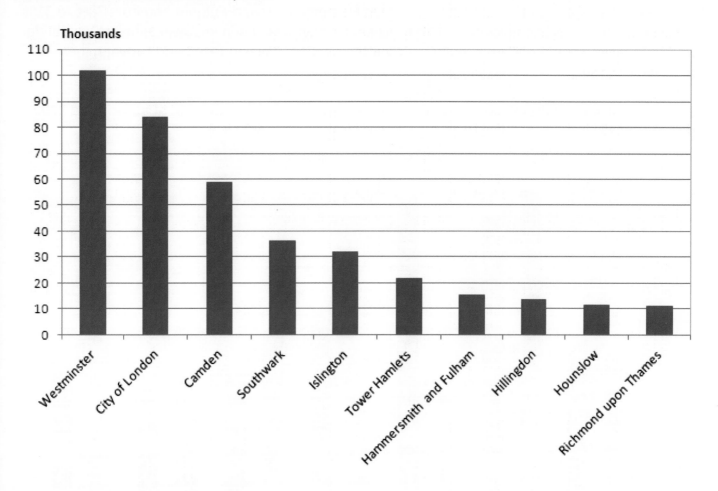

Source: Office for National Statistics

Notes:

1. Local units with zero employment and enterprises with zero employment have been excluded from this analysis.
2. The industrial sectors presented are based upon the UK Standard Industrial Classification (SIC) 2007, which can be found at www.ons.gov.uk/ons/guide-method/classifications/current-standard-classifications/standard-industrial-classification/index.html

While jobs in the professional, scientific and technical sector are concentrated in certain local authorities, in retailing they are more evenly spread across London. With the exception of Westminster, where there were 57,500 employees working in the retail sector, the number of employees in each local authority in 2012 ranged from 4,000 in Barking and Dagenham to 20,200 in Kensington and Chelsea.

Chart 7 shows how the numbers of employees have changed in the retail sector in selected local authorities over the past decade. There have been big increases in Hammersmith and Fulham and in Newham (probably linked to the opening of the Westfield shopping centres). In both these boroughs, the increase in numbers of employees has been accompanied by a decrease in the proportion working for SMEs, from 51% to 27% in Hammersmith and Fulham and from 38% to 31% in Newham. Numbers of employees in the retail sector have also risen in Tower Hamlets. Redbridge and Sutton have seen a decline in numbers over the decade, while in Brent and Croydon there has been little change.

Chart 7: Number of employees in the retail sector in selected London local authorities 2002, 2007 and 2012

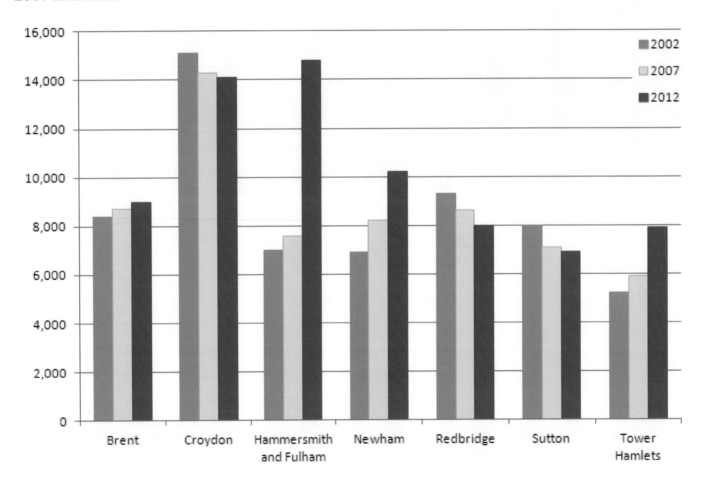

Source: Office for National Statistics

Notes:
1. Local units with zero employment and enterprises with zero employment have been excluded from this analysis.
2. The industrial sectors presented are based upon the UK Standard Industrial Classification (SIC) 2007, which can be found at www.ons.gov.uk/ons/guide-method/classifications/current-standard-classifications/standard-industrial-classification/index.html
3. Data prior to 2009 has been converted from SIC 1992 and SIC 2003 onto SIC 2007 to provide a consistent time series. See Appendix 1 for more details.

Financial and insurance activity takes place mainly in three London local authorities: City of London (with 151,300 employees in 2012), Tower Hamlets (with 75,200) and Westminster (with 37,900). Chart 8 shows that each of these local authorities has a different profile in terms of numbers of employees working for large firms in the financial and insurance sector, and that these patterns have been diverging over the past decade. There has been increasing concentration in the City and Tower Hamlets (where 76% and 94% of employees respectively worked for large enterprises in 2012), while the opposite has been happening in Westminster (where only 39% worked for large enterprises in 2012).

Chart 8: Proportion of employees in large enterprises in the financial and insurance sector in selected London local authorities: 2002, 2007 and 2012

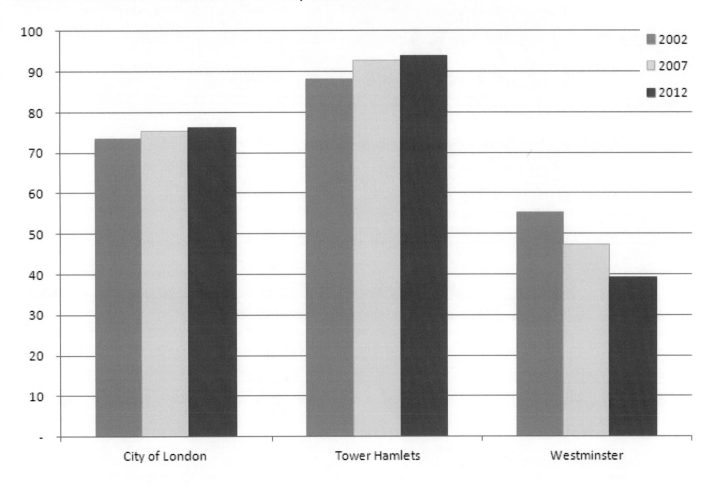

Source: Office for National Statistics

Notes:

1. Local units with zero employment and enterprises with zero employment have been excluded from this analysis.
2. The industrial sectors presented are based upon the UK Standard Industrial Classification (SIC) 2007, which can be found at www.ons.gov.uk/ons/guide-method/classifications/current-standard-classifications/standard-industrial-classification/index.html
3. Data prior to 2009 has been converted from SIC 1992 and SIC 2003 onto SIC 2007 to provide a consistent time series. See Appendix 1 for more details.

Map 9: Number of employees in SMEs in London's accommodation and food services sector, 2012

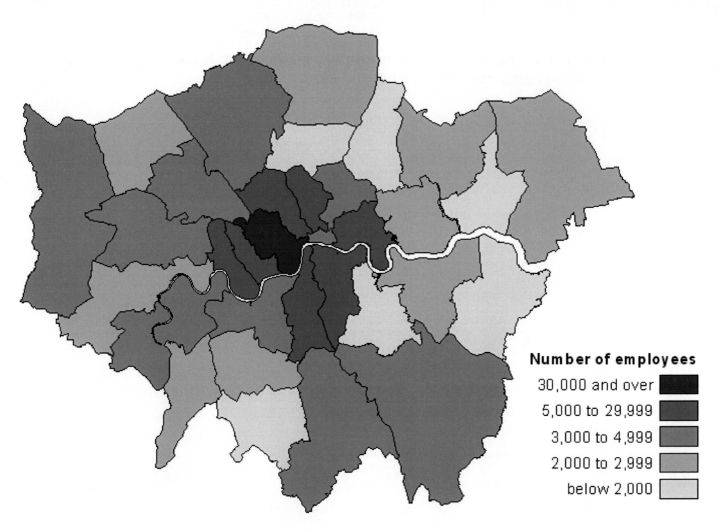

Number of employees

30,000 and over ■
5,000 to 29,999 ■
3,000 to 4,999 ■
2,000 to 2,999 ■
below 2,000 □

Source: Office for National Statistics

Notes:

1.   Local units with zero employment and enterprises with zero employment have been excluded from this analysis.

It is also possible to show this kind of information on maps. Maps 9 and 10 show the distribution of employees working for SMEs and large enterprises in London's accommodation and food services sector in 2012. In Westminster, there were large numbers of employees working for both SMEs and large enterprises. In the City of London, large enterprises were the main employers, with over

10,000 employees in 2012; there were fewer than 5,000 employees working for SMEs. By contrast, an employee working in Hammersmith and Fulham or in Southwark in 2012 would be more likely to have been working for an SME than a large firm.

Map 10: Number of employees in large enterprises in London's accommodation and food services sector, 2012

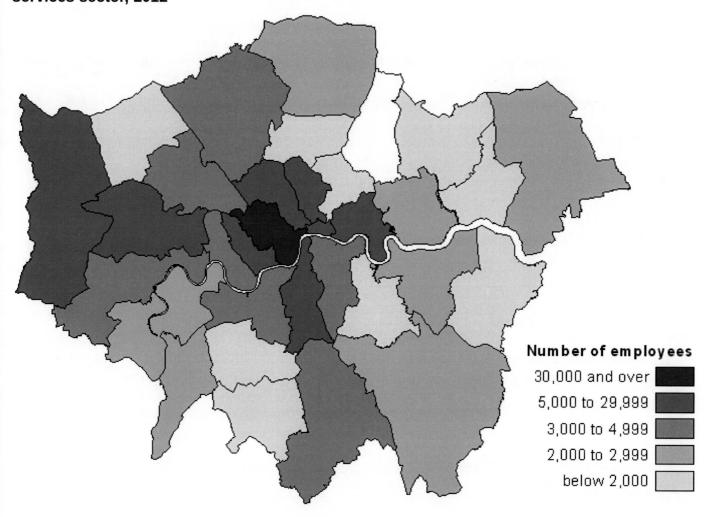

Number of employees

30,000 and over	■
5,000 to 29,999	■
3,000 to 4,999	■
2,000 to 2,999	■
below 2,000	□

Source: Office for National Statistics

Notes:

1. Local units with zero employment and enterprises with zero employment have been excluded from this analysis.

Data available with this publication

The data tables published with this article present breakdowns of IDBR data at London level and for each local authority within London. UK figures are also shown for comparison. The tables show numbers of workplaces and numbers of employees by enterprise size band and by industry sector. They answer the questions: How many businesses are there in my area? What sector of the economy do they belong to? Are they large or small? How many people do they provide employment for? How has the picture changed over time?

The following tables are available with this publication for 2001 to 2012:

Workbook entitled 'Size of firms in London and the UK by enterprise size':

- Table 1: Number of workplaces in the UK and London by size of enterprise, 2001-2012 (all seven enterprise size bands)
- Table 2: Number of employees in the UK and London by size of enterprise, 2001-2012 (all seven enterprise size bands)
- Table 3: Number of workplaces in the UK, by industry sector and by size of enterprise, 2001-2012 (three bands: <10, 10-249 and 250+ employees)
- Table 4: Number of employees in the UK, by industry sector and by size of enterprise, 2001-2012 (three bands: <10, 10-249 and 250+ employees)
- Table 5: Number of workplaces in London, by industry sector and by size of enterprise, 2001-2012 (three bands: <10, 10-249 and 250+ employees)
- Table 6: Number of employees in London, by industry sector and by size of enterprise, 2001-2012 (three bands: <10, 10-249 and 250+ employees)

Workbook entitled 'Size of firms in London local authorities by enterprise size':

- Number of workplaces and employees by enterprise size band (three bands: <10, 10-249 and 250+ employees) and by industry sector for each of the 33 London local authorities

Notes

1. For further information, see www.ons.gov.uk/ons/about-ons/who-we-are/services/unpublished-data/business-data/idbr/index.html

Part 3: Next steps

More analysis

ONS will publish another article on 8 August 2013 entitled Small and Large Firms in London, 2001 to 2012. This will contain the following analysis of MSOAs in London for 2001 to 2012:

- Number of workplaces by enterprise size band (two bands: <250 and 250+ employees) for each MSOA in London
- Number of employees by enterprise size band (two bands: <250 and 250+ employees) for each MSOA in London

Future work

Now that a standardised approach to producing analysis by enterprise size band from IDBR data exists, similar analyses could be undertaken for other parts of the UK. It would also be possible for local planners and policy makers to add estimates for the self employed to the IDBR figures, following the methodology developed by BIS (see **Part 1: Methodology**).

Better geographies

Until recently, the only low-level geographies available to analysts were based on political boundaries, such as parliamentary constituencies, or on administrative boundaries, such as local authorities, or on where people live[1]. None of these approaches is designed for analysing business data such as that contained in the IDBR. However, ONS has recently published a new classification known as 'Census Workplace Zones', which is based on information about where people work from the 2011 Census. This provides the foundation for improving geographical analysis of businesses.

The Census Workplace Zones are very small, so they cannot be used for IDBR analysis without compromising confidentiality. Nevertheless, it should also be possible to group Census Workplace Zones together to create larger business zones for which results can be presented. This is a key challenge for the future.

Different researchers may group the Census Workplace Zones together in different ways, reflecting different requirements. However, this could create problems because once results have been published for one grouping, other groupings may no longer be possible. This is because if there are overlaps between different groupings, publication of results might compromise confidentiality since information about particular businesses could be deduced by comparing the results. To prevent this happening, standardised groupings of Census Workplace Zones are needed, like those which are already available for geographies based on where people live. A project is now under way, coordinated by ONS Geography, to create such standardised groupings.

In putting together the groupings, this project must take into account the need for the areas to be suitable for analysing other business statistics sources such as the Annual Survey of Hours and Earnings (ASHE) and the BRES as well as the IDBR. It must also take into account the probable needs of different types of user, from policy makers and planners to academics and members of the business community. Furthermore, it must take into account existing residential population-based groupings such as MSOAs. Therefore, this is a complex task which is likely to take time to achieve.

Notes

1. Geographical areas based on where people live are derived from the Census and include 'output areas' and 'super output areas' such as MSOAs. Further information can be found at www.ons.gov.uk/ons/guide-method/geography/beginner-s-guide/census/index.html

Background notes

1. Details of the policy governing the release of new data are available by visiting www.statisticsauthority.gov.uk/assessment/code-of-practice/index.html or from the Media Relations Office email: media.relations@ons.gsi.gov.uk

These National Statistics are produced to high professional standards and released according to the arrangements approved by the UK Statistics Authority.

Copyright

References

1. *Business Demography*, Office for National Statistics. Web page (all releases) available at www.ons.gov.uk/ons/rel/bus-register/business-demography/index.html

2. *Business Population Estimates 2010-2012*, Department for Business, Innovation and Skills (2012) Available at https://www.gov.uk/government/publications/bis-business-population-estimates

3. *Business Population Estimates for the UK and Regions, 2012: Methodology & Quality Note*, Department for Business, Innovation and Skills (2012). Available at https://www.gov.uk/government/publications/bis-business-population-estimates

4. Business Register Employment Survey (BRES), Office for National Statistics. Web page (all releases) available at www.ons.gov.uk/ons/publications/all-releases.html?definition=tcm:77-230512

5. BRES on NOMIS is available at www.nomisweb.co.uk

6. GSS Business Statistics – interactive users guide. Available at www.ons.gov.uk/ons/guide-method/understanding-ons-statistics/business-statistics---interactive-user-guide/index.html

7. Labour Market Statistics, Office for National Statistics: Monthly release available at www.ons.gov.uk/ons/taxonomy/index.html?nscl=Labour+Market

8. Prothero, R. (2008): *Employment in London by firm size*, GLA Economics Working Paper 31 published by Greater London Authority, May 2008. Available at www.london.gov.uk/mayor/economic_unit/docs/wp_31.pdf

9. *UK Business: Activity, Size and Location*, Office for National Statistics. The latest edition (2012) is available at www.ons.gov.uk/ons/rel/bus-register/uk-business/2012/index.html

10. *UK Business: Activity, Size and Location Methodology and Metadata*, 1 October 2012. Available at www.ons.gov.uk/ons/guide-method/method-quality/specific/business-and-energy/uk-business--activity--size-and-location/uk-business--activity--size-and-location-methodology-and-metadata.pdf (85.5 Kb Pdf)

Appendix 1: Creating a time series for breakdowns by industry sector

The IDBR datasets for 2001 to 2012 contain information that was collected each year on the basis of the UK Standard Industry Classification (SIC) that was in place at the time. For the 2001 and 2002 datasets, this was SIC92. For 2003 to 2008 it was SIC03. For 2009 to 2012 it was SIC07. This presents problems for users wishing to look at change over time. Therefore, the results presented here have been converted onto a consistent (SIC07) basis.

However, this means that all breakdowns by industry sector before 2009 contain an element of modelling (required for the conversions) and users should be aware of the assumptions used in this modelling. Also, we believe that the conversion process does not succeed in putting the classification of head office activities before 2009 onto a basis that is fully comparable with SIC07. This appendix explains how the conversion process was done and also discusses head office activities.

Creating SIC07-consistent industry sectors before 2009

Originally, the conversion was done in two stages, both using information at local unit level:

1. Data collected on a SIC92 basis was converted onto a SIC03 basis using a table showing the relationship between 5-digit SIC categories. This was relatively simple because the changes were between 4-or 5-digit SIC categories and had no impact at 1-digit level, which was the level at which the data was being analysed.
2. Data on a SIC03 basis (whether originally collected on this basis or converted from SIC92) was converted onto a SIC07 basis. This was complicated because the change from SIC03 to SIC07 affected a large number of lower-digit categories and had an impact at 1-digit level. The method used involved a lookup table and a weighted correlation table. This probability-based allocation process is described in detail below (see **Converting from SIC03 to SIC07**).

The results of all probability-based conversion processes are imperfect. In order to improve the outcome, we decided that if we had the SIC07 code of a local unit after SIC07 was introduced and this local unit had been in the dataset before then, we could use this information to 'backcast' SIC07 codes for previous years. The process we adopted was: if we knew what the SIC07 code of the local unit was in 2009 to 2011 and it was the same code in all three years, we assumed that this code could be allocated to the local unit (and its employees) in previous years if the local unit existed in those years.

Thus the final results are based on a combination of two methods: a) a probability-based process of conversion from SIC03, and b) 'backcasting' SIC07 codes. Table A1 shows the proportion of employees in London for whom industry sector before 2009 is the result of backcasting.

Table A1: How industry sector on SIC07 basis was calculated, London 2001-08

	2001	2002	2003	2004	2005	2006	2007	2008
% of employees for whom industry sector is backcast	38	42	49	53	58	62	66	70
% of employees for whom industry sector is based on conversion from SIC03	62	58	51	47	42	38	34	30

Converting from SIC03 to SIC07 using the probability-based allocation process

ONS provides two tools for converting data from SIC03 to SIC07. The spreadsheet 'Correlation between SIC 2003 and 2007' is a lookup table showing the relationship between each of the 5-digit SIC03 codes and their SIC07 equivalents. However, one SIC03 code may become several SIC07 codes and some SIC07 codes cover more than one SIC03 code. Therefore it is necessary to use the 'Weighted Tables with percentages SIC03 - SIC07' workbook, which shows what proportion of each SIC03 code will end up in the SIC07 code shown in the lookup table. This is provided separately for number of local units (count %), employment and turnover. We used count % and employment % at 5-digit level, with the latter being used as a proxy for employees.

To show how this works, take the example of a workplace which was in SIC03 5-digit code 01210 and had 100 employees. According to the correlation table (count %), this SIC03 code was split such that 74% was allocated to SIC07 code 01410 and 26% was allocated to SIC07 code 01420. Therefore the workplace was split such that it was counted as 0.74 units in category 01410, and 0.26 units in category 01420.

For producing analyses of the number of employees by industry sector, the conversion from SIC03 to SIC07 needed to use the employment % in the correlation table (rather than the count %) and this had to be applied to employees individually rather than to local units, which might contain several employees. Not doing so meant that sectors with larger workplaces ended up with a higher proportion of employees than they should, while those with smaller workplaces got a lower proportion. Extending the example, according to the correlation table (employment %), 71% of employment in SIC03 code 01210 was allocated to SIC07 code 01410, and 29% to code 01420. Therefore 71 of the 100 employees in the workplace would be allocated to 01410 and 29 employees would be allocated to 01420.

This complication meant that it was necessary to do the analysis of numbers of employees by industry sector separately from the analysis of number of local units by industry sector. Therefore, when interpreting tables by industry sector that use data converted from SIC03 (before 2009), the employees in a particular cell of the 'number of employees' table do not necessarily work for the local units in the equivalent cell of the 'number of workplaces' table. Conceptually, this is because a small number of records relating to local units with more than one employee will have been split between 5-digit SIC07 categories during the SIC03 to SIC07 conversion process.

Head office activities

During the analysis, we found evidence to suggest that the probability-based conversion process is not able to identify and convert all head office activities onto a SIC07 basis. The issue arises because originally, in SIC92, head offices were recorded against the principal activity of the firm to which they belonged (they had no separate SIC code). In SIC03, this approach was retained at enterprise level, but local units which were head offices were recorded under code 7415 (management activities of holding companies). In SIC07 activities of head offices were split out from those of holding companies and given a unique code (70100) which puts them into the professional, scientific and technical sector.

The process of converting data from SIC03 to SIC07 based on lookup and weighted correlation tables should, in theory, make it possible to convert from SIC03 code 7415 to SIC07 code 70100. However, the results indicate that this was not as successful as other parts of the conversion process. Moreover, it is not possible to convert head office information from data originally collected using SIC92 because head offices were not identified by a separate SIC code under SIC92.

Therefore, before 2009, numbers of employees in the professional, scientific and technical sector are likely to be underestimated and numbers in other industry sectors may be overestimated because employees of head offices may be recorded in other industry sectors rather than in the professional, scientific and technical sector. This means that caution is advised when looking at pre-2009 breakdowns by industry sector, especially in early years when much of the data is based on the probability-based conversion process rather than on 'backcasting' (see Table A1 above). This is particularly so in places where head office activity is important (see Table A2).

Table A2: Proportion of employees in the professional, scientific and technical sector who work in head offices, by London local authority, 2012

Local Authority	%
Hillingdon	43
Hounslow	20
Westminster	19
Kensington and Chelsea	18
Lambeth	18
Brent	13
Sutton	13
Tower Hamlets	9
Hammersmith and Fulham	9
Enfield	9
Croydon	8
Kingston upon Thames	8
Barking and Dagenham	8
Richmond upon Thames	7
Ealing	7
Merton	7
Greenwich	7
Hackney	5
Barnet	5
Islington	4
Havering	4
Camden	3
Southwark	3
Bromley	3
Harrow	3
Redbridge	3
City of London	2
Wandsworth	2
Newham	0
Haringey	0
Bexley	0
Lewisham	0
Waltham Forest	0

Table source: Office for National Statistics

Small and Large Firms in London, 2001 to 2012

Author Name(s): **Sarah Levy and James Harris, Office for National Statistics (ONS)**

Abstract

This article presents results for 983 small areas in London showing the number of employees working for enterprises with fewer than 250 employees in the UK (Small and Medium-sized Enterprises, or SMEs) and for enterprises with 250 or more employees (large enterprises). The analysis uses data from the Inter-Departmental Business Register for the period 2001-12. Results include proportions of employees working for SMEs and highlight some of the changes which have taken place since 2001. The article is accompanied by data tables showing numbers of workplaces and employees in each of the 983 small areas in London in 2001-12, broken down to show SMEs and large enterprises separately.

Introduction

This is the second release in a series of two articles on the size of firms in London. The first article, published on 19 July 2013, presented analysis of numbers of workplaces and employees in London, broken down by enterprise size and industry sector, for the period 2001 to 2012. It presented this analysis at the level of London and its 33 local authorities.

The first article reported that:

- The proportion of workplaces associated with Small and Medium-sized Enterprises (SMEs) in London remained steady at around nine-tenths of all workplaces in 2001-12. Workplaces belonging to large enterprises comprised around one-tenth of London's workplaces.
- Some three-fifths of employees in London worked for large enterprises in 2001-12, while two-fifths worked for an SME.

SMEs are defined as enterprises with fewer than 250 employees and large enterprises as those with 250 or more employees.

This article presents a second set of results: for the small areas known as 'Middle-layer Super Output Areas' (MSOAs) which nest within the local authorities[1]. There are 983 MSOAs in London. The results at MSOA level are broken down to show SMEs and large enterprises separately. However, for confidentiality reasons, it is not possible to produce breakdowns by industry sector[2].

For both articles, the figures are calculated using data from the Inter-Departmental Business Register (IDBR), see **Background notes**. Although workplaces and employees are counted at local level, we use enterprise size bands that are based on numbers of employees working for the enterprise in the UK as a whole. It should be noted that 'enterprises' include private sector businesses, public sector bodies and not-for-profit organisations.

Notes

1. For a description of this geography, see www.ons.gov.uk/ons/guide-method/geography/beginner-s-guide/census/super-output-areas--soas-/index.html

2. For details of this and other methodology issues, see www.ons.gov.uk/ons/rel/regional-trends/london-analysis/size-of-firms-in-london--2001-to-2012/index.html

Part 1: The London-wide picture

Figures 1 and 2 show the number of employees working for large enterprises in 2001, the earliest year for which IDBR datasets are available, and 2012, the latest year available. The number of employees working for large enterprises in London rose by 12% over this period. This increase took place before the 2008-09 recession; thereafter, the number of employees working for large enterprises fell slightly.

Jobs in large firms are mainly concentrated in the centre of London and around Heathrow, and there are also some concentrations in town centres in outer London boroughs, for example in Croydon, Uxbridge and Romford. The pattern of where jobs are concentrated has changed little over time, but some areas have seen job creation by large enterprises while others have lost such jobs:

*   Uxbridge has seen an increase in numbers of employees working for large enterprises from 16,600 to 42,100 (MSOAs E02000508 and E02000509).
*   Croydon has seen a decline in numbers of employees working for large enterprises from 43,900 to 33,900 (MSOAs E02000213, E02000215, E02000217 and E02000220).

FIGURE 1: Number of employees working for large enterprises in London, by MSOA: 2001

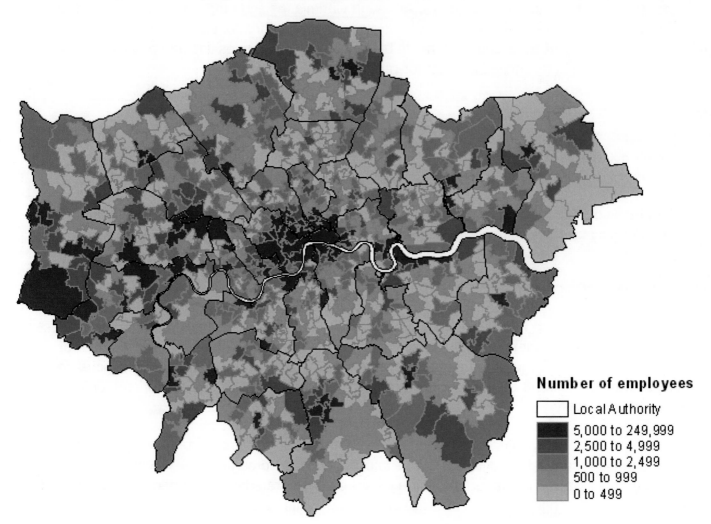

Source: Office for National Statistics

FIGURE 2: Number of employees working for large enterprises in London, by MSOA: 2012

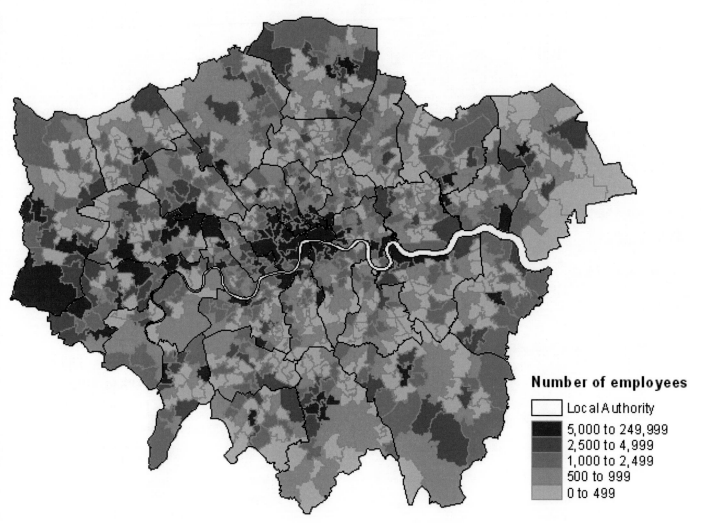

Number of employees

☐ Local Authority
5,000 to 249,999
2,500 to 4,999
1,000 to 2,499
500 to 999
0 to 499

Source: Office for National Statistics

Figures 3 and 4 show the number of employees working for SMEs in 2001 and in 2012. The number of employees working for SMEs in London rose by 25% between 2001 and 2012. However, readers should treat this figure with caution because some of the growth appears to be due to improvements in the HM Revenue and Customs data on small businesses that feeds into the IDBR, producing an artificial increase in the figures between 2011 and 2012 (see **Background notes**). Between 2001 and 2011, the number of employees working for SMEs in London rose by 15%.

SME jobs are more evenly spread across London than those in large enterprises and it is hard to distinguish from Figures 3 and 4 where growth in SME jobs has been greatest. Therefore, Part 2 of this article 'zooms in' to look at some small areas within London in greater detail. These are intended as examples. For those readers who are interested in other parts of London, similar analysis can be done using the data tables in this release.

FIGURE 3: Number of employees working for SMEs in London, by MSOA: 2001

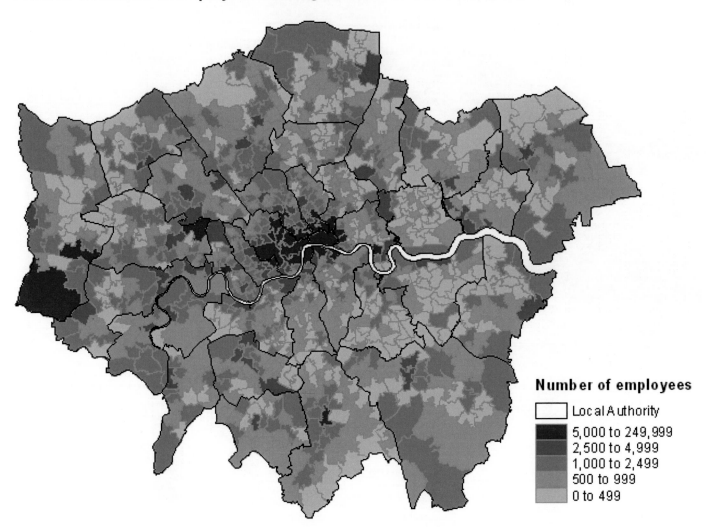

Source: Office for National Statistics

FIGURE 4: Number of employees working for SMEs in London, by MSOA: 2012

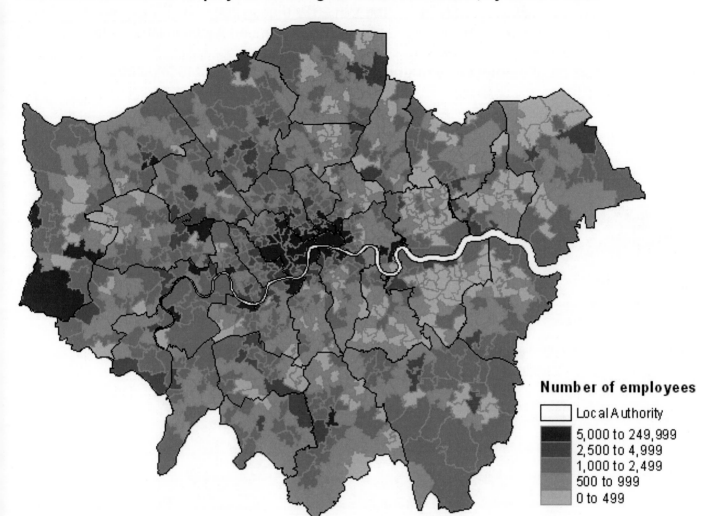

Source: Office for National Statistics

In London as a whole the proportion of employees working for SMEs is around two-fifths of the total and has changed little since 2001[1]. However, there are considerable variations between MSOAs and in some parts of London there have been big changes in the proportion of employees working for SMEs since 2001. For instance, in 2012 there were 213 MSOAs in London (out of 983) where 70% or more of all employees worked for SMEs, compared with 124 MSOAs in 2001. Figures 5 and 6 show that:

- Along the A1 / M1 corridor in the London Borough of Barnet, a higher proportion of employees worked for SMEs in 2012 than in 2001. This reflected increases in the number of employees working for SMEs in most years between 2001 and 2012, combined with a decline in the number of employees working for large enterprises in the latter half of the period (2006-12).

- In the southern part of the London Borough of Croydon, to the east of the A23 (Brighton Road), a higher proportion of employees worked for SMEs in 2012 than in 2001. This was partly because of job creation by SMEs and partly because of a fall in the number of jobs in large enterprises.

FIGURE 5: Proportion of employees working for SMEs in London, by MSOA: 2001

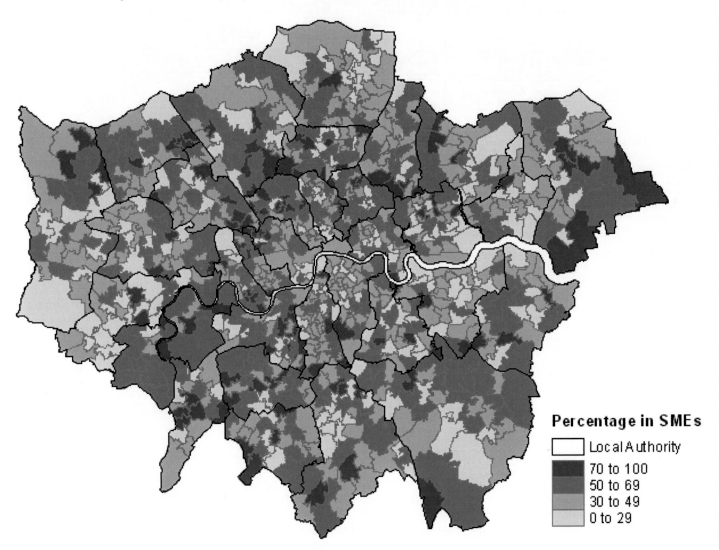

Source: Office for National Statistics

FIGURE 6: Proportion of employees working for SMEs in London, by MSOA: 2012

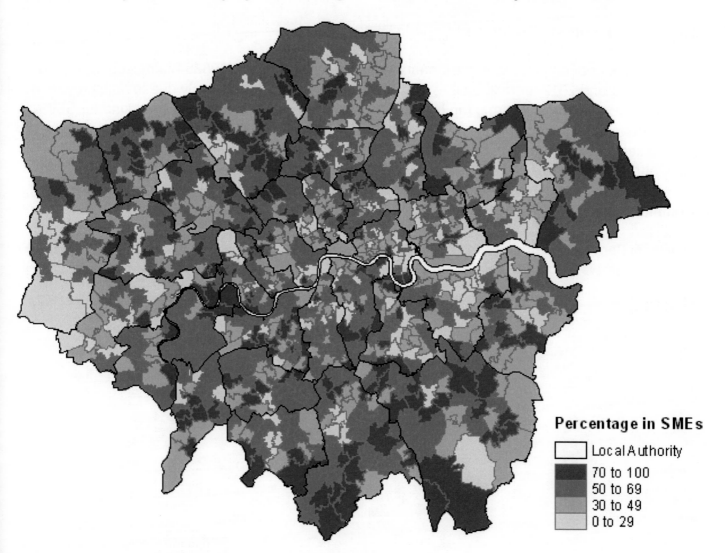

Percentage in SMEs

Local Authority

70 to 100
50 to 69
30 to 49
0 to 29

Source: Office for National Statistics

Notes

1. See www.ons.gov.uk/ons/rel/regional-trends/london-analysis/size-of-firms-in-london--2001-to-2012/index.html

Part 2: Small area examples within London

Canary Wharf, London Bridge and Canada Water

The total number of employees in the Canary Wharf area (MSOA E02006854) almost quadrupled between 2001 and 2012, from 27,400 to 100,500 (Figure 7). This was mainly due to an increase in employees working for large firms (up by 67,400), but the number of employees working for SMEs in the area doubled, from 5,100 to 10,800. The biggest driver of growth was the financial and insurance activities sector, but information and communications, the professional, scientific and technical sector, and administrative and support service activities also contributed strongly (Table 1). There were also increases in the numbers of employees working in several other sectors, notably in retail, accommodation and food services, and arts, entertainment and recreation.

FIGURE 7: Percentage change in the number of employees working in Canary Wharf and the north of Southwark, by MSOA: 2001-12

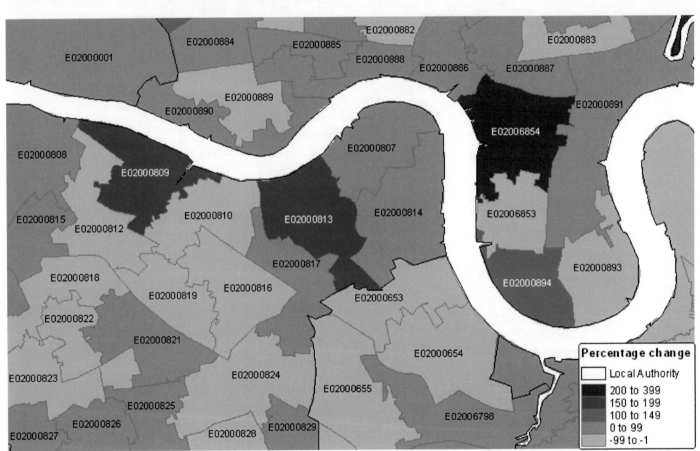

Source: Office for National Statistics

Table 1: Number of employees in the Canary Wharf area (MSOA E02006854), by industry sector: 2001 and 2012

Industrial sector	2001	2012
Primary and utilities	..	..
Manufacturing	300	100
Construction	1,200	1,200
Wholesale and motor trades	800	700
Retail	300	1,400
Transportation and storage	2,000	600
Accommodation and food service activities	1,200	3,600
Information and communication	3,500	9,200
Financial and insurance activities	14,300	58,500
Real estate	500	1,200
Professional, scientific and technical	900	7,800
Administrative and support service activities	1,700	12,600
Public administration and defence	..	..
Education	100	100
Human health and social work activities	100	500
Arts, entertainment and recreation	100	2,200
Other service activities	300	300
Activities of households as employers	0	0
Activities of extraterritorial organisations	0	0
Total in all sectors	**27,400**	**100,500**

Table source: Office for National Statistics

Table notes:
1. The symbol '..' denotes values which have been suppressed for disclosure control.
2. The industrial sectors presented are based upon the UK Standard Industrial Classification (SIC) 2007, with two changes: sectors A, B, D and E have been combined to create new classification 'Primary and utilities'; and sector

G has been split, where divisions 45 and 46 combine to form 'Wholesale and motor trades' while division 47 forms 'Retail'. Further information on SIC 2007 can be found at www.ons.gov.uk/ons/guide-method/classifications/current-standard-classifications/standard-industrial-classification/index.html

3. Data for 2001 was converted from SIC 1992 to SIC 2007 for comparability with 2012 results. For more details, see Appendix 1 of the first article in this series at www.ons.gov.uk/ons/rel/regional-trends/london-analysis/size-of-firms-in-london--2001-to-2012/index.html

Parts of the London Borough of Southwark have also seen rapid growth in employee jobs over the past decade. In particular, the area to the south-east of London Bridge Station in the north of Southwark (MSOA E02000809) saw the number of employees working for large firms nearly triple between 2001 and 2012 and the number of employees working SMEs more than double. This was largely driven by increases in jobs in the professional, scientific and technical sector, information and communications, administrative and support service activities and the human health and social work sector. In the Canada Water area, also in the north of Southwark (MSOA E02000813), most of the growth in employee jobs between 2001 and 2012 was associated with SMEs, where the number of employees rose from 800 in 2001 to 1,200 in 2010 and to 3,400 in 2012. In 2012, almost three-fifths of the SME jobs in this area were in the administrative and support services sector.

South Newham

Figure 8 shows changes in the number of employees working for SMEs between 2001 and 2012 in the southern part of the London Borough of Newham, between London Underground's District Line to the north and the Thames to the south, including London City Airport and the Royal Docks Enterprise Zone[1]. Overall, the number of employees working for SMEs in this part of Newham increased by one-third over this period, although part of this increase (between 2011 and 2012) may be due to the improvements in HM Revenue and Customs data on small businesses that feeds into the IDBR (see Part 1). Some MSOAs saw particularly large increases from low bases; for instance, the number of employees working for SMEs rose from 100 to 400 in E02000742 and from 200 to 1,100 in E02000749. This growth occurred over a range of activities, including accommodation and food services and real estate as well as education and human health and social work activities.

FIGURE 8: Percentage change in the number of employees working in SMEs in South Newham, by MSOA: 2001-12

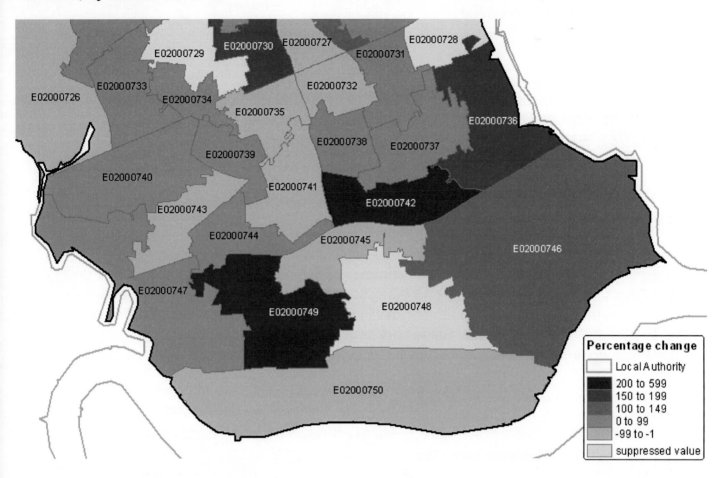

Source: Office for National Statistics

Notes:

1. Figures have been suppressed for disclosure control in some MSOAs.

Westfield shopping centres

The impact of the Westfield centre at White City/Shepherd's Bush in West London, which opened in October 2008, can be seen in MSOA E02000375. The number of employees in this area rose from 8,000 in 2008 to 15,100 in 2012, almost entirely due to increases in jobs in the retail and accommodation and food sectors. The centre provided a boost for employment in SMEs (with the number of employees rising by 110% between 2008 and 2012) as well as for large enterprises (up 86% between 2008 and 2012).

The impact of the Westfield centre at Stratford near the Olympic Park in East London, which opened on 13 September 2011, is not yet visible in the data. This is because much of the employment data in the 2012 IDBR extract is from the previous year's Business Register and Employment Survey (BRES, see **Background notes**), for which the sample was selected in August 2011 before the Westfield centre at Stratford opened.

Notes

1. This area is made up of the following MSOAs: E02000728, E02000731, E02000732, E02000735, E02000736, E02000737, E02000738, E02000739, E02000740, E02000741, E02000742, E02000743, E02000744, E02000745, E02000746, E02000747, E02000748, E02000749 and E02000750.

Background notes

1. The source of data for this article is the Inter-Departmental Business Register (IDBR), a register which covers nearly all of UK economic activity including that of public sector bodies. An organisation will be on the IDBR if it is registered for Value Added Tax (VAT), and/or pays employees through a Pay As You Earn (PAYE) scheme and/or is an incorporated business registered at Companies House. Some very small businesses, self-employed people and non-profit-making organisations are not on the IDBR as they are not registered in any of these ways.

2. The information about employees on the IDBR is drawn mainly from the Business Register and Employment Survey (BRES). Estimates from other ONS surveys are also included. For the smallest businesses, either PAYE jobs or figures imputed from VAT turnover are used. The IDBR extracts used for this analysis are taken in March each year, but the employee data that they contain relates mainly to the previous September, when the BRES data is collected.

3. The IDBR is useful for producing estimates of numbers of employees broken down by enterprise size (SMEs and large enterprises), as presented in this article. However, the IDBR does not provide official estimates of numbers of employees in London or other parts of the UK. These are published in ONS's monthly Labour Market Statistics series (available at www.ons.gov.uk/ons/taxonomy/index.html?nscl=Labour+Market). ONS also recommends using the BRES for detailed industry sector and geographical breakdowns of official employee statistics.

4. Increases in numbers of workplaces and employees between 2011 and 2012 are overstated in the IDBR because improvements to HM Revenue and Customs computer systems lead to the inclusion in 2012 of businesses that had not previously been recorded on the register. This particularly affected results for SMEs. For further details, see the first article in this series at www.ons.gov.uk/ons/rel/regional-trends/london-analysis/size-of-firms-in-london--2001-to-2012/index.html and *UK Business: Activity, Size and Location, 2012* at www.ons.gov.uk/ons/rel/bus-register/uk-business/2012/index.html

5. The MSOAs mentioned in this article can be seen against the background of a searchable map of London at www.neighbourhood.statistics.gov.uk/HTMLDocs/urbanrural.html

6. Details of the policy governing the release of new data are available by visiting www.statisticsauthority.gov.uk/assessment/code-of-practice/index.html or from the Media Relations Office email: media.relations@ons.gsi.gov.uk

These National Statistics are produced to high professional standards and released according to the arrangements approved by the UK Statistics Authority.

Copyright

Household Energy Consumption in England and Wales, 2005–11

Author Name(s): **Nigel Henretty, Office for National Statistics**

Abstract

This article uses domestic energy consumption data, produced by the Department of Energy and Climate Change and available on the Neighbourhood Statistics Service website, to explore the geographical variations in average (mean) total household energy consumption in England and Wales over time. Energy consumption statistics are an important means of assessing the impact of changes in environmental policy, structure and regulation of energy companies, public awareness of environmental issues and energy saving initiatives. This article will be of interest to those involved with environmental and energy policy-making and research, particularly at the regional and local level.

Acknowledgements

1. ONS would like to thank colleagues in the Department of Energy and Climate Change and the Welsh Government for their support in this publication.

Key points

- Average total household energy consumption in England and Wales decreased by 24.7% from 2005 to 2011.
- Household energy consumption varied regionally and was highest in the East Midlands for every year between 2005 and 2011.
- Regional differences between the highest and lowest consumers of energy per household decreased by 35% from 2005 to 2011.
- Out of the 20 local authorities that had the highest household energy consumption in 2011, 16 are in the East Midlands.
- On average, households in all regions consumed more gas than electricity, and the amount of gas as a proportion of total energy consumption varied regionally.
- The regions that had the highest total household energy consumption also had the highest Economy 7 electricity consumption as a proportion of total household energy consumption.
- Some of the areas that had lower average household energy consumption do not receive piped gas and would have used other energy sources.

Introduction

This article uses domestic energy consumption data from 2005 to 2011, produced by the Department of Energy and Climate Change and available on the <u>Neighbourhood Statistics Service</u> <u>website</u>, to explore the geographical variations in mean household energy consumption over time[1]. Domestic energy consumption is expressed as an average per electricity meter in this analysis[2]. The number of ordinary electricity meters has been used as a proxy for the number of households and so energy consumption is referred to throughout the article as average household energy consumption.

The article provides an overview of household energy consumption in 2011. It identifies energy consumption in England and Wales and how it varied across the English regions and Wales, as well as providing information about the local authorities that had the highest and lowest levels of energy consumption in 2011. Changes in household energy consumption from 2005 to 2011 by region, local authority and Middle Layer Super Output Area (MSOA) are reported. Differences in the scale and geographical variation in household energy consumption changes over the period are examined.

Small areas, Middle Layer Super Output Areas (MSOAs), are analysed in order to demonstrate the geographical distribution of household energy consumption across the English regions and Wales. To do this, the percentage of MSOAs in the English regions and Wales that fell within each quintile of overall energy consumption are reported.

Analysis is presented to show the breakdown of household energy consumption by type, identifying the proportion of gas and electricity consumed by each region as a proportion of total household energy consumption, and the proportion of Economy 7 electricity consumed as a proportion of all household energy consumption.

This article will be of interest to those involved with environmental and energy policy-making and research, particularly at the regional and local level, as well as those who require an understanding of the energy market, for example, utility companies and information groups such as UK Energy Watch which collates UK energy use and generation data.

Data used in this analysis do not include the amount of energy from wood, heating oil or other sources consumed domestically and so the total energy consumption of households may underestimate the true amount of total domestic energy consumed. According to <u>2011 Census data</u>, the percentage of households in England and Wales that used heating oil, wood or other sources of energy to provide central heating was 6.4%. Wales had the highest proportion of households that used these other sources of energy (11.5%) and the North West had the lowest (3.5%). Energy consumption from these sources is not included in the domestic energy consumption data.

Domestic gas consumption data have been adjusted to take account of regional differences in weather which may have otherwise affected the geographical distribution of energy consumption.

Notes

1. See the background notes for more information about the calculation of mean household energy consumption, the weather correction applied and the geographic coverage of the data.

2. The number of electricity meters has been used as a proxy for the number of households because the standard gas industry definition of domestic use uses a consumption threshold, with any consumer using less than 73,200 kWh of gas per year being classed as a domestic user. This classification can incorrectly allocate small businesses to the domestic sector and, conversely, a small number of larger domestic consumers to the non-domestic sector. Therefore, the number of domestic gas meters may be an overestimate. Electricity meters use a profile basis and are more stable in determining if the meter is a domestic meter.

Total Household Energy Consumption in 2011

Looking at average household energy consumption (for gas and electricity combined) in the English regions and Wales in 2011, the local authorities that had the highest and lowest household energy consumption have been identified.

In England and Wales overall, average household energy consumption was 19.7 megawatt hours (MWh) per household in 2011. Figure 1 shows the average household energy consumption for English regions and Wales in 2011.

Figure 1: Average household energy consumption, English regions and Wales, 2011

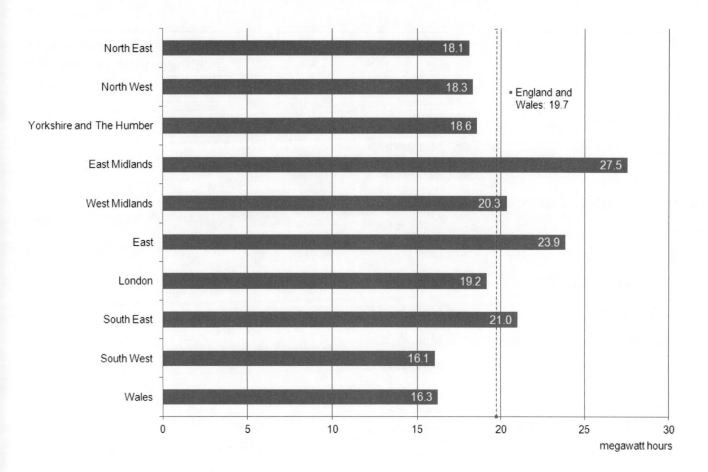

Source: Energy and Climate Change

The East Midlands had an average household energy consumption of 27.5MWh in 2011, considerably higher than the overall figure for England and Wales (19.7MWh). The South West had the lowest energy consumption in 2011 (16.1 megawatt hours per household), which is closer to the overall England and Wales figure than is the East Midlands. Wales was similar to the South West in 2011, consuming an average of 16.3MWh per household. Regions in the North of England including the North East, North West and Yorkshire and The Humber had similar levels of household energy consumption to each other, but all consumed less household energy, on average, than England and Wales overall.

Examining the household energy consumption of local authorities, Table 1 shows the 10 highest and lowest energy consuming local authorities in 2011.

Table 1: Highest and lowest average total household energy consumption, local authorities, 2011

Local authority	Region/Country	Mean household energy consumption (megawatt hours)
Highest household energy consumption		
Rutland	East Midlands	36.0
Harborough	East Midlands	35.8
Blaby	East Midlands	35.4
Rushcliffe	East Midlands	35.2
Oadby and Wigston	East Midlands	35.1
Hinckley and Bosworth	East Midlands	34.3
Derbyshire Dales	East Midlands	32.9
Charnwood	East Midlands	32.5
Melton	East Midlands	32.5
Gedling	East Midlands	32.3
Lowest household energy consumption		
Isles of Scilly	South West	11.4
Ceredigion	Wales	11.5
Tower Hamlets	London	12.2
City of London	London	12.3
Powys	Wales	12.4
Isle of Anglesey	Wales	12.4
Torridge	South West	13.1
Pembrokeshire	Wales	13.1
Carmarthenshire	Wales	13.2
Gwynedd	Wales	13.3

Table source: Energy and Climate Change

Table 1 shows that Rutland was the local authority that had the highest average household energy consumption in 2011 (36.0 MWh per household). In Rutland, household energy consumption was more than three times that of the Isles of Scilly and Ceredigion, the two local authorities which had the lowest energy consumption. All of the 10 local authorities that had the highest average household energy consumption in 2011 are in the East Midlands. In fact, 16 of the top 20 energy consuming local authorities are in the East Midlands.

In terms of lowest energy consumption, the local authorities that consumed the least energy in 2011 tended to be in more rural areas than did the highest energy consuming local authorities. The Isles of Scilly was the local authority that had the lowest household energy consumption in 2011 (11.4 MWh per household). The Isles of Scilly does not receive piped gas which means households here did not have any gas consumption recorded in the data. As a result, the average total household energy consumption would be lower than local authorities in which households receive piped gas. Two local authorities in London, Tower Hamlets and City of London, appear in the lowest household energy consumption top 10, and this goes against the general pattern of low energy consumption in more rural areas.

Local authorities in rural areas may be more likely to be in relatively isolated areas and so have a higher proportion of households without piped gas than those in less rural areas, and these households may use other sources of energy. As such, this could explain why eight of the top 10 lowest energy consuming local authorities were in Wales or the South West.

Distribution of Household Energy Consumption in Small Areas Within England and Wales

Data for household energy consumption are available at different geographical levels, including the Middle Layer Super Output Area (MSOA) level. MSOAs were designed to improve the reporting of small area statistics. They are geographical units built up from groups of Lower Layer Super Output Areas (LSOAs). Each local authority consists of between one (Isles of Scilly) and 131 (Birmingham) MSOAs[1].

Map 1 shows the average household energy consumption for each of the 7,194 MSOAs in England and Wales in 2011.

Map 1: Average household energy consumption, MSOAs, 2011

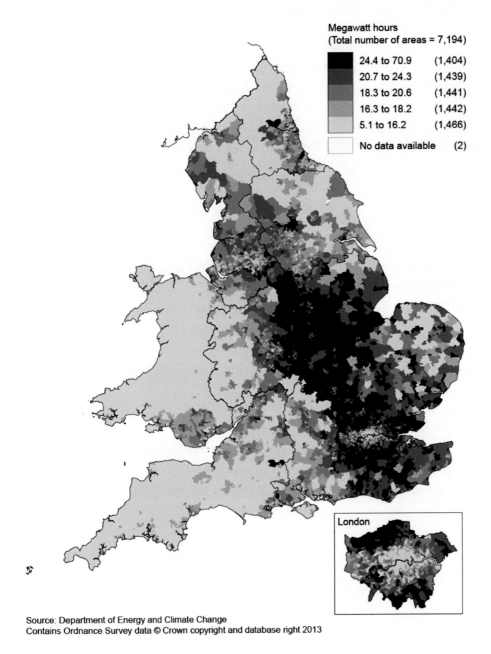

Megawatt hours
(Total number of areas = 7,194)

■	24.4 to 70.9	(1,404)
■	20.7 to 24.3	(1,439)
■	18.3 to 20.6	(1,441)
■	16.3 to 18.2	(1,442)
■	5.1 to 16.2	(1,466)
□	No data available	(2)

Source: Department of Energy and Climate Change
Contains Ordnance Survey data © Crown copyright and database right 2013

Source: Energy and Climate Change

Notes:

1. Boundaries are 2001 MSOA boundaries

Map 1 shows that many of the MSOAs that had high average household energy consumption in 2011 centre around the East Midlands. There also appear to be areas of relatively high household energy consumption in a diagonal belt between the South East and the North West, whereas households in MSOAs across Wales and the South West tended to have lower energy consumption. In London, households in MSOAs on the outskirts of the city tended to have higher average energy consumption than London overall, whereas households within inner London MSOAs generally had lower average energy consumption than the region.

The ONS produces Small Area Income Estimates for MSOAs in England and Wales, which, when viewed in conjunction with household energy consumption, show that areas that consumed more household energy also tended to have higher levels of net income after taking account of housing costs. Households in areas where income is higher may therefore be more likely to consume more energy overall.

Figure 2 shows, for the English regions and Wales, the percentage of MSOAs that lie within each quintile of energy consumption for England and Wales overall. For example, taking the whole of England and Wales, 20% of all MSOAs lie within the highest household energy consumption quintile, 20% of MSOAs lie within the second highest quintile, and so on. By comparing the percentage of MSOAs in each quintile, it is possible to compare each region and Wales with England and Wales overall. This means that, if all regions contain 20% of MSOAs in each quintile, then household energy consumption would be evenly distributed across the English regions and Wales. The five colours on the chart show the percentage of MSOAs in each of the five energy consumption quintiles, with the highest energy consumption quintile shown by the darkest colour and the percentage of MSOAs in the lowest quintile shown by the lightest colour.

Figure 2: Household energy consumption quintile distribution for MSOAs, English regions and Wales, 2011

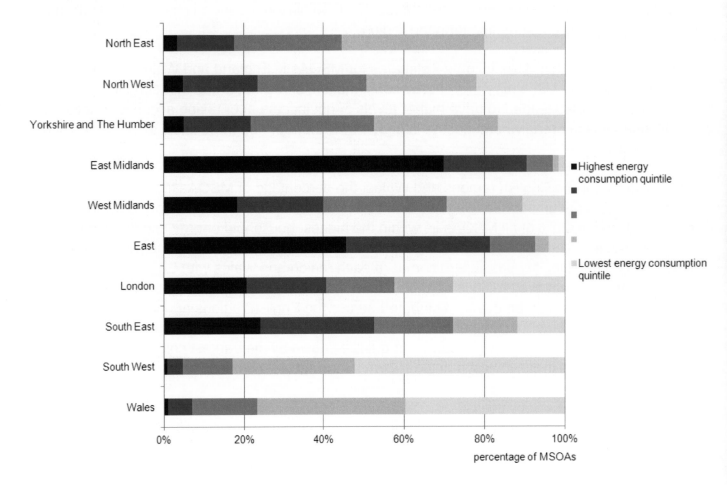

Source: Energy and Climate Change

Figure 2 shows that the East Midlands had the largest percentage of MSOAs in the highest household energy consumption quintile out of all English regions and Wales (69.9%). This continues recent trends and is more than three times the proportion for England and Wales overall and considerably more than the East of England, the next highest region with 45.7% of its MSOAs in the highest household energy consumption quintile. The South West had the lowest proportion of MSOAs in the highest household energy consumption quintile (0.9%) out of all regions and Wales, and it had the largest proportion of its MSOAs in the lowest household energy consumption quintile (52.1%).

The relatively large variation in quintile distribution demonstrates that the regions of England and Wales were disparate in terms of household energy consumption in 2011.

Notes

1. Information about Super Output Areas is available from <u>ONS Geography</u>

Changes in Household Energy Consumption, 2005–11

Historic energy consumption statistics for households in England and Wales are available for 2005 to 2011. These can be used to examine recent trends in subnational household energy consumption.

Figure 3 shows average household energy consumption for 2005 to 2011 in England and Wales, the East Midlands (the region that had the highest energy consumption per household over the period) and the South West (the region that had the lowest over the period).

Figure 3: Average household energy consumption, English regions and Wales, 2005–11

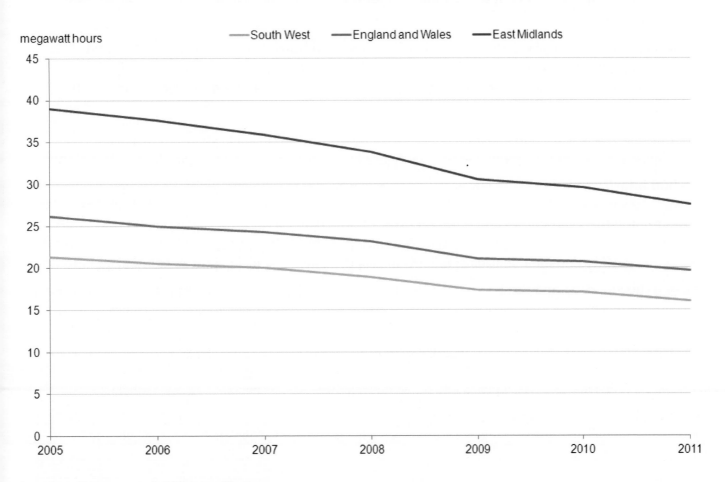

Source: Energy and Climate Change

Figure 3 shows that average household energy consumption in England and Wales decreased from 26.2 megawatt hours (MWh) in 2005 to 19.7MWh in 2011. This is a decrease of 24.7% over the period. Within England and Wales, the East Midlands had the highest household energy consumption for every year in the period, but this decreased 29.4% from 39.0MWh per household in 2005 to 27.5MWh in 2011. This was the largest decrease, in absolute terms of all the English regions and Wales (11.5MWh). However, in percentage terms, the West Midlands had the largest decrease in household energy consumption out of all the English regions and Wales (a fall of 30.0% from 29.0MWh in 2005 to 20.3MWh in 2011).

Over the seven year period, the South West had the lowest average household energy consumption for five of these years. The only two years when the South West did not record the lowest energy consumption were 2005 and 2010, when Wales had the lowest energy consumption per household.

Household energy consumption may have fallen in England and Wales in recent years for a number of reasons:

- Household improvements such as better loft and cavity wall insulation[1] have improved energy efficiency[2,3].
- Introduction of energy rating scales for properties[4] and household appliances[5], allowing consumers to make informed decisions about their purchases.
- Improved efficiency of gas boilers and condensing boilers to supply properties with both hot water and central heating[6].
- Generally increasing public awareness of energy consumption and environmental issues[7].
- The price of gas and electricity in the UK overall increased in all years apart from 2010, between 2005 and 2011[8].

However, decreases in household energy consumption in small areas within England and Wales did not occur uniformly between 2005 and 2011. Map 2 shows the percentage change in average household energy consumption for small areas (Middle Layer Super Output Areas) in England and Wales between 2005 and 2011[9].

Map 2: Change in average total household energy consumption, MSOAs, 2005–11

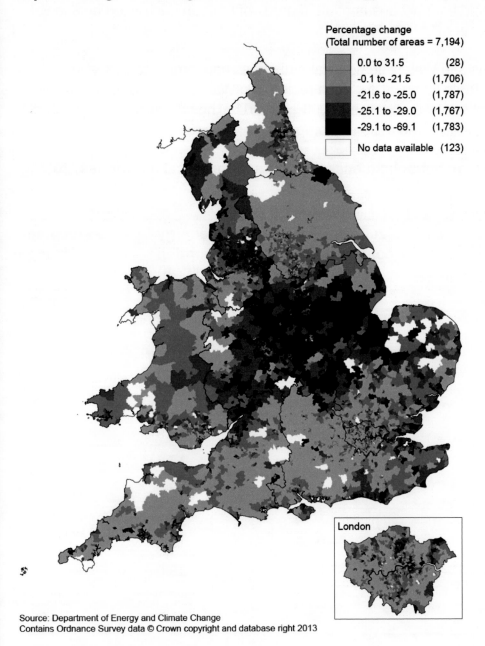

Percentage change
(Total number of areas = 7,194)

	0.0 to 31.5	(28)
	-0.1 to -21.5	(1,706)
	-21.6 to -25.0	(1,787)
	-25.1 to -29.0	(1,767)
	-29.1 to -69.1	(1,783)
	No data available	(123)

London

Source: Department of Energy and Climate Change
Contains Ordnance Survey data © Crown copyright and database right 2013

Source: Energy and Climate Change

Notes:

1. Boundaries are 2001 MSOA boundaries

Map 2 shows that the vast majority of MSOAs in England and Wales had a decrease in average household energy consumption from 2005 to 2011. In fact, only 27 MSOAs had an increase in average energy consumption over the period. Many MSOAs in the East Midlands had large decreases in household energy consumption over the period, shown by the darkest areas on the map. Generally, average household energy consumption in areas of London decreased by a lower amount than England and Wales overall.

Within each of the English regions and Wales, some local authorities had large decreases in household energy consumption. Table 2 shows, for each region and Wales, the local authority with the largest decrease in energy consumption between 2005 and 2011. The figures for England and Wales overall have also been included in the table for comparison.

Table 2: Largest change in average household energy consumption, local authorities, 2005–11

Local authority with largest change in region	Region	2005 energy consumption (MWh)	2011 energy consumption (MWh)	Percentage change
Hinckley and Bosworth	East Midlands	54.9	34.3	-37.5
Shropshire	West Midlands	23.8	15.7	-34.0
Forest Heath	East	32.3	21.5	-33.4
Gloucester	South West	25.5	17.5	-31.3
Adur	South East	34.5	23.9	-30.8
Wigan	North West	25.1	17.5	-30.5
Haringey	London	31.9	23.0	-28.0
Pembrokeshire	Wales	18.0	13.1	-27.2
Gateshead	North East	24.2	18.1	-25.3
Scarborough	Yorkshire and The Humber	23.9	18.0	-24.9
England and Wales overall		**26.2**	**19.7**	**-32.8**

Table source: Energy and Climate Change

Table 2 shows that all of the English regions and Wales contain a local authority which had an average household energy consumption decrease larger than the overall England and Wales change from 2005 to 2011. The largest household energy consumption decrease was in Hinckley and Bosworth in the East Midlands (a decrease of 37.5%). In Hinckley and Bosworth there was a reduction of household energy consumption of 20.6MWh. This reduction is greater than the amount of household energy consumption for England and Wales overall in 2011 (19.7MWh) and also greater than the amount of household energy consumption overall in seven of the English regions and Wales.

Scarborough was the local authority that had the largest household energy consumption change in Yorkshire and The Humber (a decrease of 24.9%) which was similar to the overall change in England and Wales (a decrease of 24.7%).

Notes

1. According to data from the Department of Energy and Climate Change, the estimated proportion of homes with loft insulation in the UK increased from 44.0% in April 2008 to 59.6% in October 2011.

2. For more information about the uptake of energy efficiency measures in homes, see the National Energy Efficiency Data-Framework summary of analysis.

3. In 2003, the UK Government published the Energy White Paper, which set out its strategic vision for the future of energy policy.

4. The European Parliament and Council's Directive on the energy performance of buildings came into force in 2002.

5. The European Parliament and Council's Directive on the energy performance of household appliances was first introduced in 1992 and has been amended more recently.

6. The European Parliament and Council's Directive on the energy performance of boilers was first introduced in 1992.

7. In 2006, The European Commission published the Action Plan for Energy Efficiency: Realising the Potential, which cited "increased awareness and behavioural change" as an important driver of reducing energy consumption.

8. According to data from the fuel component of the Retail Prices Index, the price of domestic gas increased from an index 100 in 2005, to 201.4 in 2011. The price of domestic electricity increased from an index of 100 in 2005, to 166.1 in 2011.

9. Information about Super Output Areas is available from ONS Geography.

Household energy consumption by type

Average household energy consumption can be broken down by the proportion of gas and electricity consumed. Figure 4 shows the proportion of household gas consumption as a percentage of total household energy consumption by region in 2011.

Figure 4: Average household energy consumption by type, 2011

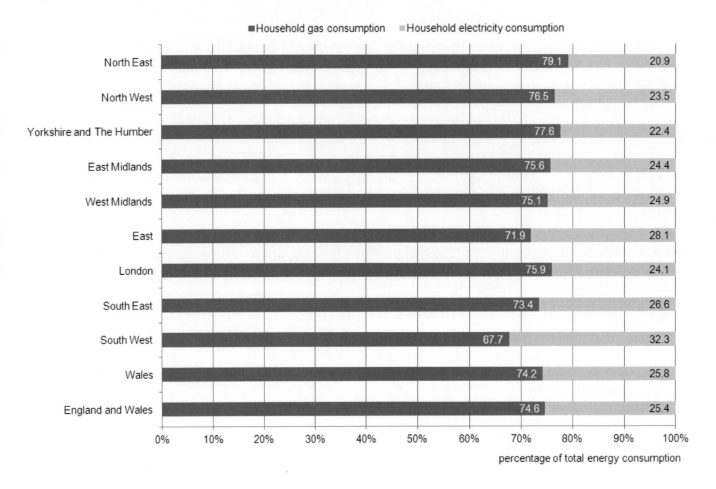

Source: Energy and Climate Change

Figure 4 shows that the North East consumed the most gas proportionally (79.1%) and the South West consumed the least (67.7%) in 2011. This could be the result of fewer households in the South West receiving piped gas compared with other regions, and therefore using less gas proportionally.

Looking at the breakdown of household electricity consumption, figure 5 shows the average household Economy 7 electricity consumption as a percentage of total average household electricity consumption[1].

Figure 5: Average household Economy 7 electricity consumption as a percentage of total energy consumption, English regions and Wales, 2011

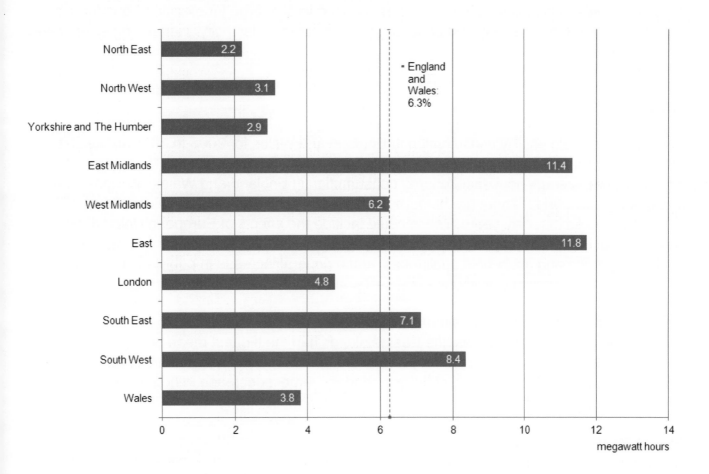

Source: Energy and Climate Change

Figure 5 shows that the East of England had the highest consumption of Economy 7 electricity as a percentage of all household energy consumption (11.8%) and the East Midlands had the second highest Economy 7 electricity consumption (11.4%). These were also the regions that consumed the most household energy overall. It could be that households which receive some electricity at a cheaper rate, may use more energy overall because it is cheaper. Having said that, Figure 4 shows, as a percentage of total average household energy consumption, the East of England consumed 71.9% of its energy from gas whereas Economy 7 electricity consumption accounted for a relatively small proportion of total household energy consumption.

The North East had the lowest consumption of Economy 7 electricity as a percentage of all household energy consumption (2.2%). Despite this, the North East had the third lowest total average household energy consumption which further suggests that Economy 7 electricity consumption does not fully account for the patterns of total average household energy consumption.

Notes

1. Economy 7 is an electricity tariff which offers a dual rate of charge for electricity, one for electricity used during the day and another, cheaper, rate for electricity used during seven hours of the night.

Summary

Statistics on household energy consumption in England and Wales for 2005 to 2011 are available from the Neighbourhood Statistics Service website for a variety of geographies. These data can be used to show that average household energy consumption in England and Wales has consistently decreased over this period. There are numerous reasons why household energy consumption may have decreased in recent years. These could include the effects of European Union directives leading to improvements in property insulation and energy efficiency, the introduction of energy ratings for properties and household appliances, and a general increase in public awareness on issues of energy efficiency and environmental sustainability.

Energy consumption data show that average household energy consumption varied geographically. Within the English regions and Wales, the East Midlands had the highest mean household energy consumption in 2011, as it had in previous years, although energy consumption there decreased by 29.4% from 2005 to 2011. The West Midlands had the largest decrease in household energy consumption of any English region and Wales over the period, at 30.0%.

Analysis of Middle Layer Super Output Areas (MSOAs) revealed that 69.9% of MSOAs in the East Midlands were in the highest energy consumption quintile in 2011. This was considerably higher than the South West where 0.9% of MSOAs were in the highest quintile in 2011.

The household energy consumption data used in this article could also be used for further analysis. Such analysis could include, but is not limited to:

*   Examining the distribution of energy consumption at the Lower Layer Super Output Area (LSOA), and how this has changed over time.
*   Assessing the geographical variation in energy consumption in terms of the rural-urban classification of areas.
*   Linking energy consumption to measures of disposable household income, fuel poverty and Indices of Multiple Deprivation.
*   Exploring the relationship between 2011 Census data on housing stock and household energy consumption.

Background notes

1. **Measuring energy consumption:**

    The Department of Energy and Climate Change produces energy consumption data that shows the total gas, electricity and Economy 7 electricity consumption in each area. To conduct analysis of energy consumption at the household level, a proxy measure of mean total fuel consumption per household, for a given year in a given area, was calculated as follows:

Calculating mean total household energy consumption

$$C = \frac{G + O + E}{M}$$

The description for this equation is currently unavailable. ONS apologises for any inconvenience caused.

Notes:

1. Where:

   - C = Mean total household energy consumption
   - G = Total household gas consumption
   - O = Total household ordinary electricity consumption
   - E = Total household Economy 7 electricity consumption
   - M = Number of ordinary domestic electricity meters

The number of domestic electricity meters has been used as a proxy for the number of households in this article. In reality though, the two cannot be used interchangeably because electricity meters in an area will generally be an overestimate of the number of households (more so in some areas than in others). For example, in 2011 the total number of electricity meters was 24.5 million which is greater than the estimated number of households according to the 2011 Census, at 24.4 million. This is for a number of reasons:

- The total number of electricity meters includes both ordinary and Economy 7 electricity meters. Households with an Economy 7 electricity meter also have an ordinary electricity meter.
- Some households can have more than one electricity meter associated with their property and therefore the number of electricity meters used may be an overestimate of the true number of households. This is particularly an issue with flats, with some supplies for communal areas such as lobbies, lifts and stairwells having a separate supply. For example, a block of six flats could have a total of seven electricity meters.
- A small number of meters do not have sufficient information associated with them to be able to allocate them to a country and are referred to as 'Unallocated' meters. Therefore, country values for the number of gas and electricity meters may be an underestimate of the true number of meters.

Further information about measuring energy consumption is included in the methodology and guidance notes on the Department of Energy and Climate Change website.

2. **Weather correction:**

The Department of Energy and Climate Change (DECC) has an agreement with all the electricity suppliers in Great Britain, whereby they agree to provide DECC with annualised consumption data for each Meter Point Administration Number (MPAN) or electricity meter. The consumption data for each MPAN is not weather corrected and represents consumption covering the 365 days commencing in late January each year. As well as the meter number and energy consumption, DECC also receive address point data for each meter.

A similar process is used to compile the gas data. Gas transporters supply DECC with the Annualised Quantity (AQ) for each Meter Point Reference Number (MPRN) or gas meter as well as addresses points data. An AQ is an estimate of annualised consumption using two meter readings at least six months apart and the closing reading is taken within the period 1 October to 30 September. The estimate is then weather corrected to reflect a 17 year trend. The MPRN data is then matched to a local authority and SOAs using the National Statistics Postcode Directory and the Postal Address File (PAF).

3. **Geographic coverage:**

    Domestic energy consumption data are available for the English regions and Wales, local authorities and MSOAs as National Statistics and can be used in a time series analysis. LSOA data are also available and currently designated as Experimental Statistics.

    There have been improvements in matching the meter point data to local authorities, MSOAs and LSOAs which will affect the comparability of data over time. Data for previous years are not revised to take account of improved matching.

    In processing this data for publication ONS has carried out checks to ensure the quality of the data.

4. Details of the policy governing the release of new data are available by visiting www.statisticsauthority.gov.uk/assessment/code-of-practice/index.html or from the Media Relations Office email: media.relations@ons.gsi.gov.uk

Copyright

A Profile of Deprivation in Larger English Seaside Destinations, 2007 and 2010

Author Name(s): **Phil Humby, Area Based Analysis, Office for National Statistics**

Abstract

There is a perception that the economies of English towns and cities which once thrived on seaside resort tourism have declined and are enduring high levels of deprivation as a result of people going abroad for their holidays. Such is the perceived extent of this decline that during the 2010 election campaign all three major political parties discussed the problems facing British seaside and coastal settlements. In this article the Office for National Statistics defines the 57 largest English seaside destinations in terms of resident population. These destinations are then analysed, put into the context of the national picture, using the English Indices of Deprivation for 2007 and 2010 to ascertain whether this widely held belief holds true. In particular, are the larger seaside destinations more deprived than the rest of England and if so how does that deprivation vary across destinations. Further analysis on seaside destinations is in development for expected publication in 2014.

Acknowledgements

1. The Office for National Statistics would like to thank colleagues in the Department for Communities and Local Government for their support for this publication.

Key Points

*   For the first time ONS has defined the 57 largest seaside destinations in England in terms of the resident population of constituent LSOAs and conducted analysis on them using the Indices of Deprivation.
*   The three most deprived seaside destinations of the 57 analysed in this article were Skegness and Ingoldmells, Blackpool and Clacton.
*   Larger seaside destinations generally had greater levels of deprivation than the rest of England in 2007 and 2010 (with the exceptions of Christchurch, Lytham St Annes, Poole, Worthing, Southport and Bognor Regis).
*   Mid-sized seaside destinations tended to have lower levels of deprivation than larger seaside destinations and a wider range of deprivation levels; the mid-sized seaside destinations featured the most deprived seaside destination (Skegness and Ingoldmells) and least deprived seaside destination (Formby) found in the analysis.

- There were large differences in the levels of deprivation faced by seaside destinations which are adjacent to each other: Blackpool was the most deprived larger English seaside destination and borders Lytham St Annes which had the second lowest deprivation level of the larger seaside destinations.
- The patterns of deprivation faced by seaside destinations in 2010 were similar to those in 2007.

Introduction

This article defines the 57 largest seaside destinations in England based on resident populations of constituent Lower Layer Super Output Areas (LSOAs). It examines the levels of deprivation experienced by seaside destinations compared with England as a whole and to each other. It specifically looks at the 31 largest seaside destinations and the 26 mid-sized seaside destinations which the Office for National Statistics has defined based on resident population. The seaside destinations defined as part of this article do not encompass all seaside destinations. Other coastal areas , which may or may not experience similar levels of deprivation, are not included in the analysis. For example, New Brighton in the Wirral is considered to be a seaside destination but does not meet the resident population threshold for either a larger or mid-sized seaside destination; while Plymouth does not have a beach, so is not considered to be a seaside destination.

Comparisons of deprivation patterns for the larger seaside destinations with England as a whole are drawn for both 2007 and 2010. The seaside destinations are compared with each other both in terms of overall Indices of Deprivation (ID) and using the individual ID domains. The variation between the seaside destinations is then explored. Mid-sized seaside destinations are compared with England, the larger seaside destinations and each other, to see if there are any differences in the patterns of deprivation.

This article will be of interest to local authorities with seaside destinations, and MPs representing constituencies with seaside destinations, to examine the levels of deprivation in their areas. The article will also appeal to special interest groups such as the British Destinations and Coastal Communities Alliance, who look at issues affecting seaside resorts and destinations. Policy makers may find this article of use in understanding the levels of deprivation in seaside destinations and identifying the most and least deprived of the areas analysed. This article is purely for statistical investigation and has no funding linked to it.

How has ONS defined seaside destinations?

ONS has defined a seaside destination as any seaside settlement to which people travel for the beach and associated activities. There is a degree of subjectivity in this as, for example, Southampton is not included as it is not a settlement people tend to travel to for the beach or associated activities, despite having a publically accessible beach at Weston Shore.

LSOA is the abbreviated name for Lower Layer Super Output Areas. LSOAs are a small area level of geography which can be aggregated to form the local authority level, that is, a local authority will have a number of LSOAs, but a LSOA will only belong to one local authority. There is no standard for the number of LSOAs within a local authority and as such the number of LSOAs within a local authority and indeed a seaside destination will vary.

Each seaside destination has been defined using its constituent LSOAs. LSOAs have been used as local authorities often cover wide areas and may contain several significant settlements and as such using local authority data as a proxy may not provide a suitable measure. For example, Southsea comprises just over a quarter of the population attributable to the local authority of Portsmouth and as such an overall statistic for Portsmouth may be unrepresentative of Southsea.

Within this article analysis is undertaken for the 57 largest seaside destinations in England split between the 31 larger seaside destinations and 26 mid-sized seaside destinations. This split has been determined based on the resident population of the LSOAs which comprise the seaside destinations. Using the 2011 Census-based mid-year population estimates for 2011, the larger English seaside destinations are those destinations with a population greater than or equal to 40,000; the mid-sized English seaside destinations are defined as those which have a population between 15,000 and 39,999.

The size of the resident population does not necessarily reflect the likely size of the tourist population on a sunny, summer weekend, nor the impact that seaside tourism plays in the local economy.

Table 1 shows the seaside destinations which have been determined as the 31 most populous in England and the population size of those destinations.

Table 1: Larger English seaside destinations and their populations, England, 2011

Map reference	Seaside destination	Population	Area (sq km)	Area as a percentage of local authority area (%)
1	Brighton	253,300	66.2	80
2	Bournemouth	183,500	46.2	100
3	Sunderland	180,900	63.3	46
4	Southend-on-Sea	174,300	41.8	100
5	Blackpool	142,100	34.9	100
6	Poole	137,700	48.3	75
7	Worthing	105,000	32.5	100
8	Eastbourne	99,300	44.2	100
9	Southport	90,400	44.2	29
10	Hastings	90,200	29.7	100
11	South Shields	83,900	20.6	32
12	Hartlepool	81,500	28.6	30

Map reference	Seaside destination	Population	Area (sq km)	Area as a percentage of local authority area (%)
13	Weston-super-Mare	73,700	23.5	6
14	Lowestoft	72,300	37.4	10
15	Torquay	65,400	26.8	43
16	Bognor Regis	64,800	34.4	16
17	Great Yarmouth	63,600	30.5	18
18	Tynemouth	59,100	18.5	22
19	Southsea	58,900	5.3	13
20	Barrow-in-Furness	56,700	45.2	58
21	Clacton	55,400	26.0	8
22	Folkestone	52,800	17.4	5
23	Scarborough	48,400	19.3	2
24	Littlehampton	48,300	17.5	8
25	Paignton	47,400	24.9	40
26	Margate	45,600	14.4	14
27	Christchurch	43,700	41.7	83
28	Bexhill	43,100	32.3	6
29	Weymouth	42,900	18.5	44
30	Lytham St Annes	42,400	21.9	13
31	Ramsgate	40,500	9.9	10

Table source: Office for National Statistics

Table notes:

1. Population of seaside destinations has been rounded within this table to the nearest 100 people. Populations used for calculations later in the article were unrounded.

Map 1 shows how the larger seaside destinations are distributed around the coastline. The references in Map 1 relate to the map reference in Table 1.

Map 1: The location of larger English seaside destinations, England and Wales, 2011

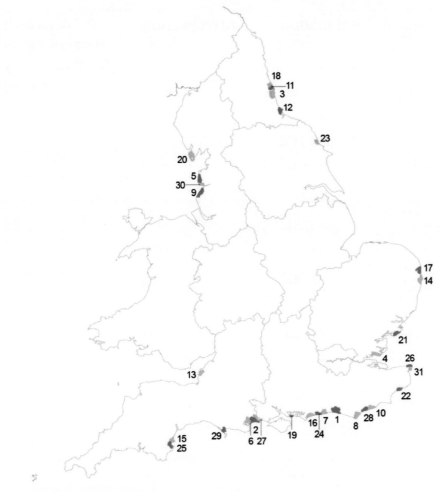

Source: Office for National Statistics
Contains Ordnance Survey data © Crown copyright and database right 2013

Source: Office for National Statistics

Table 2 shows the seaside destinations which have been determined as mid-sized seaside destinations in England and the population size of those destinations.

Table 2: Mid-sized English seaside destinations and their populations, England, 2011

Map reference	Seaside destination	Population	Area (sq km)	Area as a percentage of local authority area (%)
1	Morecambe	36,500	9.9	2
2	Cleethorpes	36,100	9.4	5
3	Redcar	35,700	40.7	17
4	Bridlington	35,600	48.7	2
5	Whitley Bay	35,000	13.5	16
6	Exmouth	34,500	18.8	2
7	Whitstable	32,800	30.0	10
8	Deal	30,100	17.0	5
9	Herne Bay	27,600	13.1	4
10	Lancing	27,400	24.5	59
11	Fleetwood	25,900	9.8	3
12	Burnham-on-Sea	24,700	44.7	8
13	Felixstowe	23,700	16.6	2
14	Broadstairs	22,700	9.0	9
15	Formby	22,400	22.0	14
16	Shoreham by sea	22,100	9.4	22
17	Skegness and Ingoldmells	22,000	32.4	2
18	Falmouth	21,800	7.8	0.2
19	Clevedon	21,300	12.8	3
20	Seaham	21,100	9.6	0.4
21	Newquay	19,900	15.0	0.4
22	Cleveleys	19,600	7.3	3
23	Harwich	18,700	8.2	2
24	Hayling Island	17,400	15.9	29
25	Teignmouth	17,200	15.6	2
26	Ryde	16,500	4.6	1

Table source: Office for National Statistics

Table notes:

1. Population of seaside destinations has been rounded within this table to the nearest 100 people. Populations used for calculations later in the article were unrounded.

2. Ingoldmells has been included with Skegness as it is home to Billy Butlin's first holiday camp: Butlin's Skegness; and as such is deemed by many tourists to be a part of Skegness.

Map 2 shows how the larger seaside destinations are distributed around the coastline. The references in Map 2 relate to the map reference in Table 2.

Map 2: The location of mid-sized English seaside destinations, England and Wales, mid-2011

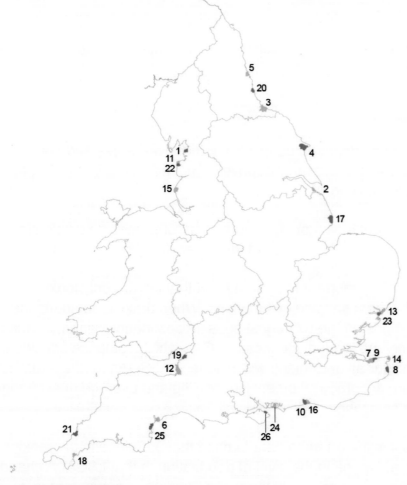

Source: Office for National Statistics

Using the Indices of Deprivation with seaside destinations

The English Indices of Deprivation (ID) were produced by the Department for Communities and Local Government, the most recent of which relate to 2007 and 2010. The ID has not been updated with information from the 2011 Census. The Indices provide an overall rank for each Lower Layer Super Output Area (LSOA) based on seven groups of indicators (called domains) as well as separate ranks for the domains themselves. The overall rank for ID is also known as the index of multiple deprivation. The most deprived LSOA is given the rank of one with higher ranks given to less deprived areas. The seven domains[1] are:

1. Income deprivation
2. Employment deprivation
3. Health deprivation and disability
4. Education, skills and training deprivation
5. Barriers to housing and services
6. Crime
7. Living environment deprivation

ID is a measure of spatial deprivation: not all deprived people live in deprived areas and not everyone living in the most deprived LSOA is necessarily deprived. The indicators in the ID reflect characteristics that are associated with deprivation.

Due to each UK country having its own set of indicators for deprivation, only seaside destinations in England have been selected for this article. Deprivation is not just a seaside phenomenon.

When looking at the rankings for the ID it is important to bear in mind that we are only looking at those LSOAs which make up the 57 largest seaside destinations. When making comparisons between the ranks for those LSOAs comprising the 57 largest seaside destinations and the ranks for all of England, the ranks for all of England will include those LSOAs which comprise seaside destinations of all sizes; that is the ranks for all of England will include the LSOAs for the larger and mid-sized seaside destinations to ensure accuracy as otherwise the England average may change and be unrepresentative of the country as a whole.

When comparing ID 2007 with ID 2010 it is important to bear in mind that a change in the ranking for a LSOA does not necessarily mean a change in the level of deprivation in that LSOA. A change in rank position between IDs simply reflects that relatively there has been an improvement or deterioration in the relative level of deprivation in that LSOA compared with all other LSOAs: the LSOA rank can improve despite there being more deprivation or worsen despite there being less deprivation, depending on what has happened in other areas.

It should be noted that when looking at seaside destinations, or indeed any sort of coastal settlement analysis, two regions: the West Midlands and London; do not have any coastline. The LSOAs for these regions are included when looking at England as a whole.

Notes

1. For a detailed explanation of the seven domains please see the ID 2010 metadata document.

How do larger seaside destinations compare with England as a whole?

Given the large number of Lower Layer Super Output Areas (LSOAs) in England (32,482), for analysis purposes the LSOA data will be looked at in quintile groups, to determine how the levels of deprivation in seaside destinations are distributed compared with those for England. It can be seen that the overall spread of deprivation for seaside destinations and how this compares with England by looking at the quintile distribution of LSOAs for the Indices of Deprivation (ID).

Figure 1 shows the quintile distribution of LSOAs across the larger English seaside destinations and England for ID and its respective domains for 2007. In the quintile distribution, for England as a whole there will be 20% of LSOAs in each quintile. If the seaside destinations are reflective of England as a whole they will have a similar proportion of LSOAs in each quintile. If there are more than 20% of LSOAs in the most deprived quintile then the larger English seaside destinations are likely to be more deprived than England as a whole. If there are less than 20% of LSOAs in the most deprived quintile then the larger English seaside destinations are likely to be less deprived than England as a whole. However, it is the overall pattern in the quintile distribution that will determine whether the larger English seaside destinations have similar or different levels of deprivation than England in general.

Figure 1: ID domain quintile distribution for the larger English seaside destinations and England, 2007

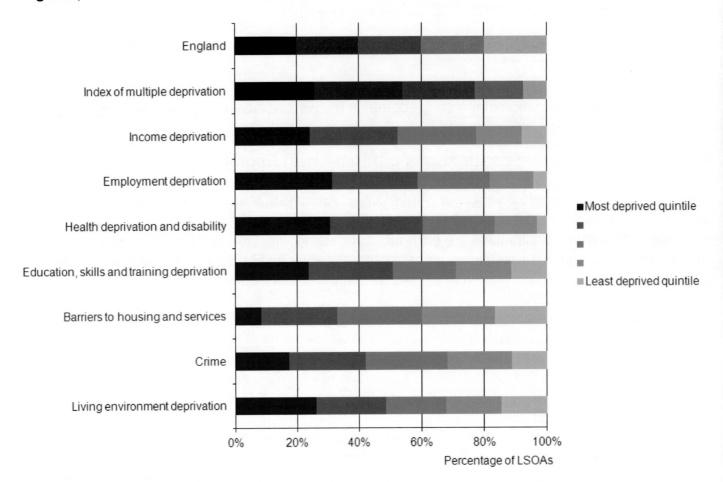

Source: Communities and Local Government

Figure 1 shows that for the index of multiple deprivation the larger English seaside destinations had higher proportions of LSOAs in the most deprived quintile than England overall, with the darker shades on the left being more spread out than the lighter shades to the right of the figure. There was a greater proportion of LSOAs in the most deprived quintile (26.0% in 2007), compared with the two least deprived quintiles (22.9%).

That said the overall deprivation pattern for the larger English seaside destinations was not consistent across all domains. The 'Health deprivation and disability' and 'Employment deprivation' domains had more than 80% of LSOAs in the first three quintiles in 2007. This means that the two least deprived quintiles made up less than 20% of LSOAs for the larger English seaside destinations, compared with 40% for England. Conversely, the 'Barriers to housing and services' domain had 33.1% of LSOAs in the two most deprived quintiles, meaning that deprivation levels for this domain were generally lower than for England as a whole. The pattern for 2010 can be seen in Figure 2.

Figure 2: ID domain quintile distribution for the larger English seaside destinations and England, 2010

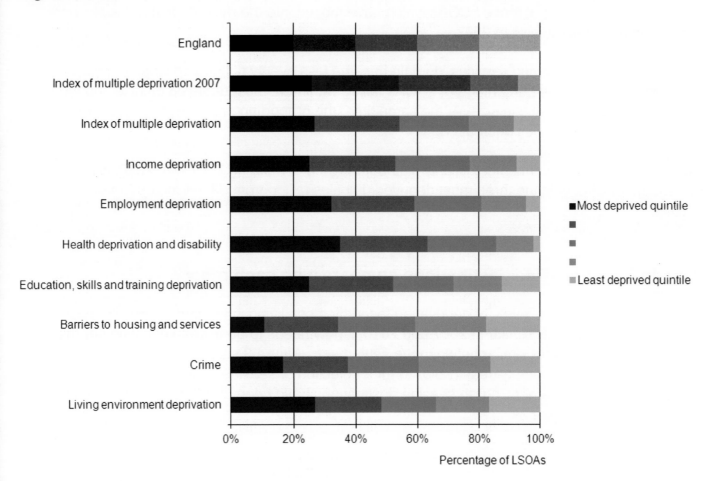

Source: Communities and Local Government

When comparing Figure 1 with Figure 2 it can be seen that the levels of deprivation in the larger seaside destinations were broadly similar. In Figure 2 the overall ID distribution of LSOAs was a little more widely spread than in Figure 1, with a greater proportion of LSOAs in the most deprived quintile (26.0% in 2007 compared with 26.9% in 2010) and the least deprived quintile (7.5% in 2007 compared with 8.7% in 2010).

The domains which had the highest proportion of LSOAs in the most deprived quintiles in both 2007 and 2010 were the 'Health deprivation and disability' domain and the 'Employment deprivation' domain. The 'Employment deprivation' domain had the greatest proportion of all domains in 2007: 31.4% compared with 30.8% for the 'Health deprivation and disability' domain; while the reverse was true in 2010: with the 'Employment deprivation' domain rising to 32.2% compared with 34.9% for the 'Health deprivation and disability' domain.

The proportion of LSOAs which fell within the most deprived quintile in the 'Health deprivation and disability' domain increased from 30.8% in 2007 to 34.9% in 2010. Although this looks like a big change, a large number of those LSOAs which have moved into the most deprived quintile were close to being in that quintile in 2007.

The 'Barriers to housing and services' domain became less evenly distributed when comparing 2007 with 2010, with the percentage of LSOAs falling within the most deprived quintile and the least deprived quintile increasing in size. At the same time, the proportion of LSOAs which fell within each of the middle three quintiles decreased.

The 'Crime' domain became more evenly distributed when comparing 2007 with 2010, with the percentage of LSOAs in the three most deprived quintiles falling from 68.3% in 2007 to 60.5% in 2010.

How do larger seaside destinations compare with each other?

Having identified that the levels of deprivation faced by those living in the larger English seaside destinations was broadly similar in 2007 and 2010, it now needs to be ascertained whether the levels of deprivation were similar between the settlements. Figure 3 shows the quintile distribution of Lower Layer Super Output Areas (LSOAs) for a selection of seaside destinations chosen to show the overall pattern; all larger English seaside destinations have been charted in Figure 3a in the data file linked to below Figure 3.

Figure 3: ID quintile distribution for selected larger seaside destinations and England, 2010

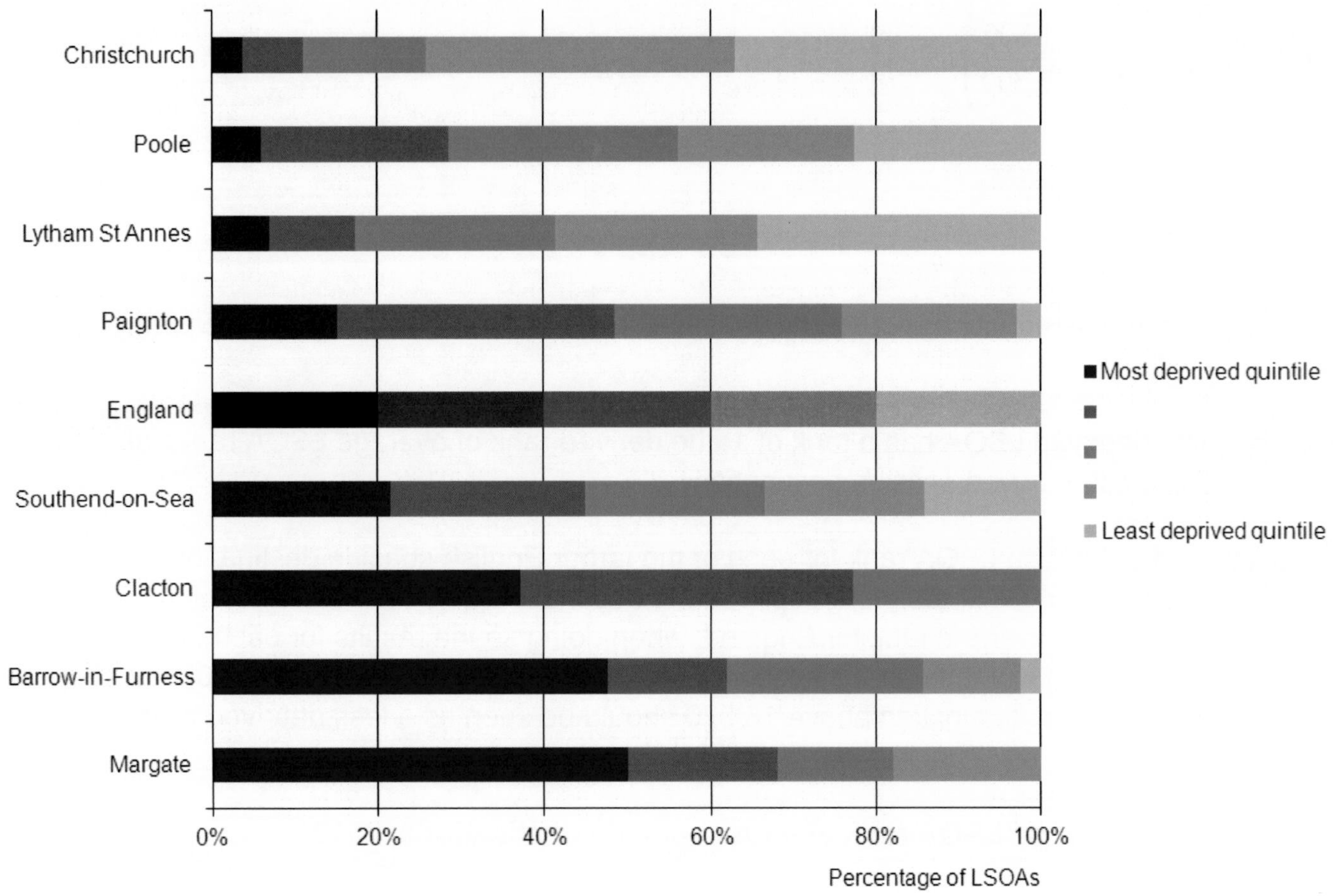

Source: Communities and Local Government

Figure 3 shows that there was no consistent pattern of deprivation among the larger English seaside destinations in 2010 for the Indices of Deprivation (ID) as a whole, in terms of the proportion of LSOAs within each settlement. This holds true when each domain is looked at separately. A single measure to readily compare the larger English seaside destinations needs to be used to enable further investigation.

One way to compare seaside destinations in terms of deprivation is to use the average LSOA rank for each domain and then rank the destinations by this average. To calculate this average the methodology used is the same as the methodology used by the Department for Communities and Local Government when calculating the ranks for local authorities. The proportion of the population for a destination within an LSOA is multiplied by the rank of that LSOA and then the results are added together for all LSOAs in that destination. In other words, if a seaside destination has two LSOAs, with ranks of 500 and 1,200 and populations of 1,500 and 1,800 respectively then the calculation would be as follows, where R is the seaside destination average rank:

Calculating average rank of deprivation

$$R = \left(\left(\frac{1,500}{3,300} \right) 500 \right) + \left(\left(\frac{1,800}{3,300} \right) 1,200 \right)$$

$$R = 227.27 + 654.55$$

$$R = 881.82$$

The description for this equation is currently unavailable. ONS apologises for any inconvenience caused.

For ID the most deprived LSOA has a rank of 1; the derived rank of average LSOA ranks allocates a rank of 1 to the most deprived seaside destination.

Table 3 shows the average LSOA rank for each of the larger English seaside destinations. The lower the average LSOA rank, the more deprived the destination. The above methodology was also applied to calculate the average rank for England, when doing so the results for each domain differ due to the LSOAs being weighted by population. For ID as a whole in England in 2010, any average LSOA rank for a seaside destination above 16,320 should be seen as a less deprived place than average.

Table 3: Rank of average LSOA rank of larger seaside destinations, 2010

Rank	Seaside destination	Average LSOA rank
1	Blackpool	7,159
2	Clacton	8,434
3	Hastings	8,903
4	Ramsgate	9,001
5	Margate	9,419
6	Hartlepool	9,426
7	Great Yarmouth	9,434
8	South Shields	9,806
9	Barrow-in-Furness	9,906
10	Sunderland	10,136
11	Torquay	10,604
12	Folkestone	11,062
13	Scarborough	11,345
14	Brighton	12,179

Rank	Seaside destination	Average LSOA rank
15	Eastbourne	12,649
16	Southsea	13,013
17	Lowestoft	13,113
18	Weymouth	13,202
19	Paignton	13,347
20	Bournemouth	14,018
21	Weston-super-Mare	14,554
22	Bexhill	14,593
23	Tynemouth	14,731
24	Southend-on-Sea	14,998
25	Littlehampton	15,607
	ENGLAND average rank	**16,320**
26	Bognor Regis	16,693
27	Southport	16,702
28	Worthing	17,825
29	Poole	18,560
30	Lytham St Annes	21,401
31	Christchurch	21,467

Table source: Communities and Local Government

Table 3 shows that while for ID as a whole the larger English seaside destinations were more susceptible to deprivation when compared with the England average, this was not always the case. Six of the destinations: Christchurch, Lytham St Annes, Poole, Worthing, Southport and Bognor Regis had average LSOA ranks above the English average, meaning that they were less deprived than the England average.

The domains that particularly stand out when this analysis is extended across all domains are 'Barriers to housing and services' and 'Living environment deprivation' as they do not follow the pattern for ID rankings for larger English seaside destinations. Figure 4 shows the rankings for the Index of Multiple Deprivation (IMD) and the 'Barriers to housing and services' and 'Living environment deprivation' domains for the 31 larger seaside destinations.

Figure 4 is a radar chart with each spine representing a different seaside destination. The ranks of average LSOA ranks for each seaside destination are displayed for IMD, the 'Barriers to housing and services' domain and the 'Living environment deprivation' domain. The seaside destinations have been ordered by IMD rank, so that IMD line on the radar chart appears to spiral outwards. If the individual domains follow the pattern for IMD then they too will spiral out, meaning that the more deprived the seaside destination is overall, the more deprived it is for that domain. If the rank for a domain is inside the spiral then the seaside destination is ranked relatively better for that domain than for IMD, if it is outside the spiral then it is ranked relatively worse for that domain than for IMD. It should be noted that these rankings are for the larger English seaside destinations and how they relate to one another and are not representative of how a seaside destination relates to England.

Figure 4: Ranking of the larger seaside destinations for ID and domains, 2010

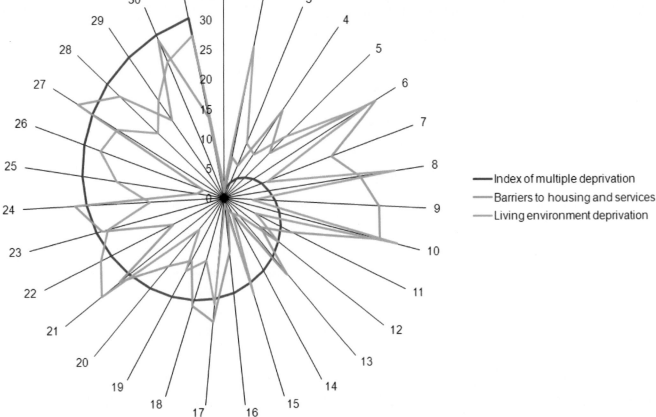

Source: Communities and Local Government

Figure 4 shows that these two domains were quite different from IMD in terms of rankings for the larger seaside destinations. On the left of the figure it is apparent that a number of seaside destinations with relatively good rankings of IMD have relatively poor rankings for 'Barriers to housing and services' and the 'Living environment deprivation'. The right of the chart shows the reverse situation. The other domains, whilst displaying some variation, were more in line with IMD with poorly ranked destinations being generally poorly ranked across the other five domains and relatively well ranked destinations being generally well ranked.

Looking at the variation in domain rankings

Having established that the rankings for the domains do not always follow the Indices of Deprivation (ID) as a whole, a selection of the larger seaside destinations can be looked at to see whether there is anything within the domains that could explain it. Four seaside destinations have been selected to investigate the variation in domain rankings; this selection has been made to demonstrate the variety in deprivation within the rankings data. The rankings for the selected seaside destinations can be seen in Figure 5.

Figure 5: Relative rankings of selected larger English seaside destinations across ID and its domains, 2010

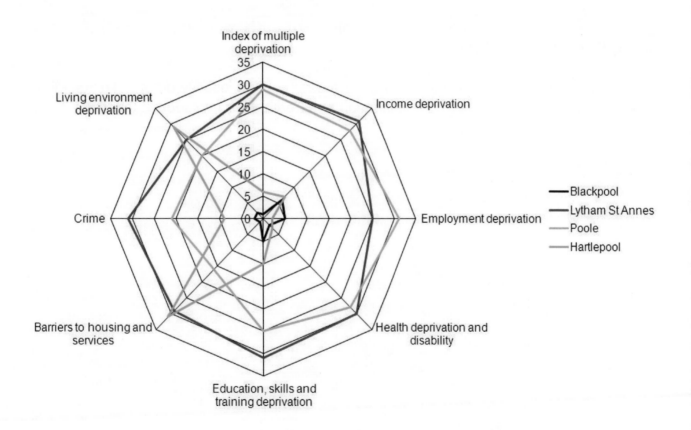

Source: Communities and Local Government

Figure 5 shows a disparity in the ranks of Blackpool and Lytham St Annes, which is particularly interesting as the two are located next to one another. Lytham St Annes is less deprived than Blackpool, while still benefiting from the seaside location. Looking at the small area income estimates for 2007/08, it is apparent that income in Lytham St Annes is higher than in Blackpool, as supported by the 'Income deprivation' domain. Out of work benefits data at LSOA level for 2010 also show that there were a greater proportion of claimants in Blackpool than in Lytham St Annes. Those living in Blackpool may be employed in lower skill work (as suggested by the 'Education, skills and training deprivation' domain) and if low paid then these workers may need to live closer to where they work to offset transport costs and higher housing costs outside of Blackpool.

Figure 5 shows that Hartlepool, which had relatively poor ID ranks overall for the larger English seaside destinations, had relatively good ranks for the 'Barriers to housing and services' and 'Living environment deprivation' domains. The domains with the lowest weighting in the calculation of the overall ID in 2010 were the 'Barriers to housing and services', 'Crime' and 'Living environment deprivation' domains, which all have a weighting of 9.3% meaning that any change in one of these domains will have a lesser effect on the overall ID than the same change in other domains.

How do larger seaside destinations compare with mid-sized seaside destinations?

As before, the Indices of Deprivation (ID) data are arranged into quintile groups. The distribution of deprivation for the mid-sized seaside destination and England can be seen in Figure 6.

Figure 6: ID domain quintile distribution of LSOAs for the mid-sized English seaside destinations, the larger seaside destinations and England, 2010

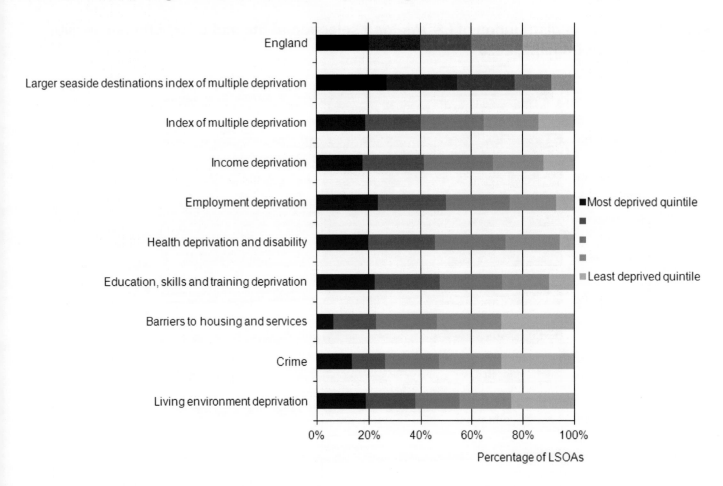

Source: Communities and Local Government

By comparing larger seaside destinations with mid-sized seaside destinations, it can be seen that the mid-sized seaside destinations have lower levels of deprivation compared with larger seaside destinations as shown by a smaller percentage of Lower Layer Super Output Areas (LSOAs) in the most deprived quintile. For ID as a whole, mid-sized seaside destinations were more similar to England as a whole than the larger seaside destinations. The patterns shown in Figure 6 for 2010 were broadly similar to those for mid-sized seaside destinations in 2007.

When looking at the data for the domains, the ones which stand out for the mid-sized seaside destinations were those with the lowest weighting: 'Barriers to housing and services', 'Crime' and 'Living environment deprivation' which had more than 20% of LSOAs in the least deprived quintile.

Having established that mid-sized seaside destinations were different from larger seaside destinations in terms of deprivation, consideration was given to whether the mid-sized seaside destinations followed the same pattern in terms of ID distribution as the larger seaside destinations. This can be seen in Figure 7.

Figure 7: ID quintile distribution of LSOAs for a selection of the mid-sized English seaside destinations and England, 2010

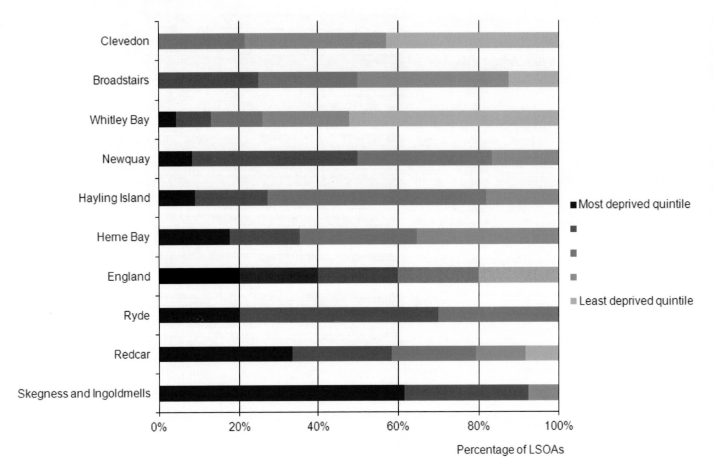

Source: Communities and Local Government

Figure 7 shows that as with the larger English seaside destinations, there was variation in the levels of deprivation in the mid-sized English seaside destinations. As can be seen in Figure 7, Clevedon had low levels of deprivation in 2010, with no constituent LSOAs being in the two most deprived quintiles. Conversely, Ryde had high levels of deprivation in 2010, with no LSOAs in the two least deprived quintiles.

Figure 7 shows that Skegness and Ingoldmells had high levels of deprivation, with 7.7% of LSOAs in the three least deprived quintiles compared with 60% for England. Skegness and Ingoldmells had 61.5% of LSOAs in the most deprived quintile, compared with just 20% for England.

For the larger seaside destinations, six of the 31 destinations had lower levels of deprivation than England average when using the average LSOA rank. The situation for the mid-sized seaside destinations can be seen in Table 4. The average LSOA rank for England was 16,320, so any destination with a higher derived average LSOA rank than England had a lower level of deprivation than England as a whole in 2010.

Table 4: Rank of average LSOA rank of mid-sized seaside destinations, 2010

Rank	Seaside destination	Average LSOA rank
1	Skegness and Ingoldmells	6,491
2	Seaham	9,038
3	Ryde	9,935
4	Fleetwood	10,011
5	Bridlington	10,196
6	Morecambe	10,976
7	Redcar	11,998
8	Newquay	12,608
9	Cleethorpes	12,683
10	Harwich	13,710
11	Falmouth	14,172
12	Lancing	14,739
13	Herne Bay	15,037
14	Hayling Island	15,565
15	Cleveleys	16,042
	ENGLAND average rank	**16,320**
16	Deal	16,434
17	Teignmouth	16,463
18	Burnham-on-Sea	16,469
19	Broadstairs	18,092
20	Exmouth	18,560
21	Shoreham by sea	18,763
22	Felixstowe	19,249
23	Whitstable	19,786
24	Clevedon	23,172

Rank	Seaside destination	Average LSOA rank
25	Whitley Bay	23,496
26	Formby	25,873

Table source: Communities and Local Government

Table 4 shows that there were 11 (out of 26) mid-sized seaside destinations which had lower levels of deprivation in 2010 than England, more than double the proportion of larger seaside destinations that year.

When comparing Table 4 with Table 3, it can be seen that one mid-sized seaside destination (Skegness and Ingoldmells) had more deprivation than any of the larger seaside destinations. There are three mid-sized seaside destinations (Formby, Whitley Bay and Clevedon) which had less deprivation than any of the larger seaside destinations. This shows greater variation in the levels of deprivation in mid-sized seaside destinations. It is interesting to note that two of the least deprived larger seaside destinations (Lytham St Annes and Christchurch) had a population of fewer than 45,000 in 2011, which is just above the threshold of mid-sized seaside destinations (40,000).

Summary

This article has used the Indices of Deprivation (ID) for 2007 and 2010 alongside ONS defined seaside destinations to establish that:

- Overall larger seaside destinations in England were more deprived than the England average in 2007 and 2010; however, some seaside destinations were less deprived than average.
- Of the larger seaside destinations, Blackpool had the highest average deprivation levels. Lytham St Annes which borders Blackpool was the seaside destination with the second lowest average deprivation levels of the 31 larger English seaside destinations. Christchurch had the lowest average deprivation levels.
- Mid-sized seaside destinations had lower levels of deprivation than larger seaside destinations and were more similar to England than the larger seaside destinations in terms of deprivation patterns. However, Skegness and Ingoldmells, a mid-sized seaside destination, had the highest average deprivation levels.
- The distribution of deprivation in the larger seaside destinations was broadly similar for 2007 and 2010.
- The patterns for the domains differ, particularly the 'Barriers to housing and services' and 'Living environment deprivation' domains with some of the most deprived seaside destinations having relatively low levels of deprivation for these domains.

Further articles looking at the characteristics of seaside destinations using results from the 2011 Census are planned for 2014. Other potential ideas for further research include:

- Comparing the larger seaside destinations with their regions, rather than England, assessing whether there were any regional patterns to the ID data.
- Investigating the cause of the disparity between Blackpool and Lytham St Annes.
- Comparing seaside destinations with other areas associated with deprivation such as inner cities and coalfield areas.

Background notes

1. Details of the policy governing the release of new data are available by visiting www.statisticsauthority.gov.uk/assessment/code-of-practice/index.html or from the Media Relations Office email: media.relations@ons.gsi.gov.uk

Copyright

This document is also available on our website at www.ons.gov.uk.

Region and Country Profiles

Statistical Regions of the United Kingdom

Regions, Counties and Unitary Authorities of the United Kingdom, 2011

North East

North West

Yorkshire and The Humber

East Midlands

West Midlands

East of England

London

South East

South West

Wales

Scotland

Northern Ireland

United Kingdom: Regions, 2012

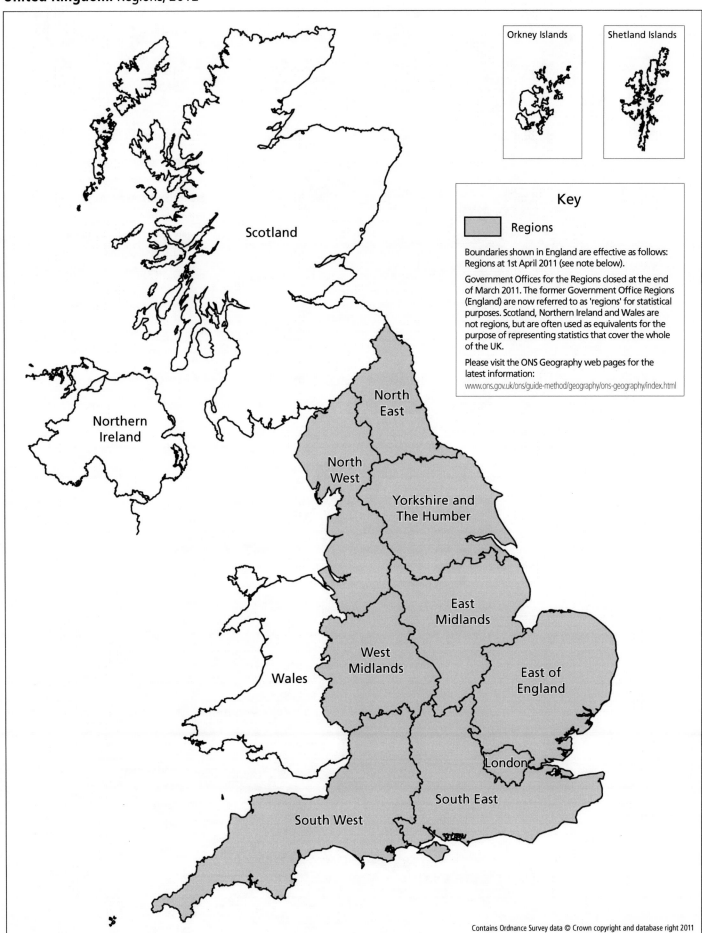

Orkney Islands

Shetland Islands

Key

Regions

Boundaries shown in England are effective as follows: Regions at 1st April 2011 (see note below).

Government Offices for the Regions closed at the end of March 2011. The former Government Office Regions (England) are now referred to as 'regions' for statistical purposes. Scotland, Northern Ireland and Wales are not regions, but are often used as equivalents for the purpose of representing statistics that cover the whole of the UK.

Please visit the ONS Geography web pages for the latest information:
www.ons.gov.uk/ons/guide-method/geography/ons-geography/index.html

Scotland

Northern Ireland

North East

North West

Yorkshire and The Humber

East Midlands

West Midlands

East of England

Wales

London

South East

South West

**Produced by ONS Geography
GIS & Mapping Unit**

United Kingdom: Regions, Counties and Unitary Authorities,[1] 2011

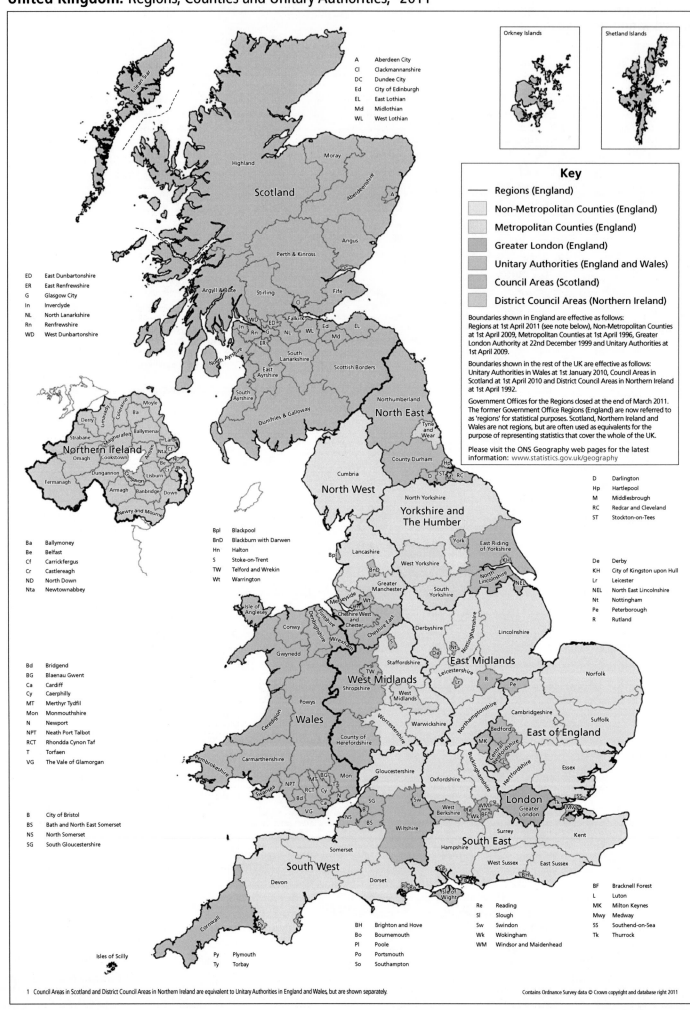

Key

— Regions (England)

Non-Metropolitan Counties (England)

Metropolitan Counties (England)

Greater London (England)

Unitary Authorities (England and Wales)

Council Areas (Scotland)

District Council Areas (Northern Ireland)

Boundaries shown in England are effective as follows: Regions at 1st April 2011 (see note below), Non-Metropolitan Counties at 1st April 2009, Metropolitan Counties at 1st April 1996, Greater London Authority at 22nd December 1999 and Unitary Authorities at 1st April 2009.

Boundaries shown in the rest of the UK are effective as follows: Unitary Authorities in Wales at 1st January 2010, Council Areas in Scotland at 1st April 2010 and District Council Areas in Northern Ireland at 1st April 1992.

Government Offices for the Regions closed at the end of March 2011. The former Government Office Regions (England) are now referred to as 'regions' for statistical purposes. Scotland, Northern Ireland and Wales are not regions, but are often used as equivalents for the purpose of representing statistics that cover the whole of the UK.

Please visit the ONS Geography web pages for the latest information: www.statistics.gov.uk/geography

A	Aberdeen City
Cl	Clackmannanshire
DC	Dundee City
Ed	City of Edinburgh
EL	East Lothian
Md	Midlothian
WL	West Lothian

ED	East Dunbartonshire
ER	East Renfrewshire
G	Glasgow City
In	Inverclyde
NL	North Lanarkshire
Rn	Renfrewshire
WD	West Dunbartonshire

Ba	Ballymoney
Be	Belfast
Cf	Carrickfergus
Cr	Castlereagh
ND	North Down
Nta	Newtownabbey

Bd	Bridgend
BG	Blaenau Gwent
Ca	Cardiff
Cy	Caerphilly
MT	Merthyr Tydfil
Mon	Monmouthshire
N	Newport
NPT	Neath Port Talbot
RCT	Rhondda Cynon Taf
T	Torfaen
VG	The Vale of Glamorgan

B	City of Bristol
BS	Bath and North East Somerset
NS	North Somerset
SG	South Gloucestershire

Bpl	Blackpool
BnD	Blackburn with Darwen
Hn	Halton
S	Stoke-on-Trent
TW	Telford and Wrekin
Wt	Warrington

D	Darlington
Hp	Hartlepool
M	Middlesbrough
RC	Redcar and Cleveland
ST	Stockton-on-Tees

De	Derby
KH	City of Kingston upon Hull
Lr	Leicester
NEL	North East Lincolnshire
Nt	Nottingham
Pe	Peterborough
R	Rutland

BF	Bracknell Forest
L	Luton
MK	Milton Keynes
Mwy	Medway
SS	Southend-on-Sea
Tk	Thurrock

Re	Reading
Sl	Slough
Sw	Swindon
Wk	Wokingham
WM	Windsor and Maidenhead

BH	Brighton and Hove
Bo	Bournemouth
Pl	Poole
Po	Portsmouth
So	Southampton

Py	Plymouth
Ty	Torbay

1 Council Areas in Scotland and District Council Areas in Northern Ireland are equivalent to Unitary Authorities in England and Wales, but are shown separately.

Contains Ordnance Survey data © Crown copyright and database right 2011

**Produced by ONS Geography
GIS & Mapping Unit**

North East had the highest regional unemployment rate in mid-2013

The 2013 ONS regional characteristics analysis for the North East

The latest ONS Region and Country Profiles analysis takes a look at the characteristics of the nine regions within England and the countries of the UK, exploring aspects such as population, age, employment, crime and house prices. The profile of the North East shows it to be the smallest in the UK in area outside London and it had the lowest growth in population. The North East contributed 3% to the UK's economic output. The population was relatively old with a median age of 41.5 years, and the incidence of crimes in the region was among the lowest in England.

The North East makes up 4% of the total UK population

As a region, the North East is the smallest in England outside London in terms of area. The North East covers 4% of the total area of the UK at 8,600 square kilometres (sq km). The urban south and east of the region is surrounded by a sparsely populated rural landscape including the Pennines and the Cheviot Hills.

The region had a population of 2.6 million at mid-2012 which was 4% of the total UK population. The increase from mid-2011 was one of the lowest increases of all the English regions at 0.2%, compared with an increase of 0.7% for the UK. Population density in the North East in mid-2012 was 304 people per sq km, below the England average of 411 but above the UK average of 263.

Regional Profile of the North East

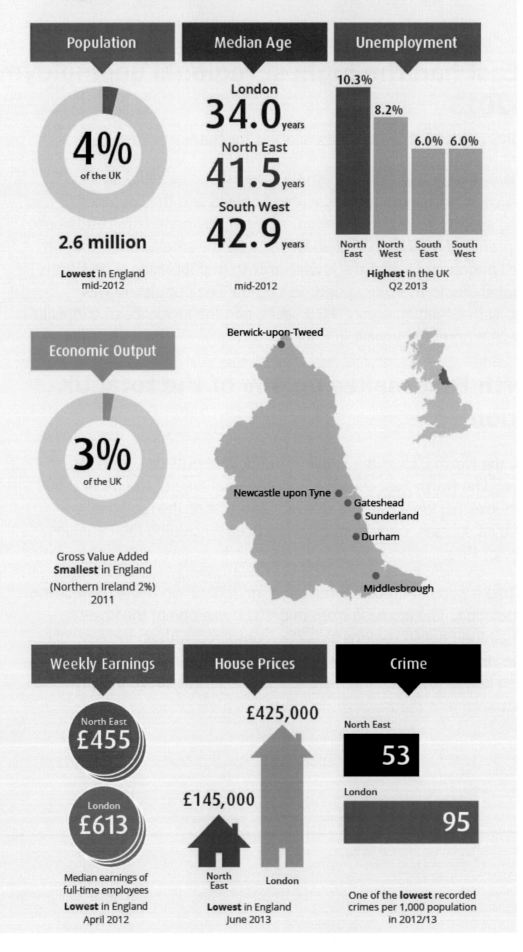

Population

4% of the UK

2.6 million

Lowest in England
mid-2012

Median Age

London
34.0 years

North East
41.5 years

South West
42.9 years

mid-2012

Unemployment

- North East 10.3%
- North West 8.2%
- South East 6.0%
- South West 6.0%

Highest in the UK
Q2 2013

Economic Output

3% of the UK

Gross Value Added
Smallest in England
(Northern Ireland 2%)
2011

Berwick-upon-Tweed

Newcastle upon Tyne
Gateshead
Sunderland
Durham
Middlesbrough

Weekly Earnings

North East
£455

London
£613

Median earnings of
full-time employees
Lowest in England
April 2012

House Prices

£425,000

£145,000

North East   London

Lowest in England
June 2013

Crime

North East
53

London
95

One of the **lowest** recorded
crimes per 1,000 population
in 2012/13

www.ons.gov.uk

Office for
National Statistics

Region had the joint lowest police-recorded crime rate in England

The population of the North East is relatively old with a median age of 41.5 years in mid-2012, which was the same as Scotland and above the UK median age of 39.7 years. Life expectancy at birth in the region in 2009 to 2011 was one of the two lowest in England at 77.5 years for males and 81.5 years for females. This compares with 78.9 and 82.9 years respectively for England.

Crime rates for the North East were among the lowest in England in 2012/13. There were 53 police-recorded crimes per 1,000 population compared with 64 per 1,000 population across England in 2012/13. The estimated rate of crimes against households reported to the Crime Survey for England and Wales (CSEW) was 187 per 1,000 households, lower than the England average (217 incidents per 1,000 households).

The North East produced 3% of the UK's economic output

The North East produced 3% of the UK's economic output (gross value added) in 2011, only Northern Ireland was lower at 2%. The region produced 8.9 tonnes of carbon dioxide (CO_2) emissions per resident in 2011, the highest of all the English regions, compared with 6.7 tonnes per resident for England.

The unemployment rate in the region was the highest in the UK at 10.3% in Q2 2013, compared with 7.8% for the UK. The employment rate stood at 66.5%, lower than the UK rate of 71.5% for the same period. Almost a fifth of children in the North East lived in workless households in Q2 2013, at 18.7% this was the highest proportion in the regions, compared with an average of 13.6% for England. In April 2012, median gross weekly earnings for full-time adult employees in the North East were £455, joint lowest with Wales and lower than the UK median of £506.

The average house price in the North East in June 2013 was £145,000, the lowest of all the English regions. Only Northern Ireland was lower, compared with the average for the UK (£242,000).

Where can I find out more about ONS regional statistics?

These statistics were analysed by the Sub-national Reporting team at the ONS using data from a range of official statistics. If you'd like to find out more about the latest regional statistics, please see our Notes on Sources, latest tables (260.5 Kb Excel sheet) and interactive mapping and charting tool or visit our Directory of Tables page. If you have any comments or suggestions, we'd like to hear them! Please email us at better.info@ons.gsi.gov.uk.

Categories: People and Places, Communities, Neighbourhoods and Communities, Agriculture and Environment, Crime and Justice, Economy, Labour Market, Housing and Households, Housing Market, Population

North West had the lowest life expectancy in England in 2009 to 2011

The 2013 ONS regional characteristics analysis for the North West

The latest ONS Region and Country Profiles analysis takes a look at the regional characteristics of the nine regions within England and countries of the UK, exploring aspects such as population, age, employment and house prices. The profile of the North West shows it to have the third largest population and the second highest population density. The North West contributed 9% to the UK's economic output. House prices are among the lowest in England.

The North West makes up 11% of the total UK population

The North West is the third largest English region in population terms, with 7.1 million people at mid-2012, 11% of the total UK population. The population increased by 0.4% between mid-2011 and mid-2012, compared with an increase of 0.7% for the UK over the same period. The region had the second highest population density in the UK (502 people per square kilometres (sq km)) in 2012.

The region covers 6% of the total area of the UK (14,100 sq km). It has two large built-up areas, Manchester and Liverpool, and the second highest proportion of its population living in urban areas (89.4%) compared with 82.4% for England in 2011. In contrast, it also has the second largest area of National Parks (including the whole of the Lake District and parts of the Yorkshire Dales and Peak District) in England.

Regional Profile of the North West

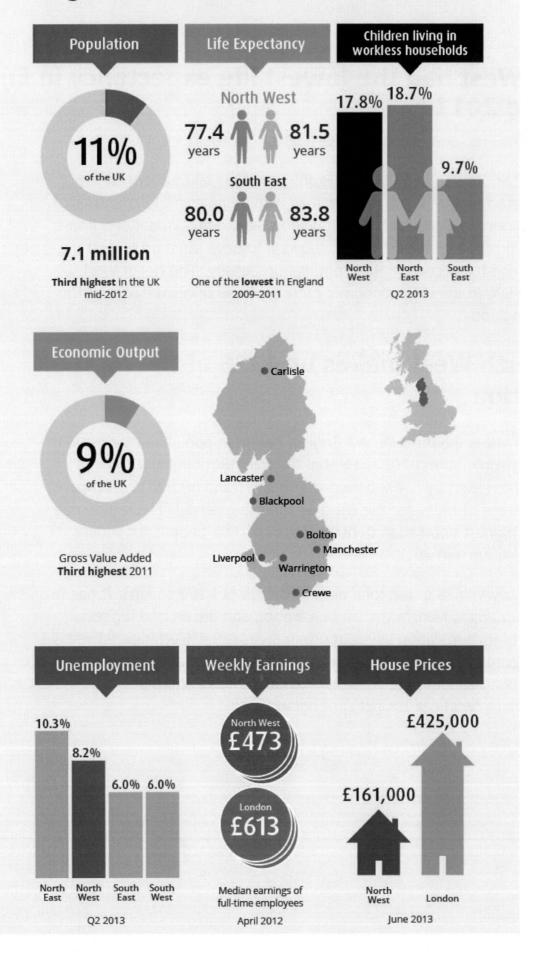

Population

11% of the UK

7.1 million

Third highest in the UK mid-2012

Life Expectancy

North West
77.4 years | 81.5 years

South East
80.0 years | 83.8 years

One of the **lowest** in England 2009–2011

Children living in workless households

17.8% — North West
18.7% — North East
9.7% — South East

Q2 2013

Economic Output

9% of the UK

Gross Value Added
Third highest 2011

Carlisle
Lancaster
Blackpool
Bolton
Manchester
Liverpool
Warrington
Crewe

Unemployment

10.3%
8.2%
6.0%   6.0%

North East | North West | South East | South West

Q2 2013

Weekly Earnings

North West **£473**

London **£613**

Median earnings of full-time employees
April 2012

House Prices

£425,000

£161,000

North West | London

June 2013

www.ons.gov.uk

Office for National Statistics

The North West had one of the highest percentages of children in workless households

The proportion of children living in workless households in the North West in Q2 2013 was 17.8%. This was one of the highest regions, compared with 13.6% for England and 18.7% in the North East.

Life expectancy at birth in the North West in 2009 to 2011 was 77.4 years for males, the lowest in England and compared with 78.9 years for England. It was 81.5 years for females, the joint lowest in England with the North East and compared with 82.9 years for England. The median age in mid-2012 for residents in the North West was 40.2 years, compared with 39.7 years for the UK.

The region produced 9% of the UK's economic output

The North West region contributed 9% of the UK's economic output (gross value added or GVA) in 2011 and the unemployment rate in Q2 2013 was 8.2%, slightly above the UK figure of 7.8%. The rate at which businesses in the region closed down in 2011 was 10.7%, the highest of all English regions and countries of the UK, compared with the UK rate of 9.8%.

The employment rate in the region stood at 69.1% in Q2 2013, slightly below the UK rate of 71.5%. The percentage of the region's population aged 16 to 64 having no qualifications in 2012 was 11.1%, above the UK average of 9.9%.

In April 2012, median gross weekly earnings for full-time adult employees in the North West were £473, lower than the UK median of £506. In 2011, gross disposable household income (GDHI) of North West residents was £14,500 per head, compared with £16,000 for the UK. The average house price in the North West in June 2013 was £161,000, the second lowest of all the English regions, compared with £242,000 for the UK and £145,000 for the North East.

Where can I find out more about ONS regional statistics?

These statistics were analysed by the Sub-national Reporting team at the ONS using data from a range of official statistics. If you'd like to find out more about the latest regional statistics, please see our Notes on Sources, latest tables (260.5 Kb Excel sheet) and interactive mapping and charting tool or visit our Directory of Tables page. If you have any comments or suggestions, we'd like to hear them! Please email us at better.info@ons.gsi.gov.uk.

Categories: People and Places, Communities, Neighbourhoods and Communities, Business and Energy, Economy, Labour Market, Housing and Households, Housing Market, Population

Yorkshire and The Humber: 11.5% of adults had no qualifications

The 2013 ONS regional characteristics analysis for Yorkshire and The Humber

The latest ONS Region and Country Profiles analysis takes a look at the regional characteristics of the nine regions within England and countries of the UK, exploring aspects such as population, age, employment, crime and house prices. The profile of Yorkshire and The Humber shows its residents to have low earnings and house prices to be stagnant. Yorkshire and The Humber contributes 7% to the UK's economic output. A relatively high percentage of the population are unqualified and labour productivity is the lowest in England.

Yorkshire and The Humber made up 8% of the total UK population

Yorkshire and The Humber had a population of 5.3 million at mid-2012, 8% of the total UK population. The increase from mid-2011 was 0.5%, compared with an increase of 0.7% for the UK. As a region, Yorkshire and The Humber covers 6% of the total area of the UK, an area of 15,400 square kilometres (sq km).

The south and west of the region are relatively urban, including two metropolitan county areas, West Yorkshire and South Yorkshire. The county of North Yorkshire includes most of the areas of the North York Moors and the Yorkshire Dales National Parks. The population density (345 people per sq km in 2012) and the proportion of residents living in urban areas (82.5% in 2011) are both close to the average for England (411 people per sq km and 82.4% respectively).

Regional Profile of Yorkshire and The Humber

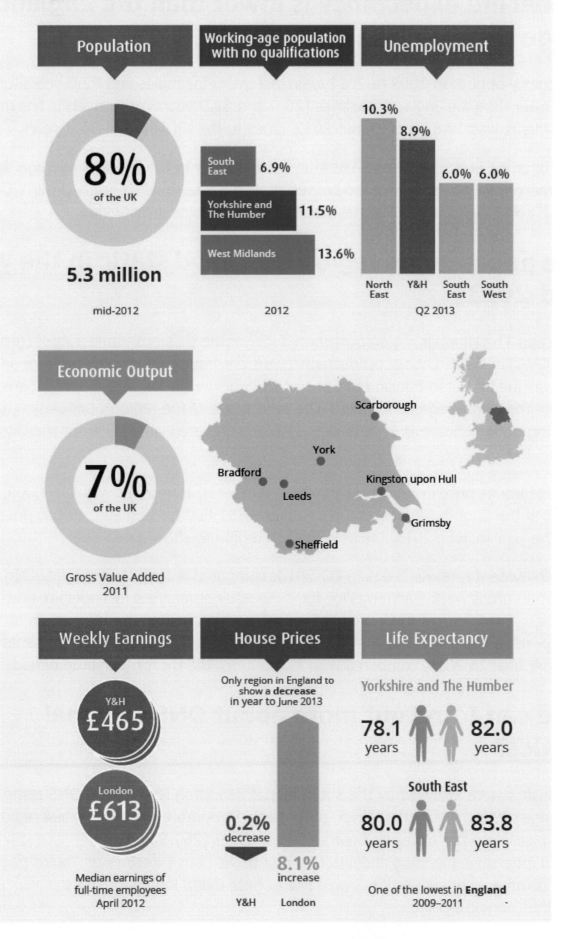

Population

8% of the UK

5.3 million

mid-2012

Working-age population with no qualifications

South East — 6.9%

Yorkshire and The Humber — 11.5%

West Midlands — 13.6%

2012

Unemployment

10.3% — North East

8.9% — Y&H

6.0% — South East

6.0% — South West

Q2 2013

Economic Output

7% of the UK

Gross Value Added 2011

Scarborough

York

Bradford

Leeds

Kingston upon Hull

Grimsby

Sheffield

Weekly Earnings

Y&H **£465**

London **£613**

Median earnings of full-time employees April 2012

House Prices

Only region in England to show a **decrease** in year to June 2013

0.2% decrease — Y&H

8.1% increase — London

Life Expectancy

Yorkshire and The Humber

78.1 years   **82.0** years

South East

80.0 years   **83.8** years

One of the lowest in **England** 2009–2011

www.ons.gov.uk

Office for National Statistics

Regional life expectancy is lower than the England average

Life expectancy at birth in 2009 to 2011 was 78.1 years for males and 82.0 years for females, lower than the England averages (78.9 and 82.9 years respectively). The median age of residents was 39.8 years in mid-2012, close to the UK figure of 39.7 years.

The level of crime in Yorkshire and The Humber is similar to the England average. In 2012/13 there were an estimated 216 crimes against households committed per 1,000 households compared with 217 crimes per 1,000 households in England.

House prices in the region remained static in the year to mid-2013

Yorkshire and The Humber region contributed 7% of the UK's economic output (gross value added or GVA) in 2011. Labour productivity (GVA per hour worked) in Yorkshire and The Humber was the lowest in England in 2011 at 12% below the UK average, compared with 29% above the UK average for London. The percentage of the region's population aged 16 to 64 having no qualifications in 2012 was 11.5%, compared with 9.9% for the UK as a whole.

The average house price in Yorkshire and The Humber in June 2013 was £164,000, among the lowest of the English regions, compared with £251,000 for England. House prices fell 0.2% in the year to June 2013, the only English region to show a decrease.

The unemployment rate was 8.9% in Q2 2013, compared with 7.8% for the UK. In April 2012, median gross weekly earnings for full-time adult employees in Yorkshire and The Humber were £465, one of the lowest in England and lower than the UK median of £506. Gross disposable household income (GDHI) of Yorkshire and The Humber residents was £13,800 per head in 2011, compared with £16,000 for the UK for the same period.

Where can I find out more about ONS regional statistics?

These statistics were analysed by the Sub-national Reporting team at the ONS using data from a range of official statistics. If you'd like to find out more about the latest regional statistics, please see our Notes on Sources, latest tables (260.5 Kb Excel sheet) and interactive mapping and charting tool or visit our Directory of Tables page. If you have any comments or suggestions, we'd like to hear them! Please email us at better.info@ons.gsi.gov.uk.

Categories: People and Places, Communities, Neighbourhoods and Communities, Crime and Justice, Economy, Labour Market, Housing and Households, Housing Market, Population

East Midlands 10-year traffic increase was one of the highest in England

The 2013 ONS regional characteristics analysis for the East Midlands

The latest ONS Region and Country Profiles analysis takes a look at the regional characteristics of the nine regions within England and countries of the UK, exploring aspects such as population, age, employment, crime and house prices. The profile of the East Midlands shows it to have a relatively small urban population that is comparatively old, with a median age of 41.0 years. The East Midlands contributes 6% to the UK's economic output, and traffic on major roads in the region has increased by nearly 5% over the past 10 years.

Proportion of the urban population of the East Midlands is lower than the UK

The East Midlands is a varied region including the Peak District National Park in the north west and the Lincolnshire Wolds in the north east with large built-up areas mainly in the central western part of the region. The percentage of the East Midlands population living in urban areas is lower than that for England (73.3% and 82.4% respectively) in 2011.

The region covers 15,600 square kilometres (sq km), which represents 6% of the total area of the UK. The East Midlands had a population of 4.6 million at mid-2012, which was 7% of the UK total. The increase from mid-2011 was the same as for the UK at 0.7%. The population density in the East Midlands in mid-2012 was 293 people per sq km, below the England average of 411 but above the UK average of 263.

Regional Profile of the East Midlands

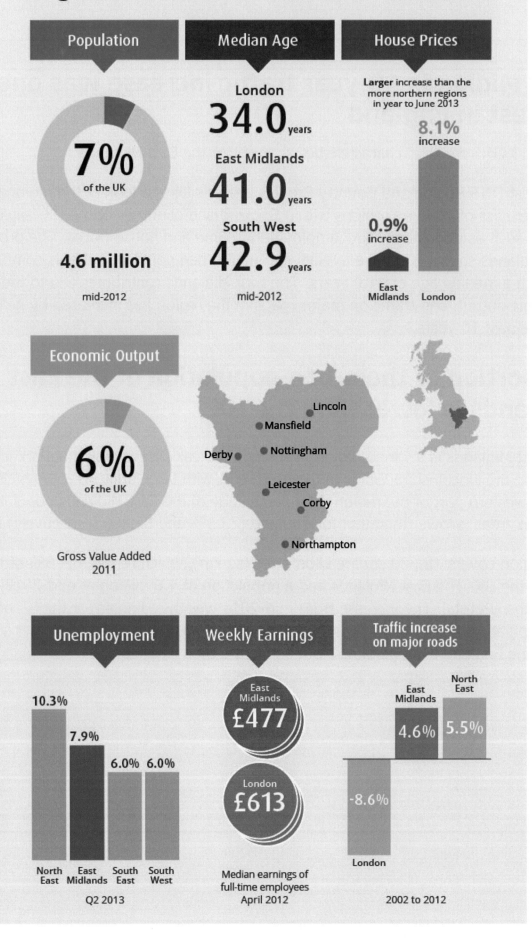

Population

7%
of the UK

4.6 million

mid-2012

Median Age

London
34.0 years

East Midlands
41.0 years

South West
42.9 years

mid-2012

House Prices

Larger increase than the more northern regions in year to June 2013

8.1%
increase

0.9%
increase

East Midlands | London

Economic Output

6%
of the UK

Gross Value Added
2011

Lincoln
Mansfield
Derby
Nottingham
Leicester
Corby
Northampton

Unemployment

10.3%
7.9%
6.0%   6.0%

North East | East Midlands | South East | South West

Q2 2013

Weekly Earnings

East Midlands
£477

London
£613

Median earnings of
full-time employees
April 2012

Traffic increase on major roads

East Midlands
4.6%

North East
5.5%

-8.6%
London

2002 to 2012

168

Regional life expectancy is close to the national average

People aged 65 and over in the region made up 17.8% of the population in 2012, compared with the UK average of 17.0%. The median age of the residents living in the East Midlands was 41.0 years, compared with the UK figure of 39.7 years. Life expectancy at birth in the region in 2009 to 2011 was 78.7 years for males and 82.8 years for females, close to the England averages of 78.9 and 82.9 years respectively.

Crime rates in 2012/13 in the East Midlands show a mixed picture. There were 58 police-recorded crimes per 1,000 population compared with 64 per 1,000 population across England. An estimated 231 crimes against households were reported to the Crime Survey for England and Wales (CSEW) per 1,000 households compared with 217 per 1,000 households for England.

East Midlands generated 6% of the UK's economic output

In 2011, over 6% of the UK's economic output (gross value added or GVA) was generated in the East Midlands. The unemployment rate in the East Midlands was 7.9% in Q2 2013, close to the UK average (7.8%). In April 2012, median gross weekly earnings for full-time adult employees in the East Midlands were £477, lower than the UK median of £506 but substantially above the North East and Yorkshire and The Humber figures.

There was a 0.9% increase in house prices in the East Midlands in the year to June 2013, compared with 3.1% for the UK as a whole. This was higher than the more northern regions and the South West, but lower than London and the surrounding regions.

Between 2002 and 2012 the increase in traffic on major roads in the East Midlands was 4.6%, above the England average at 2.0%. The rate of carbon dioxide (CO_2) emissions in the East Midlands in 2011, at 7.4 tonnes per resident, was above the UK average of 6.9 tonnes per resident.

Where can I find out more about ONS regional statistics?

These statistics were analysed by the Sub-national Reporting team at the ONS using data from a range of official statistics. If you'd like to find out more about the latest regional statistics, please see our Notes on Sources, latest tables (260.5 Kb Excel sheet) and interactive mapping and charting tool or visit our Directory of Tables page. If you have any comments or suggestions, we'd like to hear them! Please email us at better.info@ons.gsi.gov.uk.

Categories: People, Population and Community, Community, Neighbourhoods, Population and Migration, Population Estimates

West Midlands: A fifth of the population were aged under 16 in 2012

The 2013 ONS regional characteristics analysis for the West Midlands

The latest ONS Region and Country Profiles analysis takes a look at the regional characteristics of the nine regions within England and countries of the UK, exploring aspects such as population, age, employment and house prices. The West Midlands contributes 7% to the UK's economic output. As a region it has a relatively high proportion of children and the highest proportion of unqualified adults in England.

West Midlands region is home to 9% of the UK population

The West Midlands and London are the only landlocked regions in England. With an area of 13,000 square kilometres (sq km), it occupies 5% of the total area of the UK. It is centred on Birmingham and the surrounding West Midlands built-up area. In contrast, large areas of the county of Herefordshire and Shropshire are remote and sparsely populated.

It has one of the lowest proportions of its population living in rural areas at 15.1%, compared with 17.6% in England in 2011. The West Midlands had a population of 5.6 million at mid-2012, almost 9% of the UK population. The increase from mid-2011 was 0.6%, compared with an increase of 0.7% for the UK. In mid-2012, the region's population density was 434 people per sq km, close to the England average of 411.

Regional Profile of the West Midlands

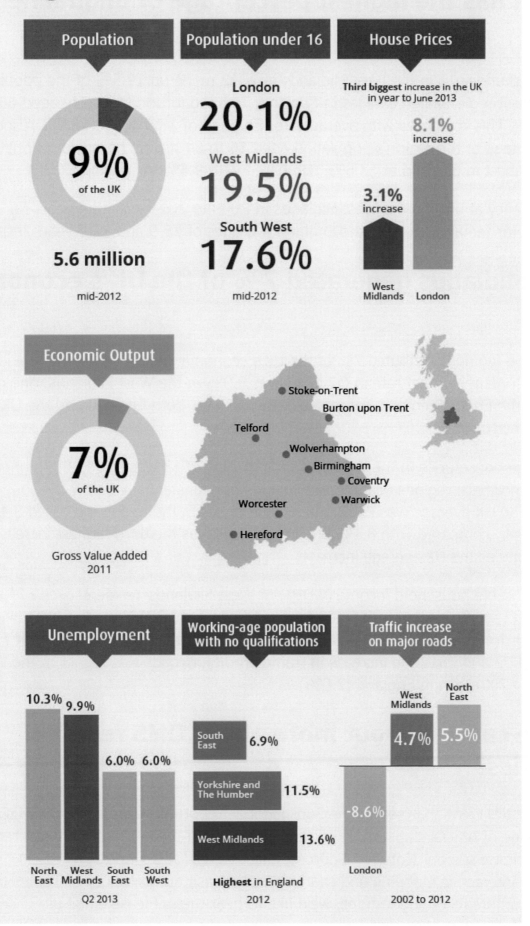

Population

9% of the UK

5.6 million

mid-2012

Population under 16

London
20.1%

West Midlands
19.5%

South West
17.6%

mid-2012

House Prices

Third biggest increase in the UK in year to June 2013

8.1% increase

3.1% increase

West Midlands   London

Economic Output

7% of the UK

Gross Value Added 2011

Stoke-on-Trent
Burton upon Trent
Telford
Wolverhampton
Birmingham
Coventry
Worcester
Warwick
Hereford

Unemployment

10.3% 9.9%

6.0% 6.0%

North East   West Midlands   South East   South West

Q2 2013

Working-age population with no qualifications

South East   6.9%

Yorkshire and The Humber   11.5%

West Midlands   13.6%

Highest in England

2012

Traffic increase on major roads

West Midlands   North East

4.7%   5.5%

-8.6%

London

2002 to 2012

www.ons.gov.uk

Office for National Statistics

Region has the highest percentage of unqualified adults

People aged under 16 in the West Midlands in 2012 made up 19.5% of the population, one of the highest regional percentages in England. The proportion that were aged 65 and over was 17.4%. This compares with averages for England of 18.9% and 16.9% respectively. The percentage of the region's population aged 16 to 64 having no qualifications in 2012 was the highest in England at 13.6%, compared with 9.5% for England.

Life expectancy at birth in the West Midlands in 2009 to 2011 was 78.4 years for males and 82.6 years for females, close to the England averages of 78.9 and 82.9 years respectively.

West Midlands generated 7% of the UK's economic output

In 2011, the region contributed 7% of the UK's economic output (gross value added or GVA). The unemployment rate in Q2 2013 was 9.9% in the West Midlands, one of the highest of the English regions, compared with 7.8% for both England and the UK, and 10.3% in the North East.

The average house price in the West Midlands in June 2013 was £184,000, higher than in any of the northern regions or the East Midlands but substantially below the south of England. The UK average was £242,000. House prices in the region increased 3.1% in the previous year, compared with 8.1% in London. This was the third highest increase in the UK and the same as the UK average increase.

Gross disposable household income (GDHI) of West Midlands' residents was £14,400 per head in 2011, compared with £16,000 for the UK. In April 2012, median gross weekly earnings for full-time adult employees were £469, lower than the UK median of £506. Between 2002 and 2012 the increase in traffic on major roads was higher in the West Midlands (4.7%) than in England (2.0%).

Where can I find out more about ONS regional statistics?

These statistics were analysed by the Sub-national Reporting team at the ONS using data from a range of official statistics. If you'd like to find out more about the latest regional statistics, please see our Notes on Sources, latest tables (260.5 Kb Excel sheet) and interactive mapping and charting tool or visit our Directory of Tables page. If you have any comments or suggestions, we'd like to hear them! Please email us at better.info@ons.gsi.gov.uk.

Categories: People and Places, Communities, Neighbourhoods and Communities, Economy, Labour Market, Housing and Households, Housing Market, Population, Travel and Transport

East of England had one of the lowest regional crime rates in 2012/13

The 2013 ONS regional characteristics analysis for the East of England

The latest ONS Region and Country Profiles analysis takes a look at the regional characteristics of the nine regions within England and countries of the UK, exploring aspects such as population, age, employment, crime and house prices. The profile of the East of England shows it to be one of the largest and most rural regions in England. The region contributes 9% to the UK's economic output; life expectancy is high and the incidence of crimes in the region is among the lowest in England.

East of England has one of the highest rural populations in the UK

The East of England is the second largest English region by area at 19,100 square kilometres (sq km) and covers 8% of the total area of the UK. The East of England had a population of 5.9 million at mid-2012, 9% of the total UK population. The population increased by 0.8% between mid-2011 and mid-2012, compared with an increase of 0.7% for the UK over the same period.

Population density in the East of England in mid-2012 was 309 people per sq km, below the England average of 411 but above the UK average of 263. The region has a diverse urban and rural make-up combining predominantly built-up areas in Essex, Hertfordshire and Bedfordshire with the scattered towns in Cambridgeshire and Suffolk and a predominantly rural area in northern Norfolk. Of its 5.9 million residents, 28.9% lived in rural areas, one of the highest regional proportions, and compared with 17.6% for England in 2011.

Regional Profile of the East of England

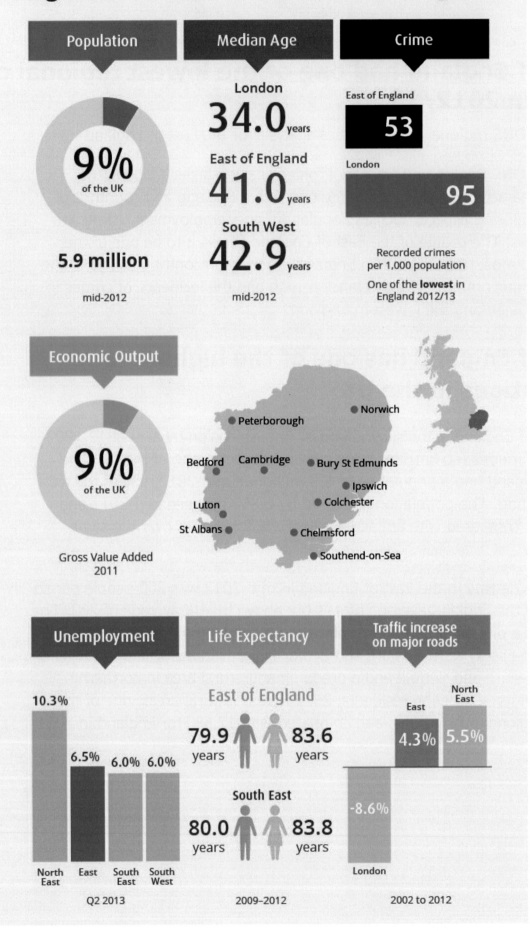

Population

9%
of the UK

5.9 million

mid-2012

Median Age

London
34.0 years

East of England
41.0 years

South West
42.9 years

mid-2012

Crime

East of England
53

London
95

Recorded crimes
per 1,000 population

One of the **lowest** in
England 2012/13

Economic Output

9%
of the UK

Gross Value Added
2011

● Norwich
● Peterborough
Bedford ● Cambridge ● Bury St Edmunds
● ● ● Ipswich
Luton ● Colchester
St Albans ● Chelmsford
● Southend-on-Sea

Unemployment

10.3%
6.5%
6.0% 6.0%

North East | East | South East | South West

Q2 2013

Life Expectancy

East of England

79.9 years   **83.6** years

South East

80.0 years   **83.8** years

2009–2012

Traffic increase on major roads

East
4.3%

North East
5.5%

London
-8.6%

2002 to 2012

Life expectancy for people in the East is among the highest in the UK

In mid-2012, the median age of the region's residents was 41.0 years, above the UK figure of 39.7 years. Life expectancy at birth in the East of England in 2009 to 2011 was 79.9 years for males and 83.6 years for females. These figures are similar to those in the South East and South West regions and higher than the England averages (78.9 and 82.9 years respectively).

The total police-recorded crime rate in 2012/13 was one of the lowest at 53 per 1,000 population compared with the England average of 64 per 1,000 population. The household crime rate was 201 offences per 1,000 households compared with 217 per 1,000 households for England as a whole.

The regional unemployment rate was one of the lowest in the UK

The region generated nearly 9% of the UK's economic output (gross value added or GVA) in 2011. The unemployment rate in the East of England was 6.5% in Q2 2013, compared with 7.8% for the UK. The employment rate for the same period stood at 75.5% and was among the highest in the UK, compared with 71.5% for the UK.

In April 2012, median gross weekly earnings for full-time adult employees were £531, slightly higher than the UK median of £506. Gross disposable household income (GDHI) of residents in the East of England, at £16,600 per head in 2011, was similar to the UK average (£16,000).

While house prices in the East of England were slightly above the England average in June 2013, the annual increase was lower than the England average, £256,000 compared with £251,000. The increase over the year was 2.2% compared with 3.3% for England. On the region's major roads there was a 4.3% increase in traffic between 2002 and 2012, higher than the England increase of 2.0%.

Where can I find out more about ONS regional statistics?

These statistics were analysed by the Sub-national Reporting team at the ONS using data from a range of official statistics. If you'd like to find out more about the latest regional statistics, please see our Notes on Sources, latest tables (260.5 Kb Excel sheet) and interactive mapping and charting tool or visit our Directory of Tables page. If you have any comments or suggestions, we'd like to hear them! Please email us at better.info@ons.gsi.gov.uk

Categories: People and Places, Communities, Neighbourhoods and Communities, Crime and Justice, Economy, Labour Market, Housing and Households, Housing Market, Population, Travel and Transport

London's population was increasing the fastest among the regions in 2012

The 2013 ONS regional characteristics analysis for London

The latest ONS Region and Country Profiles analysis takes a look at the regional characteristics of the nine regions within England and countries of the UK, exploring aspects such as population, age, employment, crime and house prices. The profile of London shows it to be the smallest region in area although it had the greatest growth in population. London contributed nearly a quarter of the UK's economic output. The population was the youngest in the UK with a median age of 34.0, and the incidence of crimes in the region was the highest in England.

London is the smallest region by area

London is the smallest region in terms of area, occupying 1,600 square kilometres (sq km), less than 1% of the total area of the UK. London had a population of 8.3 million at mid-2012, 13% of the total UK population. This was 1.3% more than in mid-2011, the highest regional increase, compared with an increase of 0.7% for the UK over the same period.

London was the most densely populated part of the UK, population density in mid-2012 standing at 5,285 people per sq km. The averages for England and the UK were 411 and 263 people per sq km respectively.

Regional Profile of London

Population

13% of the UK

8.3 million

mid-2012

Population Increase

Largest increase in UK 8.2 million to **8.3 million** in year to mid-2012

1.3% increase — London

0.2% increase — North East

Median Age

London
34.0 years

West Midlands
39.7 years

South West
42.9 years

mid-2012

Economic Output

22% of the UK

Gross Value Added
Largest in the UK 2011

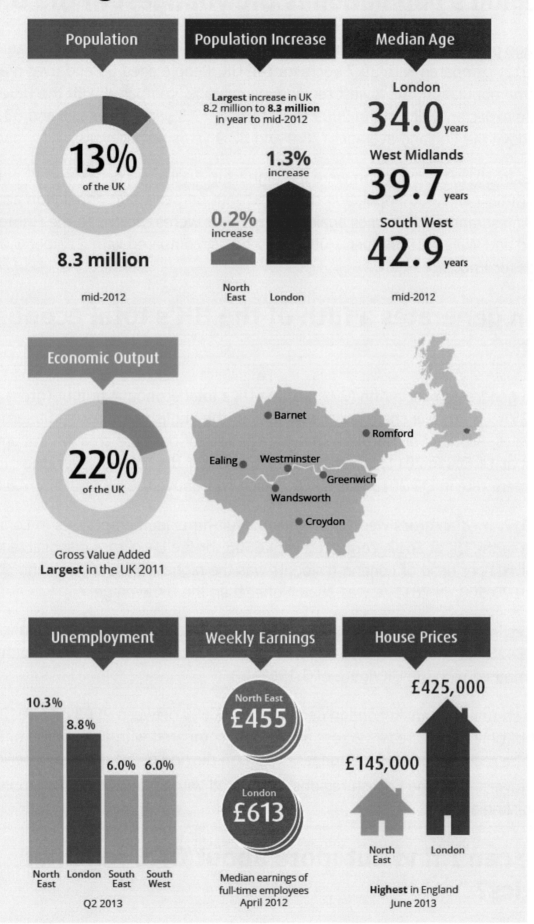

Barnet
Romford
Ealing
Westminster
Greenwich
Wandsworth
Croydon

Unemployment

10.3% North East
8.8% London
6.0% South East
6.0% South West

Q2 2013

Weekly Earnings

North East
£455

London
£613

Median earnings of full-time employees
April 2012

House Prices

£425,000

£145,000

North East — London

Highest in England
June 2013

www.ons.gov.uk

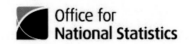

Office for
National Statistics

The region's population is the youngest in the UK

London's age profile is younger than that of the UK as a whole, with a median age of 34.0 years in 2012, compared with 39.7 years for the UK. People aged 65 and over made up 11.3% of the population, the lowest regional percentage, compared with the UK average of 17.0%. Life expectancy at birth in 2009 to 2011 was 79.3 years for males and 83.6 years for females, above the England averages (78.9 and 82.9 years respectively).

Crime rates in 2012/13 in London were the highest in England. There were 95 police-recorded crimes per 1,000 population compared with 64 per 1,000 population across England. An estimated 245 crimes against households were reported to the Crime Survey for England and Wales (CSEW) per 1,000 households, compared with 217 per 1,000 households for England.

London generates a fifth of the UK's total economic output

The region generated over a fifth (22%) of the UK's total economic output (gross value added or GVA) in 2011, a share larger than any of the English regions, and a larger share than for Wales, Scotland or Northern Ireland. The rate of business creation in London was the highest at 14.6% in 2011, compared with 11.2% for the UK. However, the unemployment rate in Q2 2013 was 8.8%, which was above the UK figure of 7.8%.

In April 2012, median gross weekly earnings for full-time adult employees in London were the highest in the UK at £613, compared with £506 for the UK. Gross disposable household income (GDHI) per head of London residents was the highest of all regions and countries of the UK. At £20,500, in 2011, it was 28% higher than the UK average.

House prices in London are notably the highest in the UK. The average house price in June 2013 was £425,000 compared with £242,000 for the UK. This was 8.1% more than a year earlier, compared with the UK figure of 3.1%.

The traffic on major roads in London decreased by 8.6% between 2002 and 2012. This was the larger of only two decreases across all regions, compared with an increase of 2.0% for England. The region produced 4.9 tonnes of carbon dioxide (CO_2) emissions per resident in 2011, the lowest of all the English regions, compared with an average of 6.7 tonnes per resident for England.

Where can I find out more about ONS regional statistics?

These statistics were analysed by the Sub-national Reporting team at the ONS using data from a range of official statistics. If you'd like to find out more about the latest regional statistics, please see our Notes on Sources, latest tables (260.5 Kb Excel sheet) and interactive mapping and charting tool or visit our Directory of Tables page. If you have any comments or suggestions, we'd like to hear them! Please email us at better.info@ons.gsi.gov.uk.

Categories: People and Places, Communities, Neighbourhoods and Communities, Agriculture and Environment, Business and Energy, Crime and Justice, Economy, Labour Market, Housing and Households, Housing Market, Population, Travel and Transport

South East had the joint lowest regional unemployment rate in mid-2013

The 2013 ONS regional characteristics analysis for the South East

The latest ONS Region and Country Profiles analysis takes a look at the regional characteristics of the nine regions within England and countries of the UK, exploring aspects such as population, age, employment and house prices. The profile of the South East shows it to be the largest region in population terms, with the longest life expectancy. The South East contributes 15% to the UK's economic output. The unemployment rate is among the lowest, and incomes are the highest outside London.

The South East makes up 14% of the total UK population

The South East is the third largest region of England, covering 19,100 square kilometres (sq km) and constituting 8% of the total area of the UK. It surrounds London to the south and west and extends as far north as Milton Keynes. A fifth (20.4%) of the region's population lived in rural areas, compared with 17.6% for England in mid-2011.

The population of 8.7 million at mid-2012 was the largest of all the regions of England and countries of the UK at almost 14% of the total UK population. This was 0.8% more than in 2011, compared with an increase of 0.7% for the UK over the same period. In mid-2012, population density in the South East was 458 people per sq km, higher than the population density for England (411 people per sq km) and the third highest of all the regions.

Regional Profile of the South East

Population

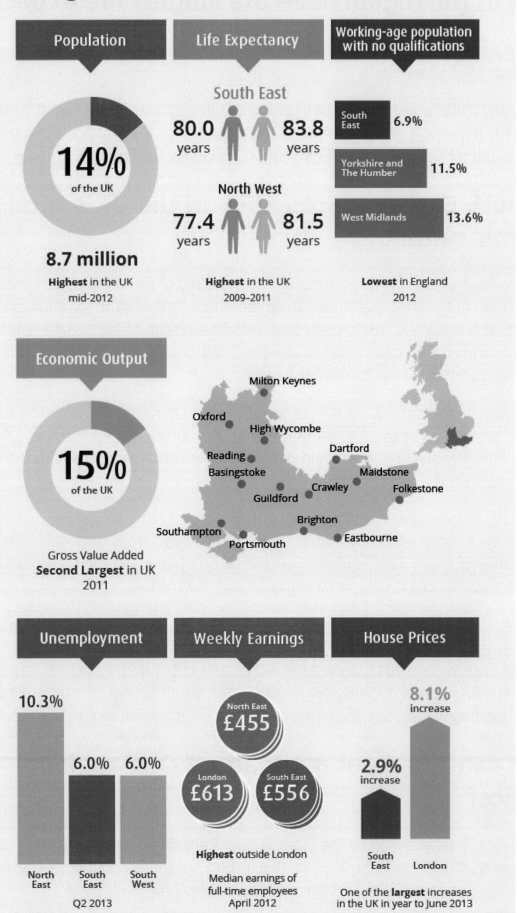

14%
of the UK

8.7 million

Highest in the UK
mid-2012

Life Expectancy

South East
80.0 years   **83.8** years

North West
77.4 years   **81.5** years

Highest in the UK
2009–2011

Working-age population with no qualifications

South East — 6.9%

Yorkshire and The Humber — 11.5%

West Midlands — 13.6%

Lowest in England
2012

Economic Output

15%
of the UK

Gross Value Added
Second Largest in UK
2011

Milton Keynes
Oxford
High Wycombe
Dartford
Reading
Basingstoke
Maidstone
Crawley
Folkestone
Guildford
Brighton
Southampton
Eastbourne
Portsmouth

Unemployment

10.3%   **6.0%**   **6.0%**

North East   South East   South West

Q2 2013

Weekly Earnings

North East **£455**

London **£613**   South East **£556**

Highest outside London

Median earnings of
full-time employees
April 2012

House Prices

8.1% increase

2.9% increase

South East   London

One of the **largest** increases
in the UK in year to June 2013

www.ons.gov.uk

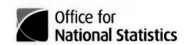

Office for National Statistics

People in the region have the longest life expectancies

The median age of the region's population in mid-2012 was 40.8 years, compared with the UK average of 39.7 years.

In 2009 to 2011, life expectancy at birth in the South East was 80.0 years for males and 83.8 years for females. This was similar to the estimate for the South West and East of England and higher than 78.9 and 82.9 years respectively for England.

The South East produces 15% of the UK's total economic output

In 2011, the South East was responsible for nearly 15% of the UK's economic output (gross value added or GVA). The South East's unemployment rate was the joint lowest with the South West, at 6.0% in Q2 2013, compared with an average of 7.8% for the UK. The lowest regional proportion of children living in workless households in Q2 2013 was in the South East at 9.7%, compared with 13.6% for England.

The employment rate stood at 75.8%, higher than the UK rate of 71.5%. The percentage of the region's population aged 16 to 64 that had no qualifications in 2012 was 6.9%, the lowest of all the regions of England and countries of the UK, compared with 9.9% for the UK and 9.5% in England.

In April 2012, median gross weekly earnings for full-time adult employees were £556, the highest outside London and above the UK median of £506. Gross disposable household income (GDHI) of South East residents was the second highest in the UK, after London, at £18,100 per head in 2011, compared with £16,000 for the UK.

House prices in the South East are the second highest in the UK. The average house price in June 2013 was £299,000, compared with £242,000 for the UK. House prices increased 2.9% in the year to June 2013, compared with 8.1% in London. Private enterprise completed construction of 17,300 new homes in the South East in 2011/12. This was the most of all the English regions and countries of the UK, contributing 16% to the UK total.

Where can I find out more about ONS regional statistics?

These statistics were analysed by the Sub-national Reporting team at the ONS using data from a range of official statistics. If you'd like to find out more about the latest regional statistics, please see our Notes on Sources, latest tables (260.5 Kb Excel sheet) and interactive mapping and charting tool or visit our Directory of Tables page. If you have any comments or suggestions, we'd like to hear them! Please email us at better.info@ons.gsi.gov.uk.

Categories: People and Places, Communities, Neighbourhoods and Communities, Economy, Labour Market, Housing and Households, Housing Market, Population

South West had the oldest population in the UK in 2012

The 2013 ONS regional characteristics analysis for the South West

The latest ONS Region and Country Profiles analysis takes a look at the regional characteristics of the nine regions within England and countries of the UK, exploring aspects such as population, age, employment, crime and house prices. The profile of the South West shows it to be the largest region in the UK and the most rural English region. The South West contributed 8% to the UK's economic output. The region's population was the oldest with a median age of 42.9 years, and the incidence of crimes in the region was among the lowest in England.

The South West is the largest English region

In terms of area the South West is the largest English region at 23,800 square kilometres (sq km), occupying 18% of the total area of England. It is also bigger in area than both Wales and Northern Ireland.

The South West had a population of 5.3 million at mid-2012, 8% of the UK total population. There had been an increase of 0.7% since mid-2011, the same as for the UK over the same period. Almost a third (31.6%) of the region's population lived in rural areas in 2011, the highest proportion of all the English regions, compared with 17.6% for England.

The South West's population density in mid-2012 was 224 people per sq km, compared with the UK and England population densities of 263 and 411 respectively. The figure is the lowest among English regions, but above that of Wales, Scotland and Northern Ireland.

Regional Profile of the South West

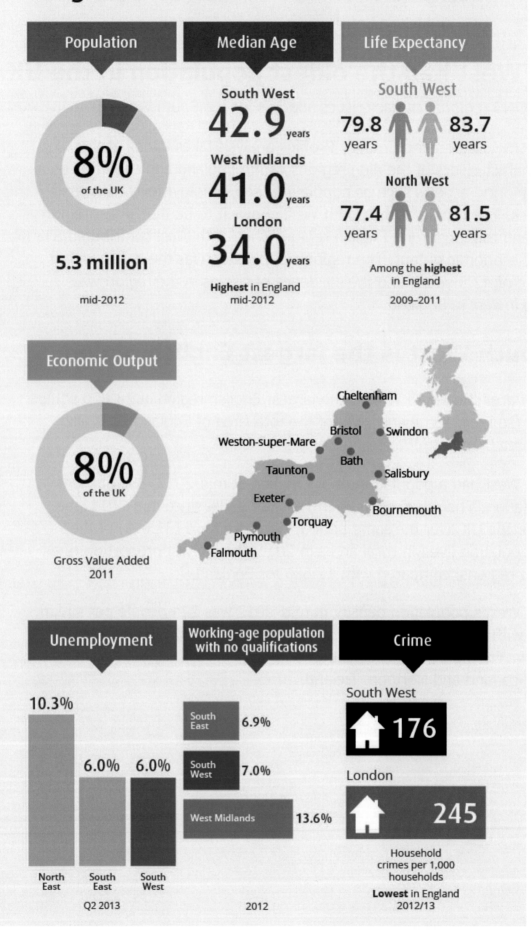

Population

8%
of the UK

5.3 million

mid-2012

Median Age

South West
42.9 years

West Midlands
41.0 years

London
34.0 years

Highest in England
mid-2012

Life Expectancy

South West

79.8 years   **83.7** years

North West

77.4 years   **81.5** years

Among the **highest**
in England
2009–2011

Economic Output

8%
of the UK

Gross Value Added
2011

Cheltenham
Bristol   Swindon
Weston-super-Mare
Bath
Taunton   Salisbury
Exeter
Torquay   Bournemouth
Plymouth
Falmouth

Unemployment

10.3%   6.0%   6.0%

North   South   South
East   East   West

Q2 2013

Working-age population with no qualifications

South East   6.9%

South West   7.0%

West Midlands   13.6%

2012

Crime

South West
🏠 176

London
🏠 245

Household
crimes per 1,000
households

Lowest in England
2012/13

www.ons.gov.uk

Office for
National Statistics

The region had the lowest household crime rate in 2012/13

Crime rates for the South West were among the lowest in England in 2012/13. There were 176 household offences per 1,000 households reported to the Crime Survey for England and Wales (CSEW), the lowest in England, which had 217 incidents per 1,000 households. There were 54 police-recorded crimes per 1,000 population, compared with 64 per 1,000 population across England in 2012/13.

The South West's age profile is older than that of the UK as a whole. With a median age of 42.9 years in mid-2012 the South West has the highest median age among all English regions and UK countries, which compares with the UK median of 39.7 years. People aged 65 and over made up the largest share of the population in the UK at 20.3%. This compares with the average for the UK of 17.0%. Life expectancy at birth in 2009 to 2011 was 79.8 years for males and 83.7 years for females. This was among the highest of the English regions, compared with 78.9 and 82.9 years respectively for England, and similar to the South East and East of England.

The South West had one of the lowest unemployment rates in mid-2013

In 2011, the South West was responsible for almost 8% of the UK's economic output (gross value added or GVA). The unemployment rate in the South West was the joint lowest in the UK, with the South East, at 6.0% in Q2 2013 compared with 7.8% for the UK.

In April 2012, median gross weekly earnings for full-time adult employees were £477, lower than the UK median of £506. The percentage of the region's population aged 16 to 64 that had no qualifications in 2012 was 7.0%, the second lowest proportion in the UK, after the South East, and compared with 9.9% for the UK.

Gross disposable household income (GDHI) of South West residents was £16,000 per head in 2011, the same as the UK average. The average house price in the South West in June 2013 was £229,000, slightly below the UK average of £242,000.

Where can I find out more about ONS regional statistics?

These statistics were analysed by the Sub-national Reporting team at the ONS using data from a range of official statistics. If you'd like to find out more about the latest regional statistics, please see our Notes on Sources, latest tables (260.5 Kb Excel sheet) and interactive mapping and charting tool or visit our Directory of Tables page. If you have any comments or suggestions, we'd like to hear them! Please email us at better.info@ons.gsi.gov.uk.

Categories: People and Places, Communities, Neighbourhoods and Communities, Crime and Justice, Economy, Labour Market, Housing and Households, Housing Market, Population

Wales had one of the oldest populations in the UK in 2012

The 2013 ONS analysis of the characteristics of Wales

The latest ONS Region and Country Profiles analysis takes a look at the regional characteristics of the nine regions within England and the countries of the UK, exploring aspects such as population, age, employment and house prices. The profile of Wales shows it to have one of the oldest populations of the UK with a median age of 41.7 years, and one of the highest percentages of the adult population (14%) with disabilities that limited their daily activities or work. Wales contributed nearly 4% of the UK's economic output and the unemployment rate in Q2 2013 was 8.2%.

Wales has the third lowest population density

Wales is the third biggest of the UK countries and English regions; smaller in area than Scotland but larger than any English region except South West; it covers 9% of the total area of the UK at 20,700 square kilometres (sq km). The region is generally mountainous, with its highest peaks in the north and central areas, especially in Snowdonia. Two-thirds (67.2%) of people lived in urban areas in 2011, concentrated mainly in the south east of the country.

Wales had a population of 3.1 million at mid-2012, which was almost 5% of the UK population. This makes it smaller than Scotland but larger than Northern Ireland and the North East region. The population of Wales had increased by 0.3% since mid-2011 compared with 0.7% for the UK over the same period. The population density for Wales in mid-2012 was 148 people per sq km compared with England (411), Scotland (68) and Northern Ireland (134).

Profile of Wales

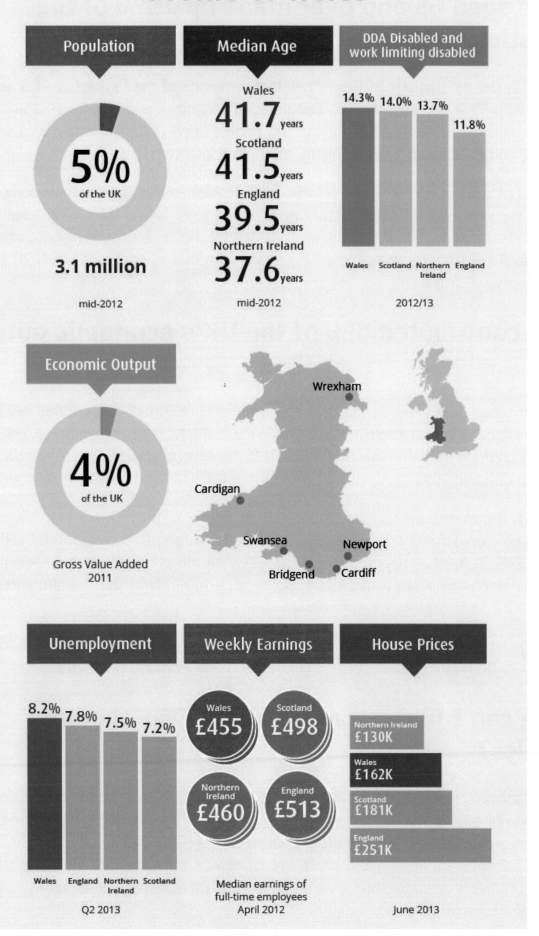

Population

5%
of the UK

3.1 million

mid-2012

Median Age

Wales
41.7 years

Scotland
41.5 years

England
39.5 years

Northern Ireland
37.6 years

mid-2012

DDA Disabled and work limiting disabled

14.3%   14.0%   13.7%   11.8%

Wales   Scotland   Northern Ireland   England

2012/13

Economic Output

4%
of the UK

Gross Value Added
2011

Wrexham

Cardigan

Swansea

Newport

Bridgend   Cardiff

Unemployment

8.2%   7.8%   7.5%   7.2%

Wales   England   Northern Ireland   Scotland

Q2 2013

Weekly Earnings

Wales
£455

Scotland
£498

Northern Ireland
£460

England
£513

Median earnings of full-time employees
April 2012

House Prices

Northern Ireland
£130K

Wales
£162K

Scotland
£181K

England
£251K

June 2013

www.ons.gov.uk

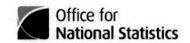

Office for National Statistics

People aged 65 and over made up 19% of the population in 2012

In mid-2012, the median age of Wales' residents was one of the highest at 41.7 years, compared with 39.7 years for the UK. People aged 65 and over made up 19.1% of the population, compared with 17.0% for the UK. People aged under 16 made up 18.1% of the population, compared with 18.8% for the total UK population.

Over 14% (14.3%) of adults aged 16 to 64 had disabilities that limited their daily activities or work in the year ending March 2013, one of the highest proportions of all countries of the UK and English regions, compared with 12.2% for the UK. Life expectancy at birth in 2008 to 2010 was 77.5 years for males and 81.7 years for females, compared with 78.1 and 82.1 years respectively for the UK.

Wales contributed 4% of the UK's economic output in 2011

Wales contributed nearly 4% of the UK's economic output (gross value added or GVA) in 2011, only higher than Northern Ireland (2.3%) and the North East region (3.2%). The rate of business creation in Wales was 9.3% in 2011, the second lowest rate of the UK countries and English regions, compared with 11.2% for the UK.

In Q2 2013, the unemployment rate in Wales was 8.2%, slightly higher than the UK average of 7.8%. The employment rate stood at 69.4% in the same period, compared with the UK rate of 71.5%. In April 2012, median gross weekly earnings for full-time adult employees were £455, which compares with £498 in Scotland, £460 in Northern Ireland and £506 in the UK.

The average house price in Wales in June 2013 was £162,000, above the figure for Northern Ireland (£130,000) and below Scotland (£181,000) and England (£251,000).

Where can I find out more about ONS regional statistics?

These statistics were analysed by the Sub-national Reporting team at the ONS using data from a range of official statistics. If you'd like to find out more about the latest regional statistics, please see our Notes on Sources, latest tables (260.5 Kb Excel sheet) and interactive mapping and charting tool or visit our Directory of Tables page. If you have any comments or suggestions, we'd like to hear them! Please email us at better.info@ons.gsi.gov.uk.

Categories: People and Places, Communities, Neighbourhoods and Communities, Business and Energy, Economy, Health and Social Care, Labour Market, Housing and Households, Housing Market, Population

Scotland's labour productivity equalled UK's in 2011

The 2013 ONS analysis of the characteristics of Scotland

The latest ONS Region and Country Profiles analysis takes a look at the regional characteristics of the nine regions within England and the countries of the UK, exploring aspects such as population, age, employment, crime and house prices. The profile of Scotland shows it to have one of the oldest populations of the UK with a median age of 41.5 years, and the lowest life expectancy at birth. Scotland contributed 8% of the UK's economic output and the unemployment rate in mid-2013 was 7.2%.

Scotland is larger in area than any English region

Scotland covers nearly a third (32%) of the total area of the UK (77,900 square kilometres (sq km)), making it larger than Wales, Northern Ireland or any of the English regions. It has the lowest population density of any country in the UK or English region with 68 people per sq km in mid-2012. Its geography is highly varied, from rural lowlands to barren uplands and from large cities to uninhabited islands.

Scotland had a population of 5.3 million at mid-2012, 8% of the UK total. The population had increased by 0.3% since mid-2011, compared with 0.7% for the UK.

Profile of Scotland

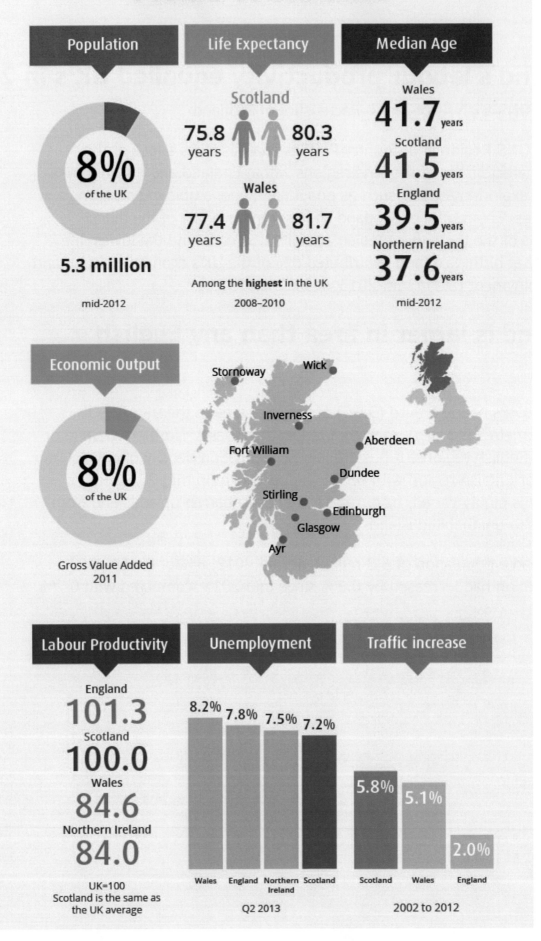

Population

8%
of the UK

5.3 million

mid-2012

Life Expectancy

Scotland

75.8 years   **80.3** years

Wales

77.4 years   **81.7** years

Among the **highest** in the UK

2008–2010

Median Age

Wales
41.7 years

Scotland
41.5 years

England
39.5 years

Northern Ireland
37.6 years

mid-2012

Economic Output

8%
of the UK

Gross Value Added
2011

Stornoway
Wick
Inverness
Aberdeen
Fort William
Dundee
Stirling
Edinburgh
Glasgow
Ayr

Labour Productivity

England
101.3
Scotland
100.0
Wales
84.6
Northern Ireland
84.0

UK=100
Scotland is the same as
the UK average

Unemployment

8.2% **7.8%** **7.5%** **7.2%**

Wales England Northern Ireland Scotland

Q2 2013

Traffic increase

5.8% **5.1%** **2.0%**

Scotland Wales England

2002 to 2012

www.ons.gov.uk

Office for
National Statistics

The country's population has the lowest life expectancy

Life expectancy at birth in 2008 to 2010 was 75.8 years for males and 80.3 years for females. This was the lowest among the UK countries, compared with 78.1 and 82.1 years respectively for the UK.

The median age of Scotland's population was 41.5 years in mid-2012, compared with 41.7 in Wales and 37.6 in Northern Ireland. This makes it one of the oldest populations among the countries of the UK and regions in England, compared with the UK figure of 39.7 years.

Scotland contributed 8% to the UK's total economic output

Scotland was responsible for 8% of the UK's economic output (gross value added or GVA) in 2011. Labour productivity (GVA per hour worked) was equal to the UK average, compared with London 29% above and Northern Ireland 16% below the UK average. In Q2 2013, the unemployment rate was 7.2%, lower than the UK average of 7.8%.

The proportion of children living in workless households in Q2 2013 was 12.0%; this is lower than England (13.6%), Wales (14.4%) and Northern Ireland (16.7%).

In April 2012, median gross weekly earnings for full-time adult employees in Scotland were £498, higher than Northern Ireland (£460) and Wales (£455), but similar to England (£513). Gross disposable household income (GDHI) of Scottish residents was £15,700 per head in 2011, compared with £16,000 for the UK. Scotland had the biggest decrease in average house prices in the year to June 2013 at 0.9%, compared with an average increase in England of 3.3%.

The traffic on major roads in Scotland increased by 5.8% between 2002 and 2012, the highest increase of any country or region in Great Britain and compared with 2.5% for Great Britain. Total greenhouse gas emissions in Scotland (excluding those from international aviation and shipping) reduced by 31% between the Kyoto Base Year and 2011. This was similar to the reduction in England and greater than the reductions in Wales (21%) and Northern Ireland (17%).

Where can I find out more about ONS regional statistics?

These statistics were analysed by the Sub-national Reporting team at the ONS using data from a range of official statistics. If you'd like to find out more about the latest regional statistics, please see our Notes on Sources, latest tables (260.5 Kb Excel sheet) and interactive mapping and charting tool or visit our Directory of Tables page. If you have any comments or suggestions, we'd like to hear them! Please email us at better.info@ons.gsi.gov.uk.

Categories: People and Places, Communities, Neighbourhoods and Communities, Agriculture and Environment, Economy, Labour Market, Housing and Households, Housing Market, Population, Travel and Transport

Northern Ireland had the largest proportion of children in 2012

The 2013 ONS analysis of the characteristics of Northern Ireland

The latest ONS Region and Country Profiles analysis takes a look at the regional characteristics of the nine regions within England and countries of the UK, exploring aspects such as population, age, employment and house prices. The profile of Northern Ireland shows it to have one of the youngest populations of the UK with a median age of 37.6 years. Northern Ireland contributed 2% of the UK's economic output and the unemployment rate in mid-2013 was 7.5%.

Northern Ireland makes up 3% of the total UK population

In terms of population, Northern Ireland is the smallest UK country and smaller than all the English regions, with 1.8 million people at mid-2012. This represents 3% of the total UK population and an increase of 0.5% since 2011.

Northern Ireland occupies the north-east of the island of Ireland, sharing a border with the Republic of Ireland (Eire). It covers 13,600 square kilometres (sq km) and covers 6% of the total area of the UK. The Belfast metropolitan area dominates in population terms, with over a third of the inhabitants of Northern Ireland. In mid-2012, Northern Ireland's population density was 134 people per sq km, the second lowest density of all UK countries.

Profile of Northern Ireland

Population

3%
of the UK

1.8 million

mid-2012

Population under 16

Northern Ireland
21.0% years

England
18.9% years

Wales
18.1% years

Scotland
17.2% years

mid-2012

Economic Inactivity

28.2%

24.3%

22.1% 22.1%

Northern Ireland | Wales | Scotland | England

Highest inactivity rate in the UK Q2 2013

Economic Output

2%
of the UK

Gross Value Added
Lowest in the UK
2011

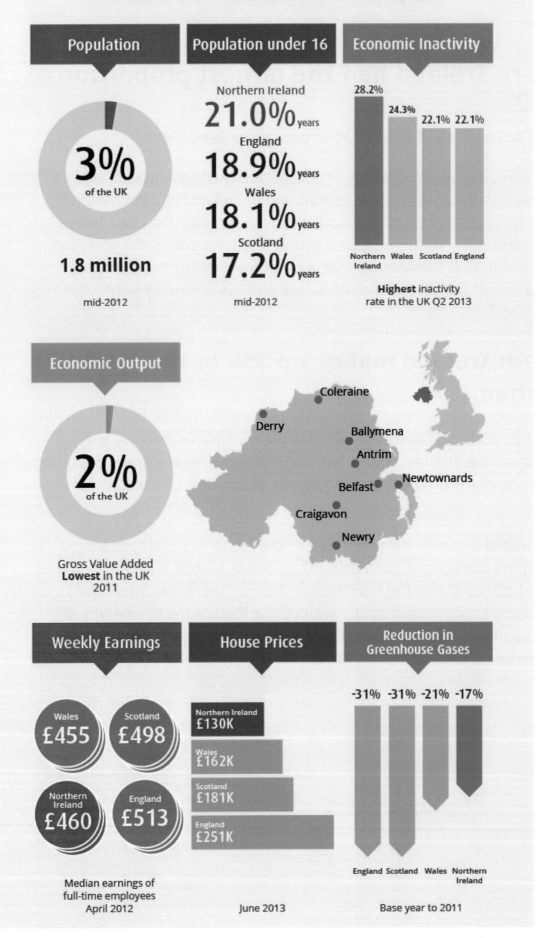

Coleraine
Derry
Ballymena
Antrim
Belfast
Newtownards
Craigavon
Newry

Weekly Earnings

Wales
£455

Scotland
£498

Northern Ireland
£460

England
£513

Median earnings of full-time employees
April 2012

House Prices

Northern Ireland
£130K

Wales
£162K

Scotland
£181K

England
£251K

June 2013

Reduction in Greenhouse Gases

-31% **-31%** **-21%** **-17%**

England | Scotland | Wales | Northern Ireland

Base year to 2011

www.ons.gov.uk

Office for National Statistics

The median age of Northern Ireland's population is 2 years less than the UK

People aged under 16 made up 21.0% of the population of Northern Ireland in mid-2012, the largest proportion in the UK, compared with 18.8% for the UK. The proportion of people aged 65 and over was 15.0%, compared with 17.0% for the UK. The median age of Northern Ireland's population was one of the youngest at 37.6 years, compared with 39.7 years for the UK.

Life expectancy at birth in 2008 to 2010 was 77.0 years for males and 81.4 years for females, compared with 78.1 and 82.1 years respectively for the UK.

Northern Ireland has the lowest house prices in the UK

Northern Ireland was responsible for 2% of the UK's economic output (gross value added or GVA), the lowest share of all the English regions and countries of the UK in 2011, compared with Wales (4%) and Scotland (8%). The rate of business creation in Northern Ireland was 6.5% in 2011, the lowest rate of the UK countries and English regions, compared with 11.2% for the UK.

The average house price in Northern Ireland in June 2013 was the lowest in the UK at £130,000; this compares with Wales (£162,000), Scotland (£181,000) and England (£251,000).

In April 2012, median gross weekly earnings for full-time adult employees in Northern Ireland were £460, lower than Scotland (£498) and England (£513), and higher than Wales (£455). Gross disposable household income (GDHI) of residents was the third lowest among the UK countries and English regions at £14,000 per head in 2011, compared with £16,000 for the UK.

The economic inactivity rate in Northern Ireland in Q2 2013 was the highest among the UK countries and English regions at 28.2%, followed by the North East with 25.7% and compared with 22.3% in the UK. The employment rate stood at 66.3%, compared with the UK rate of 71.5%. Nearly one fifth (18.4%) of people aged 16 to 64 had no qualifications in 2012. This compares with 10.7% in Scotland, 11.4% in Wales and 9.5% in England.

Northern Ireland reduced its total greenhouse gas emissions by 17% between the Kyoto Base Year and 2011, the smallest reduction of the UK countries; this compares with Wales (21%), and England and Scotland (both 31%).

Where can I find out more about ONS regional statistics?

These statistics were analysed by the Sub-national Reporting team at the ONS using data from a range of official statistics. If you'd like to find out more about the latest regional statistics, please see our Notes on Sources, latest tables (260.5 Kb Excel sheet) and interactive mapping and charting tool or visit our Directory of Tables page. If you have any comments or suggestions, we'd like to hear them! Please email us at better.info@ons.gsi.gov.uk.

Categories: People and Places, Communities, Neighbourhoods and Communities, Business and Energy, Economy, Labour Market, Housing and Households, Housing Market, Population

Data and Reference

Region and Country Profiles - Key Statistics

	Release Date 31 January 2013	Type[1]	Last updated	Latest year
1	Key statistics – population and health	NS	Dec-12	2011
2	Key statistics – social indicators	NS	Oct-12	2012
3	Key statistics – labour market and skills	NS	Jan-13	2012
4	Key statistics – education	Mixed	Oct-12	2010/11
5	Key statistics – economy	NS	Jan-13	2011
6	Key statistics – housing, transport and environment	Mixed	Jan-13	2012

1 National Statistics (NS), Non National Statistics (Non NS), or Mixed.

1 Key statistics – population and health

UK/GB/E&W	Country	Region	Old area code	New area code	Population mid-2011[1] (Thousands)	Total population growth 2001 to 2011[1] (%)	Population aged under 16 mid-2011[1] (%)	Population aged 65 and over mid-2011[1] (%)	Male life expectancy at birth, 2008 to 2010[2,3] (Years)	Female life expectancy at birth, 2008 to 2010[2,3] (Years)
United Kingdom			926	K02000001	..	..	..	..	78.1	82.1
Great Britain			925	K03000001	..	..	..	..	..	..
England and Wales			941	K04000001	56,170.9	7.3	18.8	16.5	78.3	82.3
United Kingdom	England		921	E92000001	53,107.2	7.4	18.9	16.4	78.4	82.4
United Kingdom	Wales		924	W92000004	3,063.8	5.3	18.1	18.5	77.5	81.7
United Kingdom	Scotland		923	S92000003	5,254.8	3.8	17.4	17.0	75.8	80.3
United Kingdom	Northern Ireland		922	N92000002	1,806.9	..	..	..	77.0	81.4
United Kingdom	England	North East	A	E12000001	2,596.4	2.2	17.8	17.4	77.2	81.2
United Kingdom	England	North West	B	E12000002	7,056.0	4.2	18.8	16.7	77.0	81.1
United Kingdom	England	Yorkshire and The Humber	D	E12000003	5,288.2	6.3	18.9	16.7	77.7	81.8
United Kingdom	England	East Midlands	E	E12000004	4,537.4	8.3	18.5	17.2	78.4	82.4
United Kingdom	England	West Midlands	F	E12000005	5,608.7	6.2	19.5	17.0	77.9	82.2
United Kingdom	England	East	G	E12000006	5,862.4	8.6	18.9	17.6	79.6	83.2
United Kingdom	England	London	H	E12000007	8,204.4	12.0	19.9	11.1	79.0	83.3
United Kingdom	England	South East	J	E12000008	8,652.8	7.8	19.0	17.3	79.7	83.5
United Kingdom	England	South West	K	E12000009	5,300.8	7.2	17.5	19.7	79.5	83.5

.. not available

1 The estimated mid-year resident populations of England and Wales are based on the 2011 Census. Estimates are as published on 25 September 2012.
The estimated 2011 mid-year resident population for Scotland is based on the 2001 Census data, rolled forward using information on births, deaths and migration.
The estimated mid-year resident population for Northern Ireland is based on the 2001 Census.
2 Estimates for English regions use abridged life tables as published in Reference Table: Life expectancy at birth and at age 65 by local areas in the United Kingdom, 2004-06 to 2008-10.
Estimates for UK and constituent countries use interim life tables as published in Reference Table: Period Expectation of Life at Birth and Selected Ages, UK and Constituent Countries, 1980-82 to 2008-10.
3 Guide to Life Expectancies.

Source: Office for National Statistics; National Records of Scotland; Northern Ireland Statistics and Research Agency

Additional Information

Resident population

The estimated resident population of an area includes all people who usually live there, whatever their nationality. People arriving into an area from outside the UK are only included in the population estimates if their total stay in the UK is 12 months or more. Visitors and short-term migrants (those who enter the UK for 3 to 12 months for certain purposes) are not included. Similarly, people who leave the UK are only excluded from the population estimates if they remain outside the UK for 12 months or more. This is consistent with the United Nations recommended definition of an international long-term migrant. Members of UK and non-UK armed forces stationed in the UK are included in the population and UK forces stationed outside the UK are excluded. Students are taken to be resident at their term-time address.

2 Key statistics – social indicators

UK/GB/E&W	Country	Region	Old area code	New area code	People who are DDA disabled and also work-limiting disabled[1] 2011/2012[2] (%)	Children living in workless households[3] Q2 2012 (%)	Recorded crime[4,5,6,7] 2011/12 (Recorded offences per 1,000 population)	Crimes committed against households[8,9] 2011/12 (Rates per 1,000 households)
United Kingdom			926	K02000001	12.1	15.1	..	..
Great Britain			925	K03000001	12.0	15.0	..	..
England and Wales			941	K04000001	11.9	..	72	243
United Kingdom	England		921	E92000001	11.7	14.8	71	244
United Kingdom	Wales		924	W92000004	15.4	19.1	63	214
United Kingdom	Scotland		923	S92000003	13.4	15.6	60	..
United Kingdom	Northern Ireland		922	N92000002	14.5	15.7	57	..
United Kingdom	England	North East	A	E12000001	14.5	22.5	59	261
United Kingdom	England	North West	B	E12000002	13.5	16.7	71	254
United Kingdom	England	Yorkshire and The Humber	D	E12000003	13.5	17.1	75	283
United Kingdom	England	East Midlands	E	E12000004	13.0	13.0	67	236
United Kingdom	England	West Midlands	F	E12000005	13.0	16.5	66	250
United Kingdom	England	East	G	E12000006	10.7	11.8	60	214
United Kingdom	England	London	H	E12000007	9.6	17.2	105	266
United Kingdom	England	South East	J	E12000008	9.9	11.6	63	232
United Kingdom	England	South West	K	E12000009	10.9	10.3	61	208

.. not available

1 People aged 16 to 64. Definitions of disability.

2 Source: Annual Population Survey April 2011 to March 2012.

3 Children under 16. Source: Labour Force Survey. Definition of a workless household.

Further information is on the Department for Work and Pensions website.

4 Recorded crime statistics broadly cover the more serious offences.

5 Crimes recorded by the British Transport police are not included.

6 Figures for Scotland are not comparable with those for England and Wales because of the differences in the legal systems, recording practices and classifications.

7 The Northern Ireland figure includes 'offences against the state' and 'other notifiable offences'.

8 See estimates from the Crime Survey for England and Wales for further information.

9 Estimates from the Scottish Crime and Justice Survey and Northern Ireland Crime Survey for 2011/12 have not yet been published. Estimates for 2010/11 were 225 and 131 respectively.

Scottish Crime and Justice Survey.

Northern Ireland Crime Survey.

Source: Office for National Statistics; Home Office; Scottish Government; Department of Justice, Northern Ireland

3 Key statistics – labour market and skills

UK/GB/E&W	Country	Region	Old area code	New area code	Employment rate[1], Q3 2012 (%)	Unemployment rate[2], Q3 2012 (%)	Economic inactivity rate[1] Q3 2012 (%)	Median gross weekly earnings[3] April 2012 (£)	Working-age[4] population with no qualifications 2011 (%)
United Kingdom			926	K02000001	71.2	7.8	22.6	505.90	10.9
Great Britain			925	K03000001	71.3	7.8	22.4	508.00	10.6
England and Wales			941	K04000001	..	..	..	508.90	10.5
United Kingdom	England		921	E92000001	71.5	7.8	22.3	512.70	10.4
United Kingdom	Wales		924	W92000004	69.0	8.2	24.7	455.00	12.3
United Kingdom	Scotland		923	S92000003	70.6	8.1	23.0	498.30	11.6
United Kingdom	Northern Ireland		922	N92000002	67.4	7.6	26.9	460.00	21.3
United Kingdom	England	North East	A	E12000001	67.8	9.8	24.8	455.30	12.2
United Kingdom	England	North West	B	E12000002	69.8	8.4	23.6	472.50	12.0
United Kingdom	England	Yorkshire and The Humber	D	E12000003	69.8	9.1	23.1	465.20	11.9
United Kingdom	England	East Midlands	E	E12000004	71.4	7.7	22.4	476.90	11.5
United Kingdom	England	West Midlands	F	E12000005	69.7	8.6	23.5	469.30	14.0
United Kingdom	England	East	G	E12000006	74.7	6.8	19.6	531.00	9.6
United Kingdom	England	London	H	E12000007	69.6	8.7	23.6	613.30	9.3
United Kingdom	England	South East	J	E12000008	74.5	6.5	20.2	555.80	7.9
United Kingdom	England	South West	K	E12000009	74.4	5.8	20.9	476.50	8.0

.. not available

1 Seasonally adjusted data for people aged 16-64 from the Labour Force Survey (LFS).

2 Seasonally adjusted data as a percentage of all economically active people aged 16 and over from the LFS.

3 Residence-based estimates for full-time employees on adult rates whose pay for the survey pay-period was not affected by absence. Total pay including overtime pay, shift premiums, bonuses, commission and other incentive payments.
Further information about the Annual Survey of Hours and Earnings (ASHE).

4 People aged 16-64 from the Annual Population Survey (APS), January-December.

Source: Labour Force Survey, Annual Population Survey and Annual Survey of Hours and Earnings, Office for National Statistics; Department of Finance and Personnel, Northern Ireland

UK/GB/E&W	Country	Region	Old area code	New area code	Pupils[1,2] achieving 5 or more grades A*-C including English and Mathematics GCSE or equivalent qualifications 2010/11 (%)	Programme for International Student Assessment reading score[3] 2009	Programme for International Student Assessment maths score[3] 2009	Programme for International Student Assessment science score[3] 2009
United Kingdom			926	K02000001	..	494	492	514
Great Britain			925	K03000001	..	..	..	..
England and Wales			941	K04000001	..	..	..	..
United Kingdom	England		921	E92000001	58.4	495	493	515
United Kingdom	Wales		924	W92000004	..	476	472	496
United Kingdom	Scotland		923	S92000003	..	500	499	514
United Kingdom	Northern Ireland		922	N92000002	..	499	492	511
United Kingdom	England	North East	A	E12000001	56.8	..	..	..
United Kingdom	England	North West	B	E12000002	58.4	..	..	..
United Kingdom	England	Yorkshire and The Humber	D	E12000003	54.6	..	..	..
United Kingdom	England	East Midlands	E	E12000004	57.1	..	..	..
United Kingdom	England	West Midlands	F	E12000005	57.4	..	..	..
United Kingdom	England	East	G	E12000006	59.1	..	..	..
United Kingdom	England	London	H	E12000007	61.9	..	..	..
United Kingdom	England	South East	J	E12000008	59.6	..	..	..
United Kingdom	England	South West	K	E12000009	57.9	..	..	..

.. not available

1 Revised (but not final) data published on 26 January 2012, for Local Authority Maintained schools only. Other England figures are available on the Department for Education website.

2 Pupils at the end of Key Stage 4 in the 2010/11 academic year. Due to lack of comparability of educational attainment data between countries only data for England are shown.

3 See Additional Information.

Source: Department for Education; Organisation for Economic Co-operation and Development

Additional Information

GCSE and equivalent attainment

Scottish school educational attainment statistics are available on the Scottish Government website.

Wales and Northern Ireland use GCSEs but the way the statistics are compiled varies from that in England.

Statistics for Wales are available on the Welsh Government website.

Statistics for Northern Ireland are available on the Department of Education for Northern Ireland website.

PISA

The OECD Programme for International Student Assessment (PISA) seeks to measure the extent to which students near the end of compulsory education have acquired some of the knowledge and skills that are essential for full participation in modern societies.

Its triennial surveys of key competencies of 15-year-old students are conducted in 65 OECD member and partner countries. In 2009 each participating student spent two hours carrying out pencil-and-paper tasks in reading, mathematics and science. Every PISA survey tests reading, mathematical and scientific literacy in terms of general competencies, that is, how well students can apply the knowledge and skills they have learned at school to real-life challenges. PISA does not test how well a student has mastered a school's specific curriculum.

In each test subject, the score for each participating country is the average of all student scores in that country. The average score among OECD countries is 500 points and the standard deviation is 100 points. About two-thirds of students across OECD countries score between 400 and 600 points.

Schools in each country are randomly selected by the international contractor for participation in PISA. At these schools, the test is given to students who are between age 15 years 3 months and age 16 years 2 months at the time of the test, rather than to students in a specific year of school. This average age of 15 was chosen because at this age young people in most OECD countries are nearing the end of compulsory education. PISA covers all students who have completed at least 6 years of formal schooling, regardless of the type of institution in which they are enrolled, whether they are in full-time or part-time education, whether they attend academic or vocational programmes, and whether they attend state-funded or private schools or foreign schools within the country.

The specific sample design and size for each country aimed to maximise sampling efficiency for student-level estimates. In OECD countries, sample sizes ranged from 4,410 students in Iceland to 38,250 students in Mexico. Countries with large samples have often implemented PISA both at national and regional/state levels. In the UK, results are available for each of the four countries of the UK.

5 Key statistics – economy

UK/GB/E&W	Country	Region	Old area code	New area code	Gross value added[1] as a percentage of UK[2], 2011[3] (%)	Labour productivity[4], 2011 (UK = 100)	disposable household income[5] per head, 2010[3] (£)	Business birth rate[6] 2011 (%)	Business death rate[6] 2011 (%)
United Kingdom			926	K02000001	100.0	100.0	15,727	11.2	9.8
Great Britain			925	K03000001	..	..	..	11.3	9.8
England and Wales			941	K04000001	..	..	..	11.3	9.9
United Kingdom	England		921	E92000001	85.9	101.9	15,931	11.4	9.9
United Kingdom	Wales		924	W92000004	3.6	81.5	13,783	9.3	9.5
United Kingdom	Scotland		923	S92000003	8.3	96.9	15,342	10.9	9.1
United Kingdom	Northern Ireland		922	N92000002	2.3	82.9	13,554	6.5	8.6
United Kingdom	England	North East	A	E12000001	3.2	86.2	13,329	11.2	9.9
United Kingdom	England	North West	B	E12000002	9.5	88.6	14,176	11.1	10.7
United Kingdom	England	Yorkshire and The Humber	D	E12000003	6.9	84.7	13,594	10.5	10.0
United Kingdom	England	East Midlands	E	E12000004	6.2	89.2	14,267	10.3	9.8
United Kingdom	England	West Midlands	F	E12000005	7.3	89.1	14,021	10.5	10.0
United Kingdom	England	East	G	E12000006	8.7	96.8	16,392	10.5	9.6
United Kingdom	England	London	H	E12000007	21.6	139.7	20,238	14.6	10.4
United Kingdom	England	South East	J	E12000008	14.7	108.3	17,610	10.8	9.5
United Kingdom	England	South West	K	E12000009	7.7	89.8	15,653	9.6	9.2

.. not available

1 Workplace based. For further information see: Regional Gross Value Added (Income Approach), December 2012. Regional GVA NUTS1 Table 1.1
2 UK less extra-regio. For further information see: Regional Gross Value Added (Income Approach), December 2012. Regional GVA NUTS1 Table 1.1
3 Provisional.
4 Workplace based nominal gross value added per hour worked. The annual hours figure used is an average of the four quarters and includes employees, self employed, HM Forces and Government-supported trainees.
5 Household income covers the income received by households and non-profit institutions serving households. UK figure excludes extra-regio. For further information see: Region and Country Profiles, Economy, May 2012, Table 7.
6 Birth and Death rates are expressed as a percentage of active enterprises.

Source: Office for National Statistics

Additional Information

For additional information about Regional GVA, see the Regional Accounts Methodology Guide on the Regional GVA landing page.
The figures for all UK countries and regions (NUTS1 areas) are consistent with the United Kingdom National Accounts – The Blue Book 2012.

6 Key statistics – housing, transport and environment

UK/GB/E&W	Country	Region	Old area code	New area code	Housebuilding: permanent dwellings completed by private enterprise[1] 2010/11 (Thousands)	Annual change in mix adjusted house prices[2] September 2012 (%)	Traffic[3] increase on major roads[4] between 2001 and 2011 (%)	Reduction in total greenhouse gas emissions[5] between 1990 and 2010 (%)	CO_2 emissions per resident[6] 2010 (Tonnes)
United Kingdom			926	K02000001	107.4	1.7	..	..	7.6
Great Britain			925	K03000001	..	..	4.6	..	7.6
England and Wales			941	K04000001	..	..	4.2	..	7.6
United Kingdom	England		921	E92000001	85.9	1.8	3.9	26.0	7.4
United Kingdom	Wales		924	W92000004	4.5	1.6	9.3	15.0	10.7
United Kingdom	Scotland		923.0	S92000003	10.7	0.9	8.4	22.8	7.5
United Kingdom	Northern Ireland		922	N92000002	6.4	-10.1	..	14.7	9.4
United Kingdom	England	North East	A	E12000001	3.7	2.4	7.3	..	9.4
United Kingdom	England	North West	B	E12000002	8.6	0.7	5.9	..	7.8
United Kingdom	England	Yorkshire and The Humber	D	E12000003	8.6	0.0	6.4	..	8.7
United Kingdom	England	East Midlands	E	E12000004	9.1	1.2	6.3	..	8.1
United Kingdom	England	West Midlands	F	E12000005	6.2	0.3	7.0	..	7.4
United Kingdom	England	East	G	E12000006	11.8	1.9	4.5	..	7.2
United Kingdom	England	London	H	E12000007	12.0	5.2	-8.7	..	5.7
United Kingdom	England	South East	J	E12000008	15.3	0.7	0.9	..	7.1
United Kingdom	England	South West	K	E12000009	10.2	0.0	7.1	..	7.0

.. not available

1 Includes private landlords (persons or companies) and owner-occupiers. Further information can be found on the Department for Communities and Local Government website.

Data have been revised from previous release; figures from 2007 have been revised to include data from independent Approved Inspectors as well as scheduled revisions. For more information see the Housebuilding Statistical release for December quarter 2011.

2 Mix adjusted house prices, taken from House Price Index September 2012, allow for differences between houses sold (for example type, number of rooms, location) in different months within a year. The annual rate of change shown is the percentage change between October 2011 and September 2012. Not seasonally adjusted.

3 The volume of traffic is expressed as vehicle kilometres, which is calculated by multiplying the Annual Average Daily Flow by the corresponding length of road. For further information please see the Department for Transport website.

4 Motorways and A roads.

5 Information on method of calculation can be found in the Greenhouse Gas Inventories for England, Scotland, Wales and Northern Ireland: 1990 - 2010 publication. Additional information for Scottish Greenhouse Gases can be found at the Scottish Government website.

6 The latest data can be found on the Department of Energy and Climate Change website.

Source: Department for Communities and Local Government; Welsh Government; Scottish Government; Department for Social Development, Northern Ireland; Office for National Statistics; Department for Transport; Department for Environment, Food, and Rural Affairs; Department of the Environment, Northern Ireland; Department of Energy and Climate Change

Region and Country Profiles - Key Statistics

Release Date 1 March 2013	Type[1]	Last updated	Latest year
1	Key statistics – population and health	NS	Dec-12	2011
2	Key statistics – social indicators	NS	Oct-12	2012
3	Key statistics – labour market and skills	NS	Jan-13	2012
4	Key statistics – education	Mixed	Mar-13	2011/12
5	Key statistics – economy	NS	Jan-13	2011
6	Key statistics – housing, transport and environment	Mixed	Jan-13	2012

1 National Statistics (NS), Non National Statistics (Non NS), or Mixed.

Find the latest data published as part of Region and Country Profiles for other topics:
Economy
Environment
Population and Migration
Social Indicators

1 Key statistics – population and health

UK/GB/E&W	Country	Region	Old area code	New area code	Population mid-2011[1] (Thousands)	Total population growth 2001 to 2011[1] (%)	Population aged under 16 mid-2011[1] (%)	Population aged 65 and over mid-2011[1] (%)	Male life expectancy at birth, 2008 to 2010[2,3] (Years)	Female life expectancy at birth, 2008 to 2010[2,3] (Years)
United Kingdom			926	K02000001	..	..	..	..	78.1	82.1
Great Britain			925	K03000001	..	..	..	..	..	..
England and Wales			941	K04000001	56,170.9	7.3	18.8	16.5	78.3	82.3
United Kingdom	England		921	E92000001	53,107.2	7.4	18.9	16.4	78.4	82.4
United Kingdom	Wales		924	W92000004	3,063.8	5.3	18.1	18.5	77.5	81.7
United Kingdom	Scotland		923	S92000003	5,254.8	3.8	17.4	17.0	75.8	80.3
United Kingdom	Northern Ireland		922	N92000002	1,806.9	..	..	..	77.0	81.4
United Kingdom	England	North East	A	E12000001	2,596.4	2.2	17.8	17.4	77.2	81.2
United Kingdom	England	North West	B	E12000002	7,056.0	4.2	18.8	16.7	77.0	81.1
United Kingdom	England	Yorkshire and The Humber	D	E12000003	5,288.2	6.3	18.9	16.7	77.7	81.8
United Kingdom	England	East Midlands	E	E12000004	4,537.4	8.3	18.5	17.2	78.4	82.4
United Kingdom	England	West Midlands	F	E12000005	5,608.7	6.2	19.5	17.0	77.9	82.2
United Kingdom	England	East	G	E12000006	5,862.4	8.6	18.9	17.6	79.6	83.2
United Kingdom	England	London	H	E12000007	8,204.4	12.0	19.9	11.1	79.0	83.3
United Kingdom	England	South East	J	E12000008	8,652.8	7.8	19.0	17.3	79.7	83.5
United Kingdom	England	South West	K	E12000009	5,300.8	7.2	17.5	19.7	79.5	83.5

.. not available

1 The estimated mid-year resident populations of England and Wales are based on the 2011 Census. Estimates are as published on 25 September 2012.
The estimated 2011 mid-year resident population for Scotland is based on the 2001 Census data, rolled forward using information on births, deaths and migration.
The estimated mid-year resident population for Northern Ireland is based on the 2001 Census.
2 Estimates for English regions use abridged life tables as published in Reference Table: Life expectancy at birth and at age 65 by local areas in the United Kingdom, 2004-06 to 2008-10.
Estimates for UK and constituent countries use interim life tables as published in Reference Table: Period Expectation of Life at Birth and Selected Ages, UK and Constituent Countries, 1980-82 to 2008-10.
3 Guide to Life Expectancies.

Source: Office for National Statistics; National Records of Scotland; Northern Ireland Statistics and Research Agency

Additional Information

Resident population

The estimated resident population of an area includes all people who usually live there, whatever their nationality. People arriving into an area from outside the UK are only included in the population estimates if their total stay in the UK is 12 months or more. Visitors and short-term migrants (those who enter the UK for 3 to 12 months for certain purposes) are not included. Similarly, people who leave the UK are only excluded from the population estimates if they remain outside the UK for 12 months or more. This is consistent with the United Nations recommended definition of an international long-term migrant. Members of UK and non-UK armed forces stationed in the UK are included in the population and UK forces stationed outside the UK are excluded. Students are taken to be resident at their term-time address.

2 Key statistics – social indicators

UK/GB/E&W	Country	Region	Old area code	New area code	People who are DDA disabled and also work-limiting disabled[1] 2011/2012[2] (%)	Children living in workless households[3] Q2 2012 (%)	Recorded crime[4,5,6,7] 2011/12 (Recorded offences per 1,000 population)	Crimes committed against households[8,9] 2011/12 (Rates per 1,000 households)
United Kingdom			926	K02000001	12.1	15.1	..	..
Great Britain			925	K03000001	12.0	15.0	..	..
England and Wales			941	K04000001	11.9	..	72	243
United Kingdom	England		921	E92000001	11.7	14.8	71	244
United Kingdom	Wales		924	W92000004	15.4	19.1	63	214
United Kingdom	Scotland		923	S92000003	13.4	15.6	60	..
United Kingdom	Northern Ireland		922	N92000002	14.5	15.7	57	..
United Kingdom	England	North East	A	E12000001	14.5	22.5	59	261
United Kingdom	England	North West	B	E12000002	13.5	16.7	71	254
United Kingdom	England	Yorkshire and The Humber	D	E12000003	13.5	17.1	75	283
United Kingdom	England	East Midlands	E	E12000004	13.0	13.0	67	236
United Kingdom	England	West Midlands	F	E12000005	13.0	16.5	66	250
United Kingdom	England	East	G	E12000006	10.7	11.8	60	214
United Kingdom	England	London	H	E12000007	9.6	17.2	105	266
United Kingdom	England	South East	J	E12000008	9.9	11.6	63	232
United Kingdom	England	South West	K	E12000009	10.9	10.3	61	208

.. not available

1 People aged 16 to 64. Definitions of disability.

2 Source: Annual Population Survey April 2011 to March 2012.

3 Children under 16. Source: Labour Force Survey. Definition of a workless household.

Further information is on the Department for Work and Pensions website.

4 Recorded crime statistics broadly cover the more serious offences.

5 Crimes recorded by the British Transport police are not included.

6 Figures for Scotland are not comparable with those for England and Wales because of the differences in the legal systems, recording practices and classifications.

7 The Northern Ireland figure includes 'offences against the state' and 'other notifiable offences'.

8 See estimates from the Crime Survey for England and Wales for further information.

9 Estimates from the Scottish Crime and Justice Survey and Northern Ireland Crime Survey for 2011/12 have not yet been published. Estimates for 2010/11 were 225 and 131 respectively.

Scottish Crime and Justice Survey.

Northern Ireland Crime Survey.

Source: Office for National Statistics; Home Office; Scottish Government; Department of Justice, Northern Ireland

3 Key statistics – labour market and skills

UK/GB/E&W	Country	Region	Old area code	New area code	Employment rate[1], Q3 2012 (%)	Unemployment rate[2], Q3 2012 (%)	Economic inactivity rate[1] Q3 2012 (%)	Median gross weekly earnings[3] April 2012 (£)	Working-age[4] population with no qualifications 2011 (%)
United Kingdom			926	K02000001	71.2	7.8	22.6	505.90	10.9
Great Britain			925	K03000001	71.3	7.8	22.4	508.00	10.6
England and Wales			941	K04000001	..	..	..	508.90	10.5
United Kingdom	England		921	E92000001	71.5	7.8	22.3	512.70	10.4
United Kingdom	Wales		924	W92000004	69.0	8.2	24.7	455.00	12.3
United Kingdom	Scotland		923	S92000003	70.6	8.1	23.0	498.30	11.6
United Kingdom	Northern Ireland		922	N92000002	67.4	7.6	26.9	460.00	21.3
United Kingdom	England	North East	A	E12000001	67.8	9.8	24.8	455.30	12.2
United Kingdom	England	North West	B	E12000002	69.8	8.4	23.6	472.50	12.0
United Kingdom	England	Yorkshire and The Humber	D	E12000003	69.8	9.1	23.1	465.20	11.9
United Kingdom	England	East Midlands	E	E12000004	71.4	7.7	22.4	476.90	11.5
United Kingdom	England	West Midlands	F	E12000005	69.7	8.6	23.5	469.30	14.0
United Kingdom	England	East	G	E12000006	74.7	6.8	19.6	531.00	9.6
United Kingdom	England	London	H	E12000007	69.6	8.7	23.6	613.30	9.3
United Kingdom	England	South East	J	E12000008	74.5	6.5	20.2	555.80	7.9
United Kingdom	England	South West	K	E12000009	74.4	5.8	20.9	476.50	8.0

.. not available

1 Seasonally adjusted data for people aged 16-64 from the Labour Force Survey (LFS).

2 Seasonally adjusted data as a percentage of all economically active people aged 16 and over from the LFS.

3 Residence-based estimates for full-time employees on adult rates whose pay for the survey pay-period was not affected by absence. Total pay including overtime pay, shift premiums, bonuses, commission and other incentive payments.

Further information about the Annual Survey of Hours and Earnings (ASHE).

4 People aged 16-64 from the Annual Population Survey (APS), January-December.

Source: Labour Force Survey, Annual Population Survey and Annual Survey of Hours and Earnings, Office for National Statistics; Department of Finance and Personnel, Northern Ireland

UK/GB/E&W	Country	Region	Old area code	New area code	Pupils[1,2] achieving 5 or more grades A*-C including English and Mathematics GCSE or equivalent qualifications 2011/12	Programme for International Student Assessment reading score[3] 2009	Programme for International Student Assessment maths score[3] 2009	Programme for International Student Assessment science score[3] 2009
United Kingdom			926	K02000001	..	494	492	514
Great Britain			925	K03000001	..	..	..	..
England and Wales			941	K04000001	..	..	..	..
United Kingdom	England[4]		921	E92000001	59.4	495	493	515
United Kingdom	Wales		924	W92000004	..	476	472	496
United Kingdom	Scotland		923	S92000003	..	500	499	514
United Kingdom	Northern Ireland		922	N92000002	..	499	492	511
United Kingdom	England	North East	A	E12000001	58.5	..	..	..
United Kingdom	England	North West	B	E12000002	58.9	..	..	..
United Kingdom	England	Yorkshire and The Humber	D	E12000003	57.3	..	..	..
United Kingdom	England	East Midlands	E	E12000004	57.6	..	..	..
United Kingdom	England	West Midlands	F	E12000005	58.8	..	..	..
United Kingdom	England	East	G	E12000006	58.2	..	..	..
United Kingdom	England	London	H	E12000007	62.3	..	..	..
United Kingdom	England	South East	J	E12000008	60.2	..	..	..
United Kingdom	England	South West	K	E12000009	57.5	..	..	..

.. not available

1 Revised (but not final) data published on 24 January 2013, for Local Authority Maintained schools only. Other England figures are available on the Department for Education website.

2 Pupils at the end of Key Stage 4 in the 2011/12 academic year. Due to lack of comparability of educational attainment data between countries only data for England are shown.

3 See Additional Information.

4 GCSE data for England include all pupils from state-funded schools, independent schools, independent special schools, non-maintained special schools, hospital schools and alternative provision including pupil referral units.

Source: Department for Education; Organisation for Economic Co-operation and Development

Additional Information

GCSE and equivalent attainment

Scottish school educational attainment statistics are available on the Scottish Government website.

Wales and Northern Ireland use GCSEs but the way the statistics are compiled varies from that in England.

Statistics for Wales are available on the Welsh Government website.

Statistics for Northern Ireland are available on the Department of Education for Northern Ireland website.

PISA

The OECD Programme for International Student Assessment (PISA) seeks to measure the extent to which students near the end of compulsory education have acquired some of the knowledge and skills that are essential for full participation in modern societies.

Its triennial surveys of key competencies of 15-year-old students are conducted in 65 OECD member and partner countries. In 2009 each participating student spent two hours carrying out pencil-and-paper tasks in reading, mathematics and science. Every PISA survey tests reading, mathematical and scientific literacy in terms of general competencies, that is, how well students can apply the knowledge and skills they have learned at school to real-life challenges. PISA does not test how well a student has mastered a school's specific curriculum.

In each test subject, the score for each participating country is the average of all student scores in that country. The average score among OECD countries is 500 points and the standard deviation is 100 points. About two-thirds of students across OECD countries score between 400 and 600 points.

Schools in each country are randomly selected by the international contractor for participation in PISA. At these schools, the test is given to students who are between age 15 years 3 months and age 16 years 2 months at the time of the test, rather than to students in a specific year of school. This average age of 15 was chosen because at this age young people in most OECD countries are nearing the end of compulsory education. PISA covers all students who have completed at least 6 years of formal schooling, regardless of the type of institution in which they are enrolled, whether they are in full-time or part-time education, whether they attend academic or vocational programmes, and whether they attend state-funded or private schools or foreign schools within the country.

The specific sample design and size for each country aimed to maximise sampling efficiency for student-level estimates. In OECD countries, sample sizes ranged from 4,410 students in Iceland to 38,250 students in Mexico. Countries with large samples have often implemented PISA both at national and regional/state levels. In the UK, results are available for each of the four countries of the UK.

5 Key statistics – economy

UK/GB/E&W	Country	Region	Old area code	New area code	Gross value added[1] as a percentage of UK[2], 2011[3] (%)	Labour productivity[4], 2011 (UK = 100)	Gross disposable household income[5] per head, 2010[3] (£)	Business birth rate[6] 2011 (%)	Business death rate[6] 2011 (%)
United Kingdom			926	K02000001	100.0	100.0	15,727	11.2	9.8
Great Britain			925	K03000001	..	..	..	11.3	9.8
England and Wales			941	K04000001	..	..	..	11.3	9.9
United Kingdom	England		921	E92000001	85.9	101.9	15,931	11.4	9.9
United Kingdom	Wales		924	W92000004	3.6	81.5	13,783	9.3	9.5
United Kingdom	Scotland		923	S92000003	8.3	96.9	15,342	10.9	9.1
United Kingdom	Northern Ireland		922	N92000002	2.3	82.9	13,554	6.5	8.6
United Kingdom	England	North East	A	E12000001	3.2	86.2	13,329	11.2	9.9
United Kingdom	England	North West	B	E12000002	9.5	88.6	14,176	11.1	10.7
United Kingdom	England	Yorkshire and The Humber	D	E12000003	6.9	84.7	13,594	10.5	10.0
United Kingdom	England	East Midlands	E	E12000004	6.2	89.2	14,267	10.3	9.8
United Kingdom	England	West Midlands	F	E12000005	7.3	89.1	14,021	10.5	10.0
United Kingdom	England	East	G	E12000006	8.7	96.8	16,392	10.5	9.6
United Kingdom	England	London	H	E12000007	21.6	139.7	20,238	14.6	10.4
United Kingdom	England	South East	J	E12000008	14.7	108.3	17,610	10.8	9.5
United Kingdom	England	South West	K	E12000009	7.7	89.8	15,653	9.6	9.2

.. not available

1 Workplace based. For further information see: Regional Gross Value Added (Income Approach), December 2012. Regional GVA NUTS1 Table 1.1

2 UK less extra-regio. For further information see: Regional Gross Value Added (Income Approach), December 2012. Regional GVA NUTS1 Table 1.1

3 Provisional.

4 Workplace based nominal gross value added per hour worked. The annual hours figure used is an average of the four quarters and includes employees, self employed, HM Forces and Government-supported trainees.

5 Household income covers the income received by households and non-profit institutions serving households. UK figure excludes extra-regio. For further information see: Region and Country Profiles, Economy, May 2012, Table 7.

6 Birth and Death rates are expressed as a percentage of active enterprises.

Source: Office for National Statistics

Additional Information

For additional information about Regional GVA, see the Regional Accounts Methodology Guide on the Regional GVA landing page.

The figures for all UK countries and regions (NUTS1 areas) are consistent with the United Kingdom National Accounts – The Blue Book 2012.

6 Key statistics – housing, transport and environment

UK/GB/E&W	Country	Region	Old area code	New area code	Housebuilding: permanent dwellings completed by private enterprise[1] 2010/11 (Thousands)	Annual change in mix adjusted house prices[2] September 2012 (%)	Traffic[3] increase on major roads[4] between 2001 and 2011 (%)	Reduction in total greenhouse gas emissions[5] between 1990 and 2010 (%)	CO$_2$ emissions per resident[6] 2010 (Tonnes)
United Kingdom			926	K02000001	107.4	1.7	..	..	7.6
Great Britain			925	K03000001	..	..	4.6	..	7.6
England and Wales			941	K04000001	..	..	4.2	..	7.6
United Kingdom	England		921	E92000001	85.9	1.8	3.9	26.0	7.4
United Kingdom	Wales		924	W92000004	4.5	1.6	9.3	15.0	10.7
United Kingdom	Scotland		923.0	S92000003	10.7	0.9	8.4	22.8	7.5
United Kingdom	Northern Ireland		922	N92000002	6.4	-10.1	..	14.7	9.4
United Kingdom	England	North East	A	E12000001	3.7	2.4	7.3	..	9.4
United Kingdom	England	North West	B	E12000002	8.6	0.7	5.9	..	7.8
United Kingdom	England	Yorkshire and The Humber	D	E12000003	8.6	0.0	6.4	..	8.7
United Kingdom	England	East Midlands	E	E12000004	9.1	1.2	6.3	..	8.1
United Kingdom	England	West Midlands	F	E12000005	6.2	0.3	7.0	..	7.4
United Kingdom	England	East	G	E12000006	11.8	1.9	4.5	..	7.2
United Kingdom	England	London	H	E12000007	12.0	5.2	-8.7	..	5.7
United Kingdom	England	South East	J	E12000008	15.3	0.7	0.9	..	7.1
United Kingdom	England	South West	K	E12000009	10.2	0.0	7.1	..	7.0

.. not available

1 Includes private landlords (persons or companies) and owner-occupiers. Further information can be found on the Department for Communities and Local Government website.
Data have been revised from previous release; figures from 2007 have been revised to include data from independent Approved Inspectors as well as scheduled revisions. For more information see the Housebuilding Statistical release for December quarter 2011.
2 Mix adjusted house prices, taken from House Price Index September 2012, allow for differences between houses sold (for example type, number of rooms, location) in different months within a year. The annual rate of change shown is the percentage change between October 2011 and September 2012. Not seasonally adjusted.
3 The volume of traffic is expressed as vehicle kilometres, which is calculated by multiplying the Annual Average Daily Flow by the corresponding length of road. For further information please see the Department for Transport website.
4 Motorways and A roads.
5 Information on method of calculation can be found in the Greenhouse Gas Inventories for England, Scotland, Wales and Northern Ireland: 1990 - 2010 publication. Additional information for Scottish Greenhouse Gases can be found at the Scottish Government website.
6 The latest data can be found on the Department of Energy and Climate Change website.

Source: Department for Communities and Local Government; Welsh Government; Scottish Government; Department for Social Development, Northern Ireland; Office for National Statistics; Department for Transport; Department for Environment, Food, and Rural Affairs; Department of the Environment, Northern Ireland; Department of Energy and Climate Change

Region and Country Profiles - Key Statistics

Release Date 10 April 2013	Type[1]	Last updated	Latest year
1 Key statistics – population and health	NS	Dec-12	2011
2 Key statistics – social indicators	NS	Oct-12	2012
3 Key statistics – labour market and skills	NS	Apr-13	2012
4 Key statistics – education	Mixed	Mar-13	2011/12
5 Key statistics – economy	NS	Jan-13	2011
6 Key statistics – housing, transport and environment	Mixed	Apr-13	2012

1 National Statistics (NS), Non National Statistics (Non NS), or Mixed.

Find the latest data published as part of Region and Country Profiles for other topics:
Economy
Environment
Population and Migration
Social Indicators

1 Key statistics – population and health

UK/GB/E&W	Country	Region	Old area code	New area code	Population mid-2011[1] (Thousands)	Total population growth 2001 to 2011[1] (%)	Population aged under 16 mid-2011[1] (%)	Population aged 65 and over mid-2011[1] (%)	Male life expectancy at birth, 2008 to 2010[2,3] (Years)	Female life expectancy at birth, 2008 to 2010[2,3] (Years)
United Kingdom			926	K02000001	..	..	..	..	78.1	82.1
Great Britain			925	K03000001	..	..	..	..	..	..
England and Wales			941	K04000001	56,170.9	7.3	18.8	16.5	78.3	82.3
United Kingdom	England		921	E92000001	53,107.2	7.4	18.9	16.4	78.4	82.4
United Kingdom	Wales		924	W92000004	3,063.8	5.3	18.1	18.5	77.5	81.7
United Kingdom	Scotland		923	S92000003	5,254.8	3.8	17.4	17.0	75.8	80.3
United Kingdom	Northern Ireland		922	N92000002	1,806.9	..	..	..	77.0	81.4
United Kingdom	England	North East	A	E12000001	2,596.4	2.2	17.8	17.4	77.2	81.2
United Kingdom	England	North West	B	E12000002	7,056.0	4.2	18.8	16.7	77.0	81.1
United Kingdom	England	Yorkshire and The Humber	D	E12000003	5,288.2	6.3	18.9	16.7	77.7	81.8
United Kingdom	England	East Midlands	E	E12000004	4,537.4	8.3	18.5	17.2	78.4	82.4
United Kingdom	England	West Midlands	F	E12000005	5,608.7	6.2	19.5	17.0	77.9	82.2
United Kingdom	England	East	G	E12000006	5,862.4	8.6	18.9	17.6	79.6	83.2
United Kingdom	England	London	H	E12000007	8,204.4	12.0	19.9	11.1	79.0	83.3
United Kingdom	England	South East	J	E12000008	8,652.8	7.8	19.0	17.3	79.7	83.5
United Kingdom	England	South West	K	E12000009	5,300.8	7.2	17.5	19.7	79.5	83.5

.. not available

1 The estimated mid-year resident populations of England and Wales are based on the 2011 Census. Estimates are as published on 25 September 2012.
The estimated 2011 mid-year resident population for Scotland is based on the 2001 Census data, rolled forward using information on births, deaths and migration.
The estimated mid-year resident population for Northern Ireland is based on the 2001 Census.

2 Estimates for English regions use abridged life tables as published in Reference Table: Life expectancy at birth and at age 65 by local areas in the United Kingdom, 2004-06 to 2008-10.
Estimates for UK and constituent countries use interim life tables as published in Reference Table: Period Expectation of Life at Birth and Selected Ages, UK and Constituent Countries, 1980-82 to 2008-10.

3 Guide to Life Expectancies.

Source: Office for National Statistics; National Records of Scotland; Northern Ireland Statistics and Research Agency

Additional Information

Resident population

The estimated resident population of an area includes all people who usually live there, whatever their nationality. People arriving into an area from outside the UK are only included in the population estimates if their total stay in the UK is 12 months or more. Visitors and short-term migrants (those who enter the UK for 3 to 12 months for certain purposes) are not included. Similarly, people who leave the UK are only excluded from the population estimates if they remain outside the UK for 12 months or more. This is consistent with the United Nations recommended definition of an international long-term migrant. Members of UK and non-UK armed forces stationed in the UK are included in the population and UK forces stationed outside the UK are excluded. Students are taken to be resident at their term-time address.

2 Key statistics – social indicators

UK/GB/E&W	Country	Region	Old area code	New area code	People who are DDA disabled and also work-limiting disabled[1] 2011/2012[2] (%)	Children living in workless households[3] Q2 2012 (%)	Recorded crime[4,5,6,7] 2011/12 (Recorded offences per 1,000 population)	Crimes committed against households[8,9] 2011/12 (Rates per 1,000 households)
United Kingdom			926	K02000001	12.1	15.1	..	..
Great Britain			925	K03000001	12.0	15.0	..	..
England and Wales			941	K04000001	11.9	..	72	243
United Kingdom	England		921	E92000001	11.7	14.8	71	244
United Kingdom	Wales		924	W92000004	15.4	19.1	63	214
United Kingdom	Scotland		923	S92000003	13.4	15.6	60	..
United Kingdom	Northern Ireland		922	N92000002	14.5	15.7	57	..
United Kingdom	England	North East	A	E12000001	14.5	22.5	59	261
United Kingdom	England	North West	B	E12000002	13.5	16.7	71	254
United Kingdom	England	Yorkshire and The Humber	D	E12000003	13.5	17.1	75	283
United Kingdom	England	East Midlands	E	E12000004	13.0	13.0	67	236
United Kingdom	England	West Midlands	F	E12000005	13.0	16.5	66	250
United Kingdom	England	East	G	E12000006	10.7	11.8	60	214
United Kingdom	England	London	H	E12000007	9.6	17.2	105	266
United Kingdom	England	South East	J	E12000008	9.9	11.6	63	232
United Kingdom	England	South West	K	E12000009	10.9	10.3	61	208

.. not available

1 People aged 16 to 64. Definitions of disability.
2 Source: Annual Population Survey April 2011 to March 2012.
3 Children under 16. Source: Labour Force Survey. Definition of a workless household.
Further information is on the Department for Work and Pensions website.
4 Recorded crime statistics broadly cover the more serious offences.
5 Crimes recorded by the British Transport police are not included.
6 Figures for Scotland are not comparable with those for England and Wales because of the differences in the legal systems, recording practices and classifications.
7 The Northern Ireland figure includes 'offences against the state' and 'other notifiable offences'.
8 See estimates from the Crime Survey for England and Wales for further information.
9 Estimates from the Scottish Crime and Justice Survey and Northern Ireland Crime Survey for 2011/12 have not yet been published. Estimates for 2010/11 were 225 and 131 respectively.
Scottish Crime and Justice Survey.
Northern Ireland Crime Survey.

Source: Office for National Statistics; Home Office; Scottish Government; Department of Justice, Northern Ireland

3 Key statistics – labour market and skills

UK/GB/E&W	Country	Region	Old area code	New area code	Employment rate[1],[3] Q4 2012 (%)	Unemployment rate[2],[3] Q4 2012 (%)	Economic inactivity rate[1],[3] Q4 2012 (%)	Median gross earnings April 2012[4] (£ per week)	Working-age[5] population with no qualifications 2011 (%)
United Kingdom			926	K02000001	71.5	7.8	22.3	505.90	10.9
Great Britain			925	K03000001	71.6	7.8	22.2	508.00	10.6
England and Wales			941	K04000001	..	..	..	508.90	10.5
United Kingdom	England		921	E92000001	71.9	7.7	21.9	512.70	10.4
United Kingdom	Wales		924	W92000004	68.6	8.6	24.8	455.00	12.3
United Kingdom	Scotland		923	S92000003	70.7	7.7	23.3	498.30	11.6
United Kingdom	Northern Ireland		922	N92000002	67.0	7.8	27.2	460.00	21.3
United Kingdom	England	North East	A	E12000001	67.7	9.7	24.9	455.30	12.2
United Kingdom	England	North West	B	E12000002	69.8	8.5	23.7	472.50	12.0
United Kingdom	England	Yorkshire and The Humber	D	E12000003	70.2	8.9	22.7	465.20	11.9
United Kingdom	England	East Midlands	E	E12000004	71.4	7.7	22.4	476.90	11.5
United Kingdom	England	West Midlands	F	E12000005	70.8	8.6	22.3	469.30	14.0
United Kingdom	England	East	G	E12000006	74.8	6.8	19.6	531.00	9.6
United Kingdom	England	London	H	E12000007	70.3	8.4	23.1	613.30	9.3
United Kingdom	England	South East	J	E12000008	75.0	6.5	19.7	555.80	7.9
United Kingdom	England	South West	K	E12000009	74.7	5.5	20.8	476.50	8.0

.. not available

1 Seasonally adjusted data for people aged 16-64 from the Labour Force Survey (LFS).
2 Unemployed as a percentage of all economically active people aged 16 and over from the LFS. Seasonally adjusted.
3 Regional Labour Market Statistics - February 2013 provides data and further
4 Residence-based estimates for full-time employees on adult rates whose pay for the survey pay-period was not affected by absence. Total pay including overtime pay, shift premiums, bonuses, commission and other incentive payments.
The 2012 Annual Survey of Hours and Earnings contains further information and tables.
5 Based on people aged 16-64 from the Annual Population Survey, January-December.

Source: Labour Force Survey, Annual Survey of Hours and Earnings and Annual Population Survey, Office for National Statistics; Department of Finance and Personnel, Northern Ireland

Additional Information
Glossary of Labour Market terms.
Labour Force Survey.
Annual Survey of Hours and Earnings.
Annual Population Survey.
Interpreting Labour Market Statistics.

4 Key statistics – education

UK/GB/E&W	Country	Region	Old area code	New area code	Pupils[1,2] achieving 5 or more grades A*-C including English and Mathematics GCSE or equivalent qualifications 2011/12 (%)	Programme for International Student Assessment reading score[3] 2009	Programme for International Student Assessment maths score[3] 2009	Programme for International Student Assessment science score[3] 2009
United Kingdom			926	K02000001	..	494	492	514
Great Britain			925	K03000001	..	..	..	..
England and Wales			941	K04000001	..	..	..	..
United Kingdom	England[4]		921	E92000001	59.4	495	493	515
United Kingdom	Wales		924	W92000004	..	476	472	496
United Kingdom	Scotland		923	S92000003	..	500	499	514
United Kingdom	Northern Ireland		922	N92000002	..	499	492	511
United Kingdom	England	North East	A	E12000001	58.5	..	..	..
United Kingdom	England	North West	B	E12000002	58.9	..	..	..
United Kingdom	England	Yorkshire and The Humber	D	E12000003	57.3	..	..	..
United Kingdom	England	East Midlands	E	E12000004	57.6	..	..	..
United Kingdom	England	West Midlands	F	E12000005	58.8	..	..	..
United Kingdom	England	East	G	E12000006	58.2	..	..	..
United Kingdom	England	London	H	E12000007	62.3	..	..	..
United Kingdom	England	South East	J	E12000008	60.2	..	..	..
United Kingdom	England	South West	K	E12000009	57.5	..	..	..

.. not available

1 Revised (but not final) data published on 24 January 2013, for Local Authority Maintained schools only. Other England figures are available on the Department for Education website.

2 Pupils at the end of Key Stage 4 in the 2011/12 academic year. Due to lack of comparability of educational attainment data between countries only data for England are shown.

3 See Additional Information.

4 GCSE data for England include all pupils from state-funded schools, independent schools, independent special schools, non-maintained special schools, hospital schools and alternative provision including pupil referral units.

Source: Department for Education; Organisation for Economic Co-operation and Development

Additional Information

GCSE and equivalent attainment
Scottish school educational attainment statistics are available on the Scottish Government website.
Wales and Northern Ireland use GCSEs but the way the statistics are compiled varies from that in England.
Statistics for Wales are available on the Welsh Government website.
Statistics for Northern Ireland are available on the Department of Education for Northern Ireland website.

PISA
The OECD Programme for International Student Assessment (PISA) seeks to measure the extent to which students near the end of compulsory education have acquired some of the knowledge and skills that are essential for full participation in modern societies.

Its triennial surveys of key competencies of 15-year-old students are conducted in 65 OECD member and partner countries. In 2009 each participating student spent two hours carrying out pencil-and-paper tasks in reading, mathematics and science. Every PISA survey tests reading, mathematical and scientific literacy in terms of general competencies, that is, how well students can apply the knowledge and skills they have learned at school to real-life challenges. PISA does not test how well a student has mastered a school's specific curriculum.

In each test subject, the score for each participating country is the average of all student scores in that country. The average score among OECD countries is 500 points and the standard deviation is 100 points. About two-thirds of students across OECD countries score between 400 and 600 points.

Schools in each country are randomly selected by the international contractor for participation in PISA. At these schools, the test is given to students who are between age 15 years 3 months and age 16 years 2 months at the time of the test, rather than to students in a specific year of school. This average age of 15 was chosen because at this age young people in most OECD countries are nearing the end of compulsory education. PISA covers all students who have completed at least 6 years of formal schooling, regardless of the type of institution in which they are enrolled, whether they are in full-time or part-time education, whether they attend academic or vocational programmes, and whether they attend state-funded or private schools or foreign schools within the country.

The specific sample design and size for each country aimed to maximise sampling efficiency for student-level estimates. In OECD countries, sample sizes ranged from 4,410 students in Iceland to 38,250 students in Mexico. Countries with large samples have often implemented PISA both at national and regional/state levels. In the UK, results are available for each of the four countries of the UK.

5 Key statistics – economy

UK/GB/E&W	Country	Region	Old area code	New area code	Gross value added[1] as a percentage of UK[2], 2011[3] (%)	Labour productivity[4], 2011 (UK = 100)	disposable household income[5] per head, 2010[3] (£)	Business birth rate[6] 2011 (%)	Business death rate[6] 2011 (%)
United Kingdom			926	K02000001	100.0	100.0	15,727	11.2	9.8
Great Britain			925	K03000001	..	..	..	11.3	9.8
England and Wales			941	K04000001	..	..	..	11.3	9.9
United Kingdom	England		921	E92000001	85.9	101.9	15,931	11.4	9.9
United Kingdom	Wales		924	W92000004	3.6	81.5	13,783	9.3	9.5
United Kingdom	Scotland		923	S92000003	8.3	96.9	15,342	10.9	9.1
United Kingdom	Northern Ireland		922	N92000002	2.3	82.9	13,554	6.5	8.6
United Kingdom	England	North East	A	E12000001	3.2	86.2	13,329	11.2	9.9
United Kingdom	England	North West	B	E12000002	9.5	88.6	14,176	11.1	10.7
United Kingdom	England	Yorkshire and The Humber	D	E12000003	6.9	84.7	13,594	10.5	10.0
United Kingdom	England	East Midlands	E	E12000004	6.2	89.2	14,267	10.3	9.8
United Kingdom	England	West Midlands	F	E12000005	7.3	89.1	14,021	10.5	10.0
United Kingdom	England	East	G	E12000006	8.7	96.8	16,392	10.5	9.6
United Kingdom	England	London	H	E12000007	21.6	139.7	20,238	14.6	10.4
United Kingdom	England	South East	J	E12000008	14.7	108.3	17,610	10.8	9.5
United Kingdom	England	South West	K	E12000009	7.7	89.8	15,653	9.6	9.2

.. not available

1 Workplace based. For further information see: Regional Gross Value Added (Income Approach), December 2012. Regional GVA NUTS1 Table 1.1
2 UK less extra-regio. For further information see: Regional Gross Value Added (Income Approach), December 2012. Regional GVA NUTS1 Table 1.1
3 Provisional.
4 Workplace based nominal gross value added per hour worked. The annual hours figure used is an average of the four quarters and includes employees, self employed, HM Forces and Government-supported trainees.
5 Household income covers the income received by households and non-profit institutions serving households. UK figure excludes extra-regio. For further information see: Region and Country Profiles, Economy, May 2012, Table 7.
6 Birth and Death rates are expressed as a percentage of active enterprises.

Source: Office for National Statistics

Additional Information

For additional information about Regional GVA, see the Regional Accounts Methodology Guide on the Regional GVA landing page.
The figures for all UK countries and regions (NUTS1 areas) are consistent with the United Kingdom National Accounts – The Blue Book 2012.

6 Key statistics – housing, transport and environment

UK/GB/E&W	Country	Region	Old area code	New area code	House building: permanent dwellings completed by private enterprise[1] 2011/12 (Thousands)	Annual change in mix adjusted house prices[2] December 2012 (%)	Traffic[3] increase on major roads[4] between 2001 and 2011 (%)	Reduction in total greenhouse gas emissions[5] between the base year[6] and 2010 (%)	CO$_2$ emissions per resident[7] 2010 (Tonnes)
United Kingdom			926	K02000001	109.6	3.3	..	..	7.6
Great Britain			925	K03000001	..	..	4.6	..	7.6
England and Wales			941	K04000001	..	..	4.2	..	7.6
United Kingdom	England		921	E92000001	89.1	3.4	3.9	26.0	7.4
United Kingdom	Wales		924	W92000004	4.8	2.4	9.3	15.0	10.7
United Kingdom	Scotland		923	S92000003	10.0	3.1	8.4	23.7	7.5
United Kingdom	Northern Ireland		922	N92000002	5.7	-5.7	..	14.7	9.4
United Kingdom	England	North East	A	E12000001	3.9	-0.6	7.3	..	9.4
United Kingdom	England	North West	B	E12000002	8.2	1.1	5.9	..	7.8
United Kingdom	England	Yorkshire and The Humber	D	E12000003	8.4	2.1	6.4	..	8.7
United Kingdom	England	East Midlands	E	E12000004	8.6	1.3	6.3	..	8.1
United Kingdom	England	West Midlands	F	E12000005	6.7	2.7	7.0	..	7.4
United Kingdom	England	East	G	E12000006	12.1	3.2	4.5	..	7.2
United Kingdom	England	London	H	E12000007	11.3	6.4	-8.7	..	5.7
United Kingdom	England	South East	J	E12000008	17.3	3.7	0.9	..	7.1
United Kingdom	England	South West	K	E12000009	12.3	1.4	7.1	..	7.0

.. not available

1 Includes private landlords (persons or companies) and owner-occupiers. Data and further information can be found on the Department for Communities and Local Government website.

2 Mix adjusted house prices, taken from House Price Index - December 2012, allow for differences between houses sold (for example type, number of rooms, location) in different months within a year. The annual rate of change shown is the percentage change between January 2012 and December 2012. Not seasonally adjusted.

3 The volume of traffic is expressed as vehicle kilometres, which is calculated by multiplying the Annual Average Daily Flow by the corresponding length of road. For further information please see the Department for Transport website.

4 Motorways and A roads.

5 Information on the method of calculation can be found on the Greenhouse Gas Inventories for England, Scotland, Wales and Northern Ireland: 1990 - 2010 publication.

Additional information for Scottish Greenhouse gases can be found on the Scottish Government website.

6 1995 is used as the Base Year (BY) for emissions of HFCs, PFCs and SF6 in the UK's Climate Change Programme, in accordance with Article 3.8 of the Kyoto Protocol. 1990 is used for other gases. The previous version of this table wrongly gave 1990 in the column heading instead of the base year.

7 The latest data and further information can be found on the Department of Energy and Climate Change website.

Source: Department for Communities and Local Government; Welsh Government; Scottish Government; Department for Social Development, Northern Ireland; Office for National Statistics; Department for Transport; Department for Environment, Food, and Rural Affairs; Department of the Environment, Northern Ireland; Department of Energy and Climate Change

Region and Country Profiles - Key Statistics

Release Date 19 June 2013	Type[1]	Last updated	Latest year
1 Key statistics – population and health	NS	Apr-13	2011
2 Key statistics – social indicators	NS	Apr-13	2012
3 Key statistics – labour market and skills	NS	Jun-13	2012
4 Key statistics – education	Mixed	Apr-13	2011/12
5 Key statistics – economy	NS	Jun-13	2011
6 Key statistics – housing, transport and environment	Mixed	Apr-13	2012

1 National Statistics (NS), Non National Statistics (Non NS), or Mixed.

Find the latest data published as part of Region and Country Profiles for other topics:

Economy

Environment

Population and Migration

Social Indicators

1 Key statistics – population and health

UK/GB/E&W	Country	Region	Old area code	New area code	Population mid-2011[1] (Thousands)	Total population growth 2001 to 2011[1] (%)	Population aged under 16 mid-2011[1] (%)	Population aged 65 and over mid-2011[1] (%)	Male life expectancy at birth, 2008 to 2010[2,3] (Years)	Female life expectancy at birth, 2008 to 2010[2,3] (Years)
United Kingdom			926	K02000001	..	..	..	..	78.1	82.1
Great Britain			925	K03000001	..	..	..	..	..	..
England and Wales			941	K04000001	56,170.9	7.3	18.8	16.5	78.3	82.3
United Kingdom	England		921	E92000001	53,107.2	7.4	18.9	16.4	78.4	82.4
United Kingdom	Wales		924	W92000004	3,063.8	5.3	18.1	18.5	77.5	81.7
United Kingdom	Scotland		923	S92000003	5,254.8	3.8	17.4	17.0	75.8	80.3
United Kingdom	Northern Ireland		922	N92000002	1,806.9	..	..	..	77.0	81.4
United Kingdom	England	North East	A	E12000001	2,596.4	2.2	17.8	17.4	77.2	81.2
United Kingdom	England	North West	B	E12000002	7,056.0	4.2	18.8	16.7	77.0	81.1
United Kingdom	England	Yorkshire and The Humber	D	E12000003	5,288.2	6.3	18.9	16.7	77.7	81.8
United Kingdom	England	East Midlands	E	E12000004	4,537.4	8.3	18.5	17.2	78.4	82.4
United Kingdom	England	West Midlands	F	E12000005	5,608.7	6.2	19.5	17.0	77.9	82.2
United Kingdom	England	East	G	E12000006	5,862.4	8.6	18.9	17.6	79.6	83.2
United Kingdom	England	London	H	E12000007	8,204.4	12.0	19.9	11.1	79.0	83.3
United Kingdom	England	South East	J	E12000008	8,652.8	7.8	19.0	17.3	79.7	83.5
United Kingdom	England	South West	K	E12000009	5,300.8	7.2	17.5	19.7	79.5	83.5

.. not available

1 The estimated mid-year resident populations of England and Wales are based on the 2011 Census. Estimates are as published on 25 September 2012.
The estimated 2011 mid-year resident population for Scotland is based on the 2001 Census data, rolled forward using information on births, deaths and migration.
The estimated mid-year resident population for Northern Ireland is based on the 2001 Census.
2 Estimates for English regions use abridged life tables as published in Reference Table: Life expectancy at birth and at age 65 by local areas in the United Kingdom, 2004-06 to 2008-10.
Estimates for UK and constituent countries use interim life tables as published in Reference Table: Period Expectation of Life at Birth and Selected Ages, UK and Constituent Countries, 1980-82 to 2008-10.
3 Guide to Life Expectancies.

Source: Office for National Statistics; National Records of Scotland; Northern Ireland Statistics and Research Agency

Additional Information

Resident population

The estimated resident population of an area includes all people who usually live there, whatever their nationality. People arriving into an area from outside the UK are only included in the population estimates if their total stay in the UK is 12 months or more. Visitors and short-term migrants (those who enter the UK for 3 to 12 months for certain purposes) are not included. Similarly, people who leave the UK are only excluded from the population estimates if they remain outside the UK for 12 months or more. This is consistent with the United Nations recommended definition of an international long-term migrant. Members of UK and non-UK armed forces stationed in the UK are included in the population and UK forces stationed outside the UK are excluded. Students are taken to be resident at their term-time address.

2 Key statistics – social indicators

UK/GB/E&W	Country	Region	Old area code	New area code	People who are DDA disabled and also work-limiting disabled[1] 2011/2012[2] (%)	Children living in workless households[3] Q2 2012 (%)	Recorded crime[4,5,6,7] 2011/12 (Recorded offences per 1,000 population)	Crimes committed against households[8,9] 2011/12 (Rates per 1,000 households)
United Kingdom			926	K02000001	12.1	15.1	..	..
Great Britain			925	K03000001	12.0	15.0	..	..
England and Wales			941	K04000001	11.9	..	72	243
United Kingdom	England		921	E92000001	11.7	14.8	71	244
United Kingdom	Wales		924	W92000004	15.4	19.1	63	214
United Kingdom	Scotland		923	S92000003	13.4	15.6	60	..
United Kingdom	Northern Ireland		922	N92000002	14.5	15.7	57	..
United Kingdom	England	North East	A	E12000001	14.5	22.5	59	261
United Kingdom	England	North West	B	E12000002	13.5	16.7	71	254
United Kingdom	England	Yorkshire and The Humber	D	E12000003	13.5	17.1	75	283
United Kingdom	England	East Midlands	E	E12000004	13.0	13.0	67	236
United Kingdom	England	West Midlands	F	E12000005	13.0	16.5	66	250
United Kingdom	England	East	G	E12000006	10.7	11.8	60	214
United Kingdom	England	London	H	E12000007	9.6	17.2	105	266
United Kingdom	England	South East	J	E12000008	9.9	11.6	63	232
United Kingdom	England	South West	K	E12000009	10.9	10.3	61	208

.. not available

1 People aged 16 to 64. Definitions of disability.

2 Source: Annual Population Survey April 2011 to March 2012.

3 Children under 16. Source: Labour Force Survey. Definition of a workless household.
Further information is on the Department for Work and Pensions website.

4 Recorded crime statistics broadly cover the more serious offences.

5 Crimes recorded by the British Transport police are not included.

6 Figures for Scotland are not comparable with those for England and Wales because of the differences in the legal systems, recording practices and classifications.

7 The Northern Ireland figure includes 'offences against the state' and 'other notifiable offences'.

8 See estimates from the Crime Survey for England and Wales for further information.

9 Estimates from the Scottish Crime and Justice Survey and Northern Ireland Crime Survey for 2011/12 have not yet been published. Estimates for 2010/11 were 225 and 131 respectively.
Scottish Crime and Justice Survey.
Northern Ireland Crime Survey.

Source: Office for National Statistics; Home Office; Scottish Government; Department of Justice, Northern Ireland

3 Key statistics – labour market and skills

UK/GB/E&W	Country	Region	Old area code	New area code	Employment rate[1] Q4 2012 (%)	Unemployment rate[2] Q4 2012 (%)	Economic inactivity rate[1] Q4 2012 (%)	Median gross weekly earnings[3] April 2012 (£)	Working-age[4] population with no qualifications 2012 (%)
United Kingdom			926	K02000001	71.5	7.8	22.3	505.90	9.9
Great Britain			925	K03000001	..	..	..	508.00	9.7
England and Wales			941	K04000001	..	..	..	508.90	9.6
United Kingdom	England		921	E92000001	71.9	7.7	21.9	512.70	9.5
United Kingdom	Wales		924	W92000004	68.6	8.6	24.8	455.00	11.4
United Kingdom	Scotland		923	S92000003	70.7	7.7	23.3	498.30	10.7
United Kingdom	Northern Ireland		922	N92000002	67.0	7.8	27.2	460.00	18.4
United Kingdom	England	North East	A	E12000001	67.7	9.7	24.9	455.30	11.8
United Kingdom	England	North West	B	E12000002	69.8	8.5	23.7	472.50	11.1
United Kingdom	England	Yorkshire and The Humber	D	E12000003	70.2	8.9	22.7	465.20	11.5
United Kingdom	England	East Midlands	E	E12000004	71.4	7.7	22.4	476.90	9.3
United Kingdom	England	West Midlands	F	E12000005	70.8	8.6	22.3	469.30	13.6
United Kingdom	England	East	G	E12000006	74.8	6.8	19.6	531.00	8.5
United Kingdom	England	London	H	E12000007	70.3	8.4	23.1	613.30	8.4
United Kingdom	England	South East	J	E12000008	75.0	6.5	19.7	555.80	6.9
United Kingdom	England	South West	K	E12000009	74.7	5.5	20.8	476.50	7.0

.. not available

1 Seasonally adjusted data for people aged 16-64 from Regional Labour Market Statistics - February 2013.

2 Unemployed as a percentage of all economically active people aged 16 and over. Seasonally adjusted data as published in Regional Labour Market Statistics - February 2013.

3 Residence based data relating to full-time employees on adult rates whose pay for the survey period was not affected by absence. Northern Ireland data period is 2012. The 2012 Annual Survey of Hours and Earnings contains further information and tables.

4 People aged 16-64 from the Annual Population Survey, January-December.

Source: Labour Force Survey, Annual Population Survey and Annual Survey of Hours and Earnings, Office for National Statistics; Department of Enterprise, Trade and Investment, Northern Ireland; Northern Ireland Statistics and Research Agency

Additional Information

Interpreting Labour Market Statistics
Glossary of Labour Market terms
Labour Force Survey
Labour Market Methodology
Monthly data are available from Regional Labour Market Statistics.
Annual Survey of Hours and Earnings
Annual Population Survey

4 Key statistics – education

UK/GB/E&W	Country	Region	Old area code	New area code	Pupils[1,2] achieving 5 or more grades A*-C including English and Mathematics GCSE or equivalent qualifications 2011/12 (%)	Programme for International Student Assessment reading score[3] 2009	Programme for International Student Assessment maths score[3] 2009	Programme for International Student Assessment science score[3] 2009
United Kingdom			926	K02000001	..	494	492	514
Great Britain			925	K03000001	..	..	..	..
England and Wales			941	K04000001	..	..	..	..
United Kingdom	England[4]		921	E92000001	59.4	495	493	515
United Kingdom	Wales		924	W92000004	..	476	472	496
United Kingdom	Scotland		923	S92000003	..	500	499	514
United Kingdom	Northern Ireland		922	N92000002	..	499	492	511
United Kingdom	England	North East	A	E12000001	58.5	..	..	..
United Kingdom	England	North West	B	E12000002	58.9	..	..	..
United Kingdom	England	Yorkshire and The Humber	D	E12000003	57.3	..	..	..
United Kingdom	England	East Midlands	E	E12000004	57.6	..	..	..
United Kingdom	England	West Midlands	F	E12000005	58.8	..	..	..
United Kingdom	England	East	G	E12000006	58.2	..	..	..
United Kingdom	England	London	H	E12000007	62.3	..	..	..
United Kingdom	England	South East	J	E12000008	60.2	..	..	..
United Kingdom	England	South West	K	E12000009	57.5	..	..	..

.. not available

1 Revised (but not final) data published on 24 January 2013, for Local Authority Maintained schools only. Other England figures are available on the Department for Education website.
2 Pupils at the end of Key Stage 4 in the 2011/12 academic year. Due to lack of comparability of educational attainment data between countries only data for England are shown.
3 See Additional Information.
4 GCSE data for England include all pupils from state-funded schools, independent schools, independent special schools, non-maintained special schools, hospital schools and alternative provision including pupil referral units.

Source: Department for Education; Organisation for Economic Co-operation and Development

Additional Information

GCSE and equivalent attainment
Scottish school educational attainment statistics are available on the Scottish Government website.
Wales and Northern Ireland use GCSEs but the way the statistics are compiled varies from that in England.
Statistics for Wales are available on the Welsh Government website.
Statistics for Northern Ireland are available on the Department of Education for Northern Ireland website.

PISA
The OECD Programme for International Student Assessment (PISA) seeks to measure the extent to which students near the end of compulsory education have acquired some of the knowledge and skills that are essential for full participation in modern societies.

Its triennial surveys of key competencies of 15-year-old students are conducted in 65 OECD member and partner countries. In 2009 each participating student spent two hours carrying out pencil-and-paper tasks in reading, mathematics and science. Every PISA survey tests reading, mathematical and scientific literacy in terms of general competencies, that is, how well students can apply the knowledge and skills they have learned at school to real-life challenges. PISA does not test how well a student has mastered a school's specific curriculum.

In each test subject, the score for each participating country is the average of all student scores in that country. The average score among OECD countries is 500 points and the standard deviation is 100 points. About two-thirds of students across OECD countries score between 400 and 600 points.

Schools in each country are randomly selected by the international contractor for participation in PISA. At these schools, the test is given to students who are between age 15 years 3 months and age 16 years 2 months at the time of the test, rather than to students in a specific year of school. This average age of 15 was chosen because at this age young people in most OECD countries are nearing the end of compulsory education. PISA covers all students who have completed at least 6 years of formal schooling, regardless of the type of institution in which they are enrolled, whether they are in full-time or part-time education, whether they attend academic or vocational programmes, and whether they attend state-funded or private schools or foreign schools within the country.

The specific sample design and size for each country aimed to maximise sampling efficiency for student-level estimates. In OECD countries, sample sizes ranged from 4,410 students in Iceland to 38,250 students in Mexico. Countries with large samples have often implemented PISA both at national and regional/state levels. In the UK, results are available for each of the four countries of the UK.

5 Key statistics – economy

UK/GB/E&W	Country	Region	Old area code	New area code	Gross value added[1] as a percentage of UK, 2011[2] (%)	Labour productivity, GVA per hour worked[3] 2011 (UK = 100)	Gross disposable household income[4] per head, 2011[2] (£)	Business birth rate[5] 2011 (%)	Business death rate[5] 2011[2] (%)
United Kingdom			926	K02000001	100.0	100.0	16,034	11.2	9.8
Great Britain			925	K03000001	97.7	100.5	..	11.3	9.8
England and Wales			941	K04000001	89.5	..	..	11.3	9.9
United Kingdom	England		921	E92000001	85.8	101.3	16,251	11.4	9.9
United Kingdom	Wales		924	W92000004	3.6	84.6	14,129	9.3	9.5
United Kingdom	Scotland		923	S92000003	8.2	100.0	15,654	10.9	9.1
United Kingdom	Northern Ireland		922	N92000002	2.3	84.0	13,966	6.5	8.6
United Kingdom	England	North East	A	E12000001	3.2	89.6	13,560	11.2	9.9
United Kingdom	England	North West	B	E12000002	9.4	89.7	14,476	11.1	10.7
United Kingdom	England	Yorkshire and The Humber	D	E12000003	6.9	87.9	13,819	10.5	10.0
United Kingdom	England	East Midlands	E	E12000004	6.1	89.2	14,561	10.3	9.8
United Kingdom	England	West Midlands	F	E12000005	7.3	88.8	14,362	10.5	10.0
United Kingdom	England	East	G	E12000006	8.7	97.4	16,608	10.5	9.6
United Kingdom	England	London	H	E12000007	21.9	129.4	20,509	14.6	10.4
United Kingdom	England	South East	J	E12000008	14.7	107.3	18,087	10.8	9.5
United Kingdom	England	South West	K	E12000009	7.7	93.2	16,014	9.6	9.2

.. Not available

1 Estimates of workplace based GVA allocate incomes to the region in which the economic activity takes place. The data are consistent with the workplace based raw (unsmoothed) series published in December 2012, and may differ from those included in previous versions of this table, which were headline estimates. UK figure is less Extra-Regio.

More GVA data are available in Regional Gross Value Added (Income Approach), December 2012.

2 Provisional.

3 See Labour Productivity, Q4 2012.

4 Household income covers the income received by households and non-profit institutions serving households. All household income has been allocated to regions, unlike the figures published previously. See Regional Gross Disposable Household Income (GDHI) 2011 statistical bulletin.

5 Birth and Death rates are expressed as a percentage of Active enterprises.

Source: Office for National Statistics

Additional Information

Extra-Regio comprises compensation of employees and gross operating surplus which cannot be assigned to regions. For the UK this consists mainly of offshore oil and gas extraction and the activities of UK embassies and forces overseas.

Regional Accounts Guidance and Methodology

Regional Productivity Handbook

Definitions of Active enterprises, Births and Deaths and information on estimation methods are available in the Business Demography 2011 release.

6 Key statistics – housing, transport and environment

UK/GB/E&W	Country	Region	Old area code	New area code	House building: permanent dwellings completed by private enterprise[1] 2011/12 (Thousands)	Annual change in mix adjusted house prices[2] December 2012 (%)	Traffic[3] increase on major roads[4] between 2001 and 2011 (%)	Reduction in total greenhouse gas emissions[5] between the base year[6] and 2010 (%)	CO_2 emissions per resident[7] 2010 (Tonnes)
United Kingdom			926	K02000001	109.6	3.3	..	..	7.6
Great Britain			925	K03000001	..	..	4.6	..	7.6
England and Wales			941	K04000001	..	..	4.2	..	7.6
United Kingdom	England		921	E92000001	89.1	3.4	3.9	26.0	7.4
United Kingdom	Wales		924	W92000004	4.8	2.4	9.3	15.0	10.7
United Kingdom	Scotland		923	S92000003	10.0	3.1	8.4	23.7	7.5
United Kingdom	Northern Ireland		922	N92000002	5.7	-5.7	..	14.7	9.4
United Kingdom	England	North East	A	E12000001	3.9	-0.6	7.3	..	9.4
United Kingdom	England	North West	B	E12000002	8.2	1.1	5.9	..	7.8
United Kingdom	England	Yorkshire and The Humber	D	E12000003	8.4	2.1	6.4	..	8.7
United Kingdom	England	East Midlands	E	E12000004	8.6	1.3	6.3	..	8.1
United Kingdom	England	West Midlands	F	E12000005	6.7	2.7	7.0	..	7.4
United Kingdom	England	East	G	E12000006	12.1	3.2	4.5	..	7.2
United Kingdom	England	London	H	E12000007	11.3	6.4	-8.7	..	5.7
United Kingdom	England	South East	J	E12000008	17.3	3.7	0.9	..	7.1
United Kingdom	England	South West	K	E12000009	12.3	1.4	7.1	..	7.0

.. not available

1 Includes private landlords (persons or companies) and owner-occupiers. Data and further information can be found on the Department for Communities and Local Government website.

2 Mix adjusted house prices, taken from House Price Index - December 2012, allow for differences between houses sold (for example type, number of rooms, location) in different months within a year. The annual rate of change shown is the percentage change between January 2012 and December 2012. Not seasonally adjusted.

3 The volume of traffic is expressed as vehicle kilometres, which is calculated by multiplying the Annual Average Daily Flow by the corresponding length of road. For further information please see the Department for Transport website.

4 Motorways and A roads.

5 Information on the method of calculation can be found on the Greenhouse Gas Inventories for England, Scotland, Wales and Northern Ireland: 1990 - 2010 publication. Additional information for Scottish Greenhouse gases can be found on the Scottish Government website.

6 1995 is used as the Base Year (BY) for emissions of HFCs, PFCs and SF6 in the UK's Climate Change Programme, in accordance with Article 3.8 of the Kyoto Protocol. 1990 is used for other gases. The previous version of this table wrongly gave 1990 in the column heading instead of the base year.

7 The latest data and further information can be found on the Department of Energy and Climate Change website.

Source: Department for Communities and Local Government; Welsh Government; Scottish Government; Department for Social Development, Northern Ireland; Office for National Statistics; Department for Transport; Department for Environment, Food, and Rural Affairs; Department of the Environment, Northern Ireland; Department of Energy and Climate Change

Region and Country Profiles - Key Statistics

	Release Date 12 August 2013	Type[1]	Last updated	Latest year
1	Key statistics – population and health	NS	Aug-13	2012
2	Key statistics – social indicators	NS	Aug-13	2012
3	Key statistics – labour market and skills	NS	Aug-13	2013
4	Key statistics – education	Mixed	Mar-13	2011/12
5	Key statistics – economy	NS	Jun-13	2011
6	Key statistics – housing, transport and environment	Mixed	Aug-13	2012

1 National Statistics (NS), Non National Statistics (Non NS), or Mixed.

Find the latest data published as part of Region and Country Profiles for other topics:

Economy

Environment

Population and Migration

Social Indicators

You may use or re-use this information (not including logos) free of charge in any format or medium, under the terms of the Open Government Licence

or write to the Information Policy Team, The National Archives, Kew, London TW9 4DU, or email:

psi@nationalarchives.gsi.gov.uk

Details of the policy governing the release of new data are available by visiting the Code of Practice.

or from the Media Relations Office email: media.relations@ons.gsi.gov.uk

This document is also available on our website.

1 Key statistics – population

UK/GB/E&W	Country	Region	Old area code	New area code	Population mid-2012[1] (Thousands)	Total population growth 2002 to 2012[1] (%)	Population aged under 16 mid-2012[1] (%)	Population aged 65 and over mid-2012[1] (%)	Area (Sq km)	Population density mid-2012 (People per sq km)
United Kingdom			926	K02000001	63,705.0	..	18.8	17.0	242,509	263
Great Britain			925	K03000001	61,881.4	..	18.7	17.1	228,947	270
England and Wales			941	K04000001	56,567.8	7.5	18.9	17.0	151,014	375
United Kingdom	England		921	E92000001	53,493.7	7.7	18.9	16.9	130,279	411
United Kingdom	Wales		924	W92000004	3,074.1	5.2	18.1	19.1	20,735	148
United Kingdom	Scotland		923	S92000003	5,313.6	..	17.2	17.4	77,933	68
United Kingdom	Northern Ireland		922	N92000002	1,823.6	7.4	21.0	15.0	13,562	134
United Kingdom	England	North East	A	E12000001	2,602.3	2.4	17.8	18.0	8,573	304
United Kingdom	England	North West	B	E12000002	7,084.3	4.4	18.8	17.2	14,105	502
United Kingdom	England	Yorkshire and The Humber	D	E12000003	5,316.7	6.3	18.9	17.2	15,408	345
United Kingdom	England	East Midlands	E	E12000004	4,567.7	8.2	18.5	17.8	15,606	293
United Kingdom	England	West Midlands	F	E12000005	5,642.6	6.4	19.5	17.4	12,998	434
United Kingdom	England	East	G	E12000006	5,907.3	8.7	19.0	18.2	19,109	309
United Kingdom	England	London	H	E12000007	8,308.4	12.6	20.1	11.3	1,572	5,285
United Kingdom	England	South East	J	E12000008	8,724.7	8.4	19.1	17.9	19,070	458
United Kingdom	England	South West	K	E12000009	5,339.6	7.3	17.6	20.3	23,837	224

.. not available

1 The estimated mid-year resident population. Estimates are as published on 26 June 2013, except for Scotland which are as published 8 August 2013. See Additional Information in Region and Country Profiles, Population and Migration - March 2013, Table: Resident Population by sex.

Source: Office for National Statistics; National Records of Scotland; Northern Ireland Statistics and Research Agency

2 Key statistics – social indicators

UK/GB/E&W	Country	Region	Old area code	New area code	Male life expectancy at birth, 2008 to 2010[1,2] (Years)	Female life expectancy at birth, 2008 to 2010[1,2] (Years)	People who are DDA disabled and also work-limiting disabled[3] 2011/2012[4] (%)	Children living in workless households[5] Q2 2012 (%)	Recorded crime[6,7,8,9] 2011/12 (Recorded offences per 1,000 population)	Crimes committed against households[10,11] 2011/12 (Rates per 1,000 households)
United Kingdom			926	K02000001	78.1	82.1	12.1	15.1	..	..
Great Britain			925	K03000001	..	..	12.0	15.0	..	..
England and Wales			941	K04000001	78.3	82.3	11.9	..	72	243
United Kingdom	England		921	E92000001	78.4	82.4	11.7	14.8	71	244
United Kingdom	Wales		924	W92000004	77.5	81.7	15.4	19.1	63	214
United Kingdom	Scotland		923	S92000003	75.8	80.3	13.4	15.6	60	..
United Kingdom	Northern Ireland		922	N92000002	77.0	81.4	14.5	15.7	57	131
United Kingdom	England	North East	A	E12000001	77.2	81.2	14.5	22.5	59	261
United Kingdom	England	North West	B	E12000002	77.0	81.1	13.5	16.7	71	254
United Kingdom	England	Yorkshire and The Humber	D	E12000003	77.7	81.8	13.5	17.1	75	283
United Kingdom	England	East Midlands	E	E12000004	78.4	82.4	13.0	13.0	67	236
United Kingdom	England	West Midlands	F	E12000005	77.9	82.2	13.0	16.5	66	250
United Kingdom	England	East	G	E12000006	79.6	83.2	10.7	11.8	60	214
United Kingdom	England	London	H	E12000007	79.0	83.3	9.6	17.2	105	266
United Kingdom	England	South East	J	E12000008	79.7	83.5	9.9	11.6	63	232
United Kingdom	England	South West	K	E12000009	79.5	83.5	10.9	10.3	61	208

.. not available

1 Estimates for English regions use abridged life tables and are published in Reference Table: Life expectancy at birth and at age 65 by local areas in the United Kingdom, 2004-06 to 2008-10.

Estimates for UK and constituent countries use interim life tables and are published in Reference Table: Period Expectation of Life at Birth and Selected Ages, UK and Constituent Countries, 1980-82 to 2008-10.

2 Guide to Life Expectancies.

3 People aged 16 to 64. Definitions of disability.

4 Source: Annual Population Survey April 2011 to March 2012.

5 Children under 16. Source: Labour Force Survey. Definition of a workless household.

6 Recorded crime statistics broadly cover the more serious offences.

7 Crimes recorded by the British Transport police are not included.

8 Figures for Scotland are not comparable with those for England and Wales because of the differences in the legal systems, recording practices and classifications.

9 The Northern Ireland figure includes 'offences against the state' and 'other notifiable offences'.

10 See estimates from the Crime Survey for England and Wales for further information.

See estimates from the Northern Ireland Crime Survey for further information.

11 Estimates from the Scottish Crime and Justice Survey for 2011/12 are not available. The estimate for 2010/11 was 225.

Source: Office for National Statistics; Home Office; National Records of Scotland; Scottish Government; Northern Ireland Statistics and Research Agency; Department of Justice, Northern Ireland

3 Key statistics – labour market and skills

UK/GB/E&W	Country	Region	Old area code	New area code	Employment rate[1] Q1 2013 (%)	Unemployment rate[2] Q1 2013 (%)	Economic inactivity rate[1] Q1 2013 (%)	Median gross weekly earnings[3] April 2012 (£)	Working-age[4] population with no qualifications 2012 (%)
United Kingdom			926	K02000001	71.4	7.8	22.4	505.90	9.9
Great Britain			925	K03000001	..	..	..	508.00	9.7
England and Wales			941	K04000001	..	..	..	508.90	9.6
United Kingdom	England		921	E92000001	71.6	7.8	22.1	512.70	9.5
United Kingdom	Wales		924	W92000004	69.5	8.2	24.2	455.00	11.4
United Kingdom	Scotland		923	S92000003	71.8	7.3	22.4	498.30	10.7
United Kingdom	Northern Ireland		922	N92000002	66.6	8.1	27.4	460.00	18.4
United Kingdom	England	North East	A	E12000001	66.6	9.8	26.0	455.30	11.8
United Kingdom	England	North West	B	E12000002	69.3	8.0	24.5	472.50	11.1
United Kingdom	England	Yorkshire and The Humber	D	E12000003	70.6	9.0	22.2	465.20	11.5
United Kingdom	England	East Midlands	E	E12000004	70.8	7.8	23.1	476.90	9.3
United Kingdom	England	West Midlands	F	E12000005	69.9	9.2	22.8	469.30	13.6
United Kingdom	England	East	G	E12000006	74.7	6.8	19.8	531.00	8.5
United Kingdom	England	London	H	E12000007	70.4	8.5	22.9	613.30	8.4
United Kingdom	England	South East	J	E12000008	74.6	6.6	19.9	555.80	6.9
United Kingdom	England	South West	K	E12000009	74.6	6.1	20.3	476.50	7.0

.. not available

1 Seasonally adjusted data for people aged 16-64 from Regional Labour Market Statistics - June 2013.

2 Unemployed as a percentage of all economically active people aged 16 and over. Seasonally adjusted data as published in Regional Labour Market Statistics - June 2013.

3 Residence based data relating to full-time employees on adult rates whose pay for the survey period was not affected by absence. Northern Ireland data period is 2012.
The 2012 Annual Survey of Hours and Earnings contains further information and tables.

4 People aged 16-64 from the Annual Population Survey, January-December.

Source: Labour Force Survey, Annual Population Survey and Annual Survey of Hours and Earnings, Office for National Statistics; Department of Finance and Personnel, Northern Ireland; Northern Ireland Statistics and Research Agency

Additional Information

Interpreting Labour Market Statistics
Glossary of Labour Market terms
Labour Force Survey
Labour Market Methodology
Monthly data are available from Regional Labour Market Statistics.
Annual Survey of Hours and Earnings
Annual Population Survey

4 Key statistics – education

UK/GB/E&W	Country	Region	Old area code	New area code	Pupils[1,2] achieving 5 or more grades A*-C including English and Mathematics GCSE or equivalent qualifications 2011/12 (%)	Programme for International Student Assessment reading score[3] 2009	Programme for International Student Assessment maths score[3] 2009	Programme for International Student Assessment science score[3] 2009
United Kingdom			926	K02000001	..	494	492	514
Great Britain			925	K03000001	..	..	..	..
England and Wales			941	K04000001	..	..	..	..
United Kingdom	England[4]		921	E92000001	59.4	495	493	515
United Kingdom	Wales		924	W92000004	..	476	472	496
United Kingdom	Scotland		923	S92000003	..	500	499	514
United Kingdom	Northern Ireland		922	N92000002	..	499	492	511
United Kingdom	England	North East	A	E12000001	58.5	..	..	..
United Kingdom	England	North West	B	E12000002	58.9	..	..	..
United Kingdom	England	Yorkshire and The Humber	D	E12000003	57.3	..	..	..
United Kingdom	England	East Midlands	E	E12000004	57.6	..	..	..
United Kingdom	England	West Midlands	F	E12000005	58.8	..	..	..
United Kingdom	England	East	G	E12000006	58.2	..	..	..
United Kingdom	England	London	H	E12000007	62.3	..	..	..
United Kingdom	England	South East	J	E12000008	60.2	..	..	..
United Kingdom	England	South West	K	E12000009	57.5	..	..	..

.. not available

1 Revised (but not final) data published on 24 January 2013, for Local Authority Maintained schools only. Other England figures are available on the gov.uk website.

2 Pupils at the end of Key Stage 4 in the 2011/12 academic year. Due to lack of comparability of educational attainment data between countries only data for England are shown.

3 See Additional Information.

4 GCSE data for England include all pupils from state-funded schools, independent schools, independent special schools, non-maintained special schools, hospital schools and alternative provision including pupil referral units.

Source: Department for Education; Organisation for Economic Co-operation and Development

Additional Information

GCSE and equivalent attainment

Scottish school educational attainment statistics are available on the Scottish Government website.

Wales and Northern Ireland use GCSEs but the way the statistics are compiled varies from that in England.

Statistics for Wales are available on the Welsh Government website.

Statistics for Northern Ireland are available on the Department of Education for Northern Ireland website.

PISA

The OECD Programme for International Student Assessment (PISA) seeks to measure the extent to which students near the end of compulsory education have acquired some of the knowledge and skills that are essential for full participation in modern societies.

Its triennial surveys of key competencies of 15-year-old students are conducted in 65 OECD member and partner countries. In 2009 each participating student spent two hours carrying out pencil-and-paper tasks in reading, mathematics and science. Every PISA survey tests reading, mathematical and scientific literacy in terms of general competencies, that is, how well students can apply the knowledge and skills they have learned at school to real-life challenges. PISA does not test how well a student has mastered a school's specific curriculum.

In each test subject, the score for each participating country is the average of all student scores in that country. The average score among OECD countries is 500 points and the standard deviation is 100 points. About two-thirds of students across OECD countries score between 400 and 600 points.

Schools in each country are randomly selected by the international contractor for participation in PISA. At these schools, the test is given to students who are between age 15 years 3 months and age 16 years 2 months at the time of the test, rather than to students in a specific year of school. This average age of 15 was chosen because at this age young people in most OECD countries are nearing the end of compulsory education. PISA covers all students who have completed at least 6 years of formal schooling, regardless of the type of institution in which they are enrolled, whether they are in full-time or part-time education, whether they attend academic or vocational programmes, and whether they attend state-funded or private schools or foreign schools within the country.

The specific sample design and size for each country aimed to maximise sampling efficiency for student-level estimates. In OECD countries, sample sizes ranged from 4,410 students in Iceland to 38,250 students in Mexico. Countries with large samples have often implemented PISA both at national and regional/state levels. In the UK, results are available for each of the four countries of the UK.

5 Key statistics – economy

UK/GB/E&W	Country	Region	Old area code	New area code	Gross value added[1] as a percentage of UK, 2011[2] (%)	Labour productivity, GVA per hour worked[3] 2011 (UK = 100)	Gross disposable household income[4] per head, 2011[2] (£)	Business birth rate[5] 2011 (%)	Business death rate[5] 2011[2] (%)
United Kingdom			926	K02000001	100.0	100.0	16,034	11.2	9.8
Great Britain			925	K03000001	97.7	100.5	..	11.3	9.8
England and Wales			941	K04000001	89.5	..	..	11.3	9.9
United Kingdom	England		921	E92000001	85.8	101.3	16,251	11.4	9.9
United Kingdom	Wales		924	W92000004	3.6	84.6	14,129	9.3	9.5
United Kingdom	Scotland		923	S92000003	8.2	100.0	15,654	10.9	9.1
United Kingdom	Northern Ireland		922	N92000002	2.3	84.0	13,966	6.5	8.6
United Kingdom	England	North East	A	E12000001	3.2	89.6	13,560	11.2	9.9
United Kingdom	England	North West	B	E12000002	9.4	89.7	14,476	11.1	10.7
United Kingdom	England	Yorkshire and The Humber	D	E12000003	6.9	87.9	13,819	10.5	10.0
United Kingdom	England	East Midlands	E	E12000004	6.1	89.2	14,561	10.3	9.8
United Kingdom	England	West Midlands	F	E12000005	7.3	88.8	14,362	10.5	10.0
United Kingdom	England	East	G	E12000006	8.7	97.4	16,608	10.5	9.6
United Kingdom	England	London	H	E12000007	21.9	129.4	20,509	14.6	10.4
United Kingdom	England	South East	J	E12000008	14.7	107.3	18,087	10.8	9.5
United Kingdom	England	South West	K	E12000009	7.7	93.2	16,014	9.6	9.2

.. Not available

1 Estimates of workplace based GVA allocate incomes to the region in which the economic activity takes place. The data are consistent with the workplace based raw (unsmoothed) series published in December 2012, and may differ from those included in previous versions of this table, which were headline estimates. UK figure is less Extra-Regio.
More GVA data are available in Regional Gross Value Added (Income Approach), December 2012.

2 Provisional.

3 See Labour Productivity, Q4 2012.

4 Household income covers the income received by households and non-profit institutions serving households. All household income has been allocated to regions, unlike the figures published previously. See Regional Gross Disposable Household Income (GDHI) 2011 statistical bulletin.

5 Birth and Death rates are expressed as a percentage of Active enterprises.

Source: Office for National Statistics

Additional Information

Extra-Regio comprises compensation of employees and gross operating surplus which cannot be assigned to regions. For the UK this consists mainly of offshore oil and gas extraction and the activities of UK embassies and forces overseas.

Regional Accounts Guidance and Methodology.

Regional Productivity Handbook.

Definitions of Active enterprises, Births and Deaths and information on estimation methods are available in the Business Demography 2011 release.

6 Key statistics – housing, transport and environment

UK/GB/E&W	Country	Region	Old area code	New area code	House building: permanent dwellings completed by private enterprise[1] 2011/12 (Thousands)	Annual change in mix adjusted house prices[2] December 2012 (%)	Traffic[3] increase on major roads[4] between 2002 and 2012 (%)	Reduction in total net greenhouse gas emissions[5] between the base year[6] and 2010 (%)	CO_2 emissions per resident[7] 2010 (Tonnes)
United Kingdom			926	K02000001	109.6	3.3	..	..	7.6
Great Britain			925	K03000001	..	..	2.5	..	7.6
England and Wales			941	K04000001	..	..	2.2	..	7.6
United Kingdom	England		921	E92000001	89.1	3.4	2.0	26.0	7.4
United Kingdom	Wales		924	W92000004	4.7	2.4	5.1	15.0	10.7
United Kingdom	Scotland		923	S92000003	10.0	3.1	5.8	23.7	7.5
United Kingdom	Northern Ireland		922	N92000002	5.7	-5.7	..	14.7	9.4
United Kingdom	England	North East	A	E12000001	3.9	-0.6	5.5	..	9.4
United Kingdom	England	North West	B	E12000002	8.2	1.1	3.0	..	7.8
United Kingdom	England	Yorkshire and The Humber	D	E12000003	8.4	2.1	2.5	..	8.7
United Kingdom	England	East Midlands	E	E12000004	8.6	1.3	4.6	..	8.1
United Kingdom	England	West Midlands	F	E12000005	6.7	2.7	4.7	..	7.4
United Kingdom	England	East	G	E12000006	12.1	3.2	4.3	..	7.2
United Kingdom	England	London	H	E12000007	11.3	6.4	-8.6	..	5.7
United Kingdom	England	South East	J	E12000008	17.3	3.7	-0.6	..	7.1
United Kingdom	England	South West	K	E12000009	12.3	1.4	3.8	..	7.0

.. not available

1 Includes private landlords (persons or companies) and owner-occupiers. Data and further information can be found on the gov.uk website.

2 Mix adjusted house prices, taken from House Price Index - December 2012, allow for differences between houses sold (for example type, number of rooms, location) in different months within a year. The annual rate of change shown is the percentage change between January 2012 and December 2012. Not seasonally adjusted.

3 The volume of traffic is expressed as vehicle kilometres, which is calculated by multiplying the Annual Average Daily Flow by the corresponding length of road. For further information please see the gov.uk website.

4 Motorways and A roads.

5 Information on the method of calculation can be found on the Greenhouse Gas Inventories for England, Scotland, Wales and Northern Ireland: 1990 - 2010 publication. Additional information for Scottish Greenhouse gases can be found on the Scottish Government website.

6 1995 is used as the Base Year (BY) for emissions of HFCs, PFCs and SF6 in the UK's Climate Change Programme, in accordance with Article 3.8 of the Kyoto Protocol. 1990 is used for other gases. The previous version of this table wrongly gave 1990 in the column heading instead of the base year.

7 The latest data and further information can be found on the gov.uk website.

Source: Department for Communities and Local Government; Welsh Government; Scottish Government; Department for Social Development, Northern Ireland; Office for National Statistics; Department for Transport; Department for Environment, Food, and Rural Affairs; Department of the Environment, Northern Ireland; Department of Energy and Climate Change

Region and Country Profiles - Key Statistics

	Release Date 17 October 2013	Type[1]	Last updated	Latest year
1	Key statistics – population	NS	Oct-13	2012
2	Key statistics – social indicators	NS	Oct-13	2013
3	Key statistics – labour market and skills	NS	Oct-13	2013
4	Key statistics – education	Mixed	Mar-13	2011/12
5	Key statistics – economy	NS	Jun-13	2011
6	Key statistics – housing, transport and environment	Mixed	Oct-13	2013

1 National Statistics (NS), Non National Statistics (Non NS), or Mixed.

Find the latest data published as part of Region and Country Profiles for other topics:

Economy

Environment

Population and Migration

Social Indicators

You may use or re-use this information (not including logos) free of charge in any format or medium, under the terms of the Open Government Licence

or write to the Information Policy Team, The National Archives, Kew, London TW9 4DU, or email:

psi@nationalarchives.gsi.gov.uk

Details of the policy governing the release of new data are available by visiting the Code of Practice.

or from the Media Relations Office email: media.relations@ons.gsi.gov.uk

This document is also available on our website.

1 Key statistics – population

UK/GB/E&W	Country	Region	Old area code	New area code	Population mid-2012[1] (Thousands)	Total population growth 2011 to 2012[1] (%)	Median age mid-2012[1] (Years)	Population aged under 16 mid-2012[1] (%)	Population aged 65 and over mid-2012[1] (%)	Area (Sq km)	Population density mid-2012[1] (People per sq km)
United Kingdom			926	K02000001	63,705.0	0.7	39.7	18.8	17.0	242,509	263
Great Britain			925	K03000001	61,881.4	0.7	..	18.7	17.1	228,947	270
England and Wales			941	K04000001	56,567.8	0.7	..	18.9	17.0	151,014	375
United Kingdom	England		921	E92000001	53,493.7	0.7	39.5	18.9	16.9	130,279	411
United Kingdom	Wales		924	W92000004	3,074.1	0.3	41.7	18.1	19.1	20,735	148
United Kingdom	Scotland		923	S92000003	5,313.6	0.3	41.5	17.2	17.4	77,933	68
United Kingdom	Northern Ireland		922	N92000002	1,823.6	0.5	37.6	21.0	15.0	13,562	134
United Kingdom	England	North East	A	E12000001	2,602.3	0.2	41.5	17.8	18.0	8,573	304
United Kingdom	England	North West	B	E12000002	7,084.3	0.4	40.2	18.8	17.2	14,105	502
United Kingdom	England	Yorkshire and The Humber	D	E12000003	5,316.7	0.5	39.8	18.9	17.2	15,408	345
United Kingdom	England	East Midlands	E	E12000004	4,567.7	0.7	41.0	18.5	17.8	15,606	293
United Kingdom	England	West Midlands	F	E12000005	5,642.6	0.6	39.7	19.5	17.4	12,998	434
United Kingdom	England	East	G	E12000006	5,907.3	0.8	41.0	19.0	18.2	19,109	309
United Kingdom	England	London	H	E12000007	8,308.4	1.3	34.0	20.1	11.3	1,572	5,285
United Kingdom	England	South East	J	E12000008	8,724.7	0.8	40.8	19.1	17.9	19,070	458
United Kingdom	England	South West	K	E12000009	5,339.6	0.7	42.9	17.6	20.3	23,837	224

.. not available

1 The estimated mid-year resident population as published in Population Estimates for UK, England and Wales, Scotland and Northern Ireland, Mid-2011 to Mid-2012.
For definitions see Additional Information in Region and Country Profiles, Population and Migration - March 2013, Table: Resident Population by sex.

Source: Office for National Statistics; National Records of Scotland; Northern Ireland Statistics and Research Agency

2 Key statistics – social indicators

UK/GB/E&W	Country	Region	Old area code	New area code	Male life expectancy at birth[1], 2009 to 2011[2] (Years)	Female life expectancy at birth[1], 2009 to 2011[2] (Years)	People who are DDA disabled and also work-limiting disabled[3] 2012/2013 (%)	Children living in workless households[4] Q2 2013 (%)	Recorded crime[5,6,7,8] 2012/13 (Recorded offences per 1,000 population)	Crimes committed against households[9,10] 2012/13 (Rates per 1,000 households)
United Kingdom			926	K02000001	78.1	82.1	12.2	13.6	..	..
Great Britain			925	K03000001	..	..	12.1	13.5	..	..
England and Wales			941	K04000001	78.3	82.3	11.9	..	66	..
United Kingdom	England		921	E92000001	78.4	82.4	11.8	13.6	64	217
United Kingdom	Wales		924	W92000004	77.5	81.7	14.3	14.4	57	208
United Kingdom	Scotland		923	S92000003	75.8	80.3	14.0	12.0	52	..
United Kingdom	Northern Ireland		922	N92000002	77.0	81.4	13.7	16.7	55	..
United Kingdom	England	North East	A	E12000001	77.5	81.5	14.4	18.7	53	187
United Kingdom	England	North West	B	E12000002	77.4	81.5	13.4	17.8	63	222
United Kingdom	England	Yorkshire and The Humber	D	E12000003	78.1	82.0	12.9	14.1	68	216
United Kingdom	England	East Midlands	E	E12000004	78.7	82.8	13.2	13.6	58	231
United Kingdom	England	West Midlands	F	E12000005	78.4	82.6	13.0	15.6	62	220
United Kingdom	England	East	G	E12000006	79.9	83.6	10.7	11.1	53	201
United Kingdom	England	London	H	E12000007	79.3	83.6	10.0	13.8	95	245
United Kingdom	England	South East	J	E12000008	80.0	83.8	10.1	9.7	56	227
United Kingdom	England	South West	K	E12000009	79.8	83.7	11.6	11.6	54	176

.. not available

1 Estimates for the English regions use abridged life tables (see Additional Information) and are published in Reference Table: Life expectancy at birth and at age 65 by local areas in the England and Wales, 2009-11. Comparable figures for England for 2009 to 2011 are Male 78.9 years and Female 82.9 years.

2 Estimates for UK and constituent countries use interim life tables (see Additional Information) and are for 2008 to 2010. Reference Table: Period Expectation of Life at Birth and Selected Ages, UK and Constituent Countries, 1980-82 to 2008-10.

Provisional estimates for 2009-2011 for Scotland, rolled forward from the 2011 Census, are available at Life Expectancy at Scotland level.

Final estimates for the UK and all constituent countries for 2009 to 2011 will be published in winter 2013.

3 People aged 16 to 64 from the Annual Population Survey April 2012 to March 2013.

4 Children under 16. Published in Working and workless households, 2013.

Definition of a workless household

5 Recorded crime statistics broadly cover the more serious offences.

6 Crimes recorded by the British Transport police are not included.

7 Figures for Scotland are not comparable with those for England and Wales because of the differences in the legal systems, recording practices and classifications.

8 The Northern Ireland figure includes 'offences against the state' and 'other notifiable offences'.

9 See the Crime Survey for England and Wales for further information.

10 Estimates from the Scottish Crime and Justice Survey for 2011/12 are not available and for 2012/13 they have not yet been published. The estimate for 2010/11 was 225. Estimates from the Northern Ireland Crime Survey for 2012/13 have not yet been published. The Northern Ireland figure for 2011/12 is 131.

Source: Office for National Statistics; Home Office; National Records of Scotland; Scottish Government; Northern Ireland Statistics and Research Agency; Department of Justice, Northern Ireland

Additional Information
Guide to Life Expectancies.

3 Key statistics – labour market and skills

UK/GB/E&W	Country	Region	Old area code	New area code	Employment rate[1] Q2 2013 (%)	Unemployment rate[2] Q2 2013 (%)	Economic inactivity rate[1] Q2 2013 (%)	Median gross weekly earnings[3] April 2012 (£)	Working-age[4] population with no qualifications 2012 (%)
United Kingdom			926	K02000001	71.5	7.8	22.3	505.90	9.9
Great Britain			925	K03000001	..	..	..	508.00	9.7
England and Wales			941	K04000001	..	..	..	508.90	9.6
United Kingdom	England		921	E92000001	71.7	7.8	22.1	512.70	9.5
United Kingdom	Wales		924	W92000004	69.4	8.2	24.3	455.00	11.4
United Kingdom	Scotland		923	S92000003	72.1	7.2	22.1	498.30	10.7
United Kingdom	Northern Ireland		922	N92000002	66.3	7.5	28.2	460.00	18.4
United Kingdom	England	North East	A	E12000001	66.5	10.3	25.7	455.30	11.8
United Kingdom	England	North West	B	E12000002	69.1	8.2	24.5	472.50	11.1
United Kingdom	England	Yorkshire and The Humber	D	E12000003	70.2	8.9	22.8	465.20	11.5
United Kingdom	England	East Midlands	E	E12000004	71.2	7.9	22.6	476.90	9.3
United Kingdom	England	West Midlands	F	E12000005	69.2	9.9	23.0	469.30	13.6
United Kingdom	England	East	G	E12000006	75.5	6.5	19.1	531.00	8.5
United Kingdom	England	London	H	E12000007	70.0	8.8	23.2	613.30	8.4
United Kingdom	England	South East	J	E12000008	75.8	6.0	19.3	555.80	6.9
United Kingdom	England	South West	K	E12000009	74.3	6.0	20.9	476.50	7.0

.. not available

1 Seasonally adjusted data for people aged 16-64 from Regional Labour Market Statistics - August 2013.

2 Unemployed as a percentage of all economically active people aged 16 and over. Seasonally adjusted data as published in Regional Labour Market Statistics - August 2013.

3 Residence based data relating to full-time employees on adult rates whose pay for the survey period was not affected by absence. Northern Ireland data period is 2012. The 2012 Annual Survey of Hours and Earnings contains further information and tables.

4 People aged 16-64 from the Annual Population Survey, January-December.

Source: Labour Force Survey, Annual Population Survey and Annual Survey of Hours and Earnings, Office for National Statistics; Department of Finance and Personnel, Northern Ireland; Northern Ireland Statistics and Research Agency

Additional Information

Interpreting Labour Market Statistics
Glossary of Labour Market terms
Labour Force Survey
Labour Market Methodology
Monthly data are available from Regional Labour Market Statistics.
Annual Survey of Hours and Earnings
Annual Population Survey

4 Key statistics – education

UK/GB/E&W	Country	Region	Old area code	New area code	Pupils[1,2] achieving 5 or more grades A*-C including English and Mathematics GCSE or equivalent qualifications 2011/12 (%)	Programme for International Student Assessment reading score[3] 2009	Programme for International Student Assessment maths score[3] 2009	Programme for International Student Assessment science score[3] 2009
United Kingdom			926	K02000001	..	494	492	514
Great Britain			925	K03000001	..	..	..	..
England and Wales			941	K04000001	..	..	..	..
United Kingdom	England[4]		921	E92000001	59.4	495	493	515
United Kingdom	Wales		924	W92000004	..	476	472	496
United Kingdom	Scotland		923	S92000003	..	500	499	514
United Kingdom	Northern Ireland		922	N92000002	..	499	492	511
United Kingdom	England	North East	A	E12000001	58.5	..	..	..
United Kingdom	England	North West	B	E12000002	58.9	..	..	..
United Kingdom	England	Yorkshire and The Humber	D	E12000003	57.3	..	..	..
United Kingdom	England	East Midlands	E	E12000004	57.6	..	..	..
United Kingdom	England	West Midlands	F	E12000005	58.8	..	..	..
United Kingdom	England	East	G	E12000006	58.2	..	..	..
United Kingdom	England	London	H	E12000007	62.3	..	..	..
United Kingdom	England	South East	J	E12000008	60.2	..	..	..
United Kingdom	England	South West	K	E12000009	57.5	..	..	..

.. not available

1 Revised (but not final) data published on 24 January 2013, for Local Authority Maintained schools only. Other England figures are available on the gov.uk website.

2 Pupils at the end of Key Stage 4 in the 2011/12 academic year. Due to lack of comparability of educational attainment data between countries only data for England are shown.

3 See Additional Information.

4 GCSE data for England include all pupils from state-funded schools, independent schools, independent special schools, non-maintained special schools, hospital schools and alternative provision including pupil referral units.

Source: Department for Education; Organisation for Economic Co-operation and Development

Additional Information

GCSE and equivalent attainment

Scottish school educational attainment statistics are available on the Scottish Government website.

Wales and Northern Ireland use GCSEs but the way the statistics are compiled varies from that in England.

Statistics for Wales are available on the Welsh Government website.

Statistics for Northern Ireland are available on the Department of Education for Northern Ireland website.

PISA

The OECD Programme for International Student Assessment (PISA) seeks to measure the extent to which students near the end of compulsory education have acquired some of the knowledge and skills that are essential for full participation in modern societies.

Its triennial surveys of key competencies of 15-year-old students are conducted in 65 OECD member and partner countries. In 2009 each participating student spent two hours carrying out pencil-and-paper tasks in reading, mathematics and science. Every PISA survey tests reading, mathematical and scientific literacy in terms of general competencies, that is, how well students can apply the knowledge and skills they have learned at school to real-life challenges. PISA does not test how well a student has mastered a school's specific curriculum.

In each test subject, the score for each participating country is the average of all student scores in that country. The average score among OECD countries is 500 points and the standard deviation is 100 points. About two-thirds of students across OECD countries score between 400 and 600 points.

Schools in each country are randomly selected by the international contractor for participation in PISA. At these schools, the test is given to students who are between age 15 years 3 months and age 16 years 2 months at the time of the test, rather than to students in a specific year of school. This average age of 15 was chosen because at this age young people in most OECD countries are nearing the end of compulsory education. PISA covers all students who have completed at least 6 years of formal schooling, regardless of the type of institution in which they are enrolled, whether they are in full-time or part-time education, whether they attend academic or vocational programmes, and whether they attend state-funded or private schools or foreign schools within the country.

The specific sample design and size for each country aimed to maximise sampling efficiency for student-level estimates. In OECD countries, sample sizes ranged from 4,410 students in Iceland to 38,250 students in Mexico. Countries with large samples have often implemented PISA both at national and regional/state levels. In the UK, results are available for each of the four countries of the UK.

For 2009 the differences between England, Scotland and Northern Ireland were not statistically significant.

UK/GB/E&W	Country	Region	Old area code	New area code	Gross value added[1] as a percentage of UK, 2011[2] (%)	Labour productivity, GVA per hour worked[3] 2011 (UK = 100)	Gross disposable household income[4] per head, 2011[2] (£)	Business birth rate[5] 2011 (%)	Business death rate[5] 2011[2] (%)
United Kingdom			926	K02000001	100.0	100.0	16,034	11.2	9.8
Great Britain			925	K03000001	97.7	100.5	..	11.3	9.8
England and Wales			941	K04000001	89.5	..	..	11.3	9.9
United Kingdom	England		921	E92000001	85.8	101.3	16,251	11.4	9.9
United Kingdom	Wales		924	W92000004	3.6	84.6	14,129	9.3	9.5
United Kingdom	Scotland		923	S92000003	8.2	100.0	15,654	10.9	9.1
United Kingdom	Northern Ireland		922	N92000002	2.3	84.0	13,966	6.5	8.6
United Kingdom	England	North East	A	E12000001	3.2	89.6	13,560	11.2	9.9
United Kingdom	England	North West	B	E12000002	9.4	89.7	14,476	11.1	10.7
United Kingdom	England	Yorkshire and The Humber	D	E12000003	6.9	87.9	13,819	10.5	10.0
United Kingdom	England	East Midlands	E	E12000004	6.1	89.2	14,561	10.3	9.8
United Kingdom	England	West Midlands	F	E12000005	7.3	88.8	14,362	10.5	10.0
United Kingdom	England	East	G	E12000006	8.7	97.4	16,608	10.5	9.6
United Kingdom	England	London	H	E12000007	21.9	129.4	20,509	14.6	10.4
United Kingdom	England	South East	J	E12000008	14.7	107.3	18,087	10.8	9.5
United Kingdom	England	South West	K	E12000009	7.7	93.2	16,014	9.6	9.2

.. not available

1 Estimates of workplace based GVA allocate incomes to the region in which the economic activity takes place. The data are consistent with the workplace based raw (unsmoothed) series published in December 2012, and may differ from those included in previous versions of this table, which were headline estimates. UK figure is less Extra-Regio.

More GVA data are available in Regional Gross Value Added (Income Approach), December 2012.

2 Provisional.

3 See Labour Productivity, Q4 2012.

4 Household income covers the income received by households and non-profit institutions serving households. All household income has been allocated to regions, unlike the figures published previously. See Regional Gross Disposable Household Income (GDHI) 2011 statistical bulletin.

5 Birth and Death rates are expressed as a percentage of Active enterprises.

Source: Office for National Statistics

Additional Information

Extra-Regio comprises compensation of employees and gross operating surplus which cannot be assigned to regions. For the UK this consists mainly of offshore oil and gas extraction and the activities of UK embassies and forces overseas.

Regional Accounts Guidance and Methodology.

Regional Productivity Handbook.

Definitions of Active enterprises, Births and Deaths and information on estimation methods are available in the Business Demography 2011 release.

6 Key statistics – housing, transport and environment

UK/GB/E&W	Country	Region	Old area code	New area code	House building: permanent dwellings completed by private enterprise[1] 2011/12 (Thousands)	Mix adjusted house prices[2,3] June 2013 (£)	Annual change in mix adjusted house prices[3,4] June 2013 (%)	Traffic[5] increase on major roads[6] between 2002 and 2012 (%)	Reduction in total greenhouse gas emissions[7] between the base year[8] and 2011 (%)	CO$_2$ emissions per resident[9] 2011 (Tonnes)
United Kingdom			926	K02000001	109.0	242,000	3.1	..	..	6.9
Great Britain			925	K03000001	..	243,000	..	2.5	..	..
England and Wales			941	K04000001	..	247,000	..	2.2	..	..
United Kingdom	England		921	E92000001	88.5	251,000	3.3	2.0	-30.9	6.7
United Kingdom	Wales		924	W92000004	4.8	162,000	4.3	5.1	-20.6	9.5
United Kingdom	Scotland		923	S92000003	10.1	181,000	-0.9	5.8	-30.8	6.8
United Kingdom	Northern Ireland		922	N92000002	5.7	130,000	-0.4	..	-17.5	8.4
United Kingdom	England	North East	A	E12000001	3.9	145,000	0.4	5.5	..	8.9
United Kingdom	England	North West	B	E12000002	8.2	161,000	0.1	3.0	..	7.0
United Kingdom	England	Yorkshire and The Humber	D	E12000003	8.4	164,000	-0.2	2.5	..	8.2
United Kingdom	England	East Midlands	E	E12000004	8.6	172,000	0.9	4.6	..	7.4
United Kingdom	England	West Midlands	F	E12000005	6.7	184,000	3.1	4.7	..	6.7
United Kingdom	England	East	G	E12000006	12.1	256,000	2.2	4.3	..	6.6
United Kingdom	England	London	H	E12000007	11.3	425,000	8.1	-8.6	..	4.9
United Kingdom	England	South East	J	E12000008	17.3	299,000	2.9	-0.6	..	6.3
United Kingdom	England	South West	K	E12000009	12.3	229,000	0.0	3.8	..	6.5

.. not available

1 Includes private landlords (persons or companies) and owner-occupiers. Data and further information can be found on the Gov.uk website.

2 Data from September 2005 are collected via the Regulated Mortgage Survey. Prices are rounded to the nearest £1,000. Not seasonally adjusted.

3 Mix adjusted house prices, taken from House Price Index - June 2013, allow for differences between houses sold (for example type, number of rooms, location) in different months within a year.

4 The annual rate of change shown is the percentage change between July 2012 and June 2013. Not seasonally adjusted.

5 The volume of traffic is expressed as vehicle kilometres, which is calculated by multiplying the Annual Average Daily Flow by the corresponding length of road. For further information please see the Gov.uk website.

6 Motorways and A roads.

7 Information on the method of calculation can be found on the Gov.uk website. The figures exclude estimated emissions from international aviation and shipping. Additional information for Scottish Greenhouse gases, including the adjustments necessary to report performance against the Climate Change (Scotland) Act 2009, can be found on The Scottish Government website.

8 1995 is used as the Base Year (BY) for emissions of HFCs, PFCs and SF6 in the UK's Climate Change Programme, in accordance with Article 3.8 of the Kyoto Protocol. 1990 is used for other gases. A previous version of this table wrongly gave 1990 in the column heading instead of the base year.

9 The latest data and further information can be found on the Gov.uk website.

Source: Department for Communities and Local Government; Welsh Government; Scottish Government; Department for Social Development, Northern Ireland; Office for National Statistics; Department for Transport; Department for Environment, Food, and Rural Affairs; Department of the Environment, Northern Ireland; Department of Energy and Climate Change

Region and Country Profiles - Key Statistics

Release Date 19 December 2013	Type[1]	Last updated	Latest year
1	Key statistics – population	NS	Dec-13	2012
2	Key statistics – social indicators	NS	Oct-13	2013
3	Key statistics – labour market and skills	NS	Dec-13	2013
4	Key statistics – education	Mixed	Dec-13	2011/12
5	Key statistics – economy	NS	Jun-13	2011
6	Key statistics – housing, transport and environment	Mixed	Dec-13	2013

1 National Statistics (NS), Non National Statistics (Non NS), or Mixed.

Find the latest data published as part of Region and Country Profiles for other topics:

Economy

Environment

Population and Migration

Social Indicators

You may use or re-use this information (not including logos) free of charge in any format or medium, under the terms of the Open Government Licence

or write to the Information Policy Team, The National Archives, Kew, London TW9 4DU, or email:

psi@nationalarchives.gsi.gov.uk

Details of the policy governing the release of new data are available by visiting the Code of Practice.

or from the Media Relations Office email: media.relations@ons.gsi.gov.uk

This document is also available on our website.

1 Key statistics – population

UK/GB/E&W	Country	Region	Old area code	New area code	Population mid-2012[1] (Thousands)	Total population growth 2011–2012[1] (%)	Median age mid-2012[1] (Years)	Population aged under 16 mid-2012[1] (%)	Population aged 65 and over mid-2012[1] (%)	Area (Sq km)	Population density mid-2012[1] (People per sq km)
United Kingdom			926	K02000001	63,705.0	0.7	39.7	18.8	17.0	..	..
Great Britain			925	K03000001	61,881.4	0.7	..	18.7	17.1	..	..
England and Wales			941	K04000001	56,567.8	0.7	..	18.9	17.0	151,012	375
United Kingdom	England		921	E92000001	53,493.7	0.7	39.5	18.9	16.9	130,279	411
United Kingdom	Wales		924	W92000004	3,074.1	0.3	41.7	18.1	19.1	20,733	148
United Kingdom	Scotland		923	S92000003	5,313.6	0.3	41.5	17.2	17.4	77,933	68
United Kingdom	Northern Ireland		922	N92000002	1,823.6	0.5	37.6	21.0	15.0	13,562	134
United Kingdom	England	North East	A	E12000001	2,602.3	0.2	41.5	17.8	18.0	8,573	304
United Kingdom	England	North West	B	E12000002	7,084.3	0.4	40.2	18.8	17.2	14,106	502
United Kingdom	England	Yorkshire and The Humber	D	E12000003	5,316.7	0.5	39.8	18.9	17.2	15,408	345
United Kingdom	England	East Midlands	E	E12000004	4,567.7	0.7	41.0	18.5	17.8	15,607	293
United Kingdom	England	West Midlands	F	E12000005	5,642.6	0.6	39.7	19.5	17.4	12,998	434
United Kingdom	England	East	G	E12000006	5,907.3	0.8	41.0	19.0	18.2	19,109	309
United Kingdom	England	London	H	E12000007	8,308.4	1.3	34.0	20.1	11.3	1,572	5,285
United Kingdom	England	South East	J	E12000008	8,724.7	0.8	40.8	19.1	17.9	19,069	458
United Kingdom	England	South West	K	E12000009	5,339.6	0.7	42.9	17.6	20.3	23,837	224

.. not available

1 The estimated mid-year resident populations are based on the 2011 Census. Estimates are as published on 8 August 2013.
For definitions see Additional Information in Region and Country Profiles, Population and Migration - March 2013, Table: Resident Population by sex.

Source: Office for National Statistics; National Records of Scotland; Northern Ireland Statistics and Research Agency

2 Key statistics – social indicators

UK/GB/E&W	Country	Region	Old area code	New area code	Male life expectancy at birth[1], 2009–11[2] (Years)	Female life expectancy at birth[1], 2009–11[2] (Years)	People who are DDA disabled and also work-limiting disabled[3] 2012/2013 (%)	Children living in workless households[4] Q2 2013 (%)	Recorded crime[5,6,7,8] 2012/13 (Recorded offences per 1,000 population)	Crimes committed against households[9,10] 2012/13 (Rates per 1,000 households)
United Kingdom			926	K02000001	78.1	82.1	12.2	13.6	..	..
Great Britain			925	K03000001	..	..	12.1	13.5	..	..
England and Wales			941	K04000001	78.3	82.3	11.9	..	66	..
United Kingdom	England		921	E92000001	78.4	82.4	11.8	13.6	64	217
United Kingdom	Wales		924	W92000004	77.5	81.7	14.3	14.4	57	208
United Kingdom	Scotland		923	S92000003	75.8	80.3	14.0	12.0	52	..
United Kingdom	Northern Ireland		922	N92000002	77.0	81.4	13.7	16.7	55	..
United Kingdom	England	North East	A	E12000001	77.5	81.5	14.4	18.7	53	187
United Kingdom	England	North West	B	E12000002	77.4	81.5	13.4	17.8	63	222
United Kingdom	England	Yorkshire and The Humber	D	E12000003	78.1	82.0	12.9	14.1	68	216
United Kingdom	England	East Midlands	E	E12000004	78.7	82.8	13.2	13.6	58	231
United Kingdom	England	West Midlands	F	E12000005	78.4	82.6	13.0	15.6	57	220
United Kingdom	England	East	G	E12000006	79.9	83.6	10.7	11.1	53	201
United Kingdom	England	London	H	E12000007	79.3	83.6	10.0	13.8	95	245
United Kingdom	England	South East	J	E12000008	80.0	83.8	10.1	9.7	56	227
United Kingdom	England	South West	K	E12000009	79.8	83.7	11.6	11.6	54	176

.. not available

1 Estimates for the English regions use abridged life tables (see Additional Information) and are published in Reference Table: Life expectancy at birth and at age 65 by local areas in the England and Wales, 2009-11. Comparable figures from the interim life tables for England for 2009–11 are Male 78.9 years and Female 82.9 years.

2 Estimates for UK and constituent countries use interim life tables (see Additional Information) and are for 2008–10 (the last available). Reference Table: Period Expectation of Life at Birth and Selected Ages, UK and Constituent Countries, 1980-82 to 2008-10.

Provisional estimates for 2009 to 2011 for Scotland, rolled forward from the 2011 Census, are available at Life Expectancy at Scotland level.

3 People aged 16 to 64 from the Annual Population Survey April 2012 to March 2013.

4 Children under 16. Published in Working and workless households, 2013.

Definition of a workless household

5 For more information on Recorded crime statistics.

6 Crimes recorded by the British Transport police are not included.

7 Figures for Scotland are not comparable with those for England and Wales because of the differences in the legal systems, recording practices and classifications.

8 The Northern Ireland figure includes 'offences against the state' and 'other notifiable offences'.

9 See the Crime Survey for England and Wales for further information.

10 Estimates from the Scottish Crime and Justice Survey for 2011/12 are not available and for 2012/13 they have not yet been published. The estimate for 2010/11 is 225. Estimates from the Northern Ireland Crime Survey for 2012/13 have not yet been published. The Northern Ireland figure for 2011/12 is 131.

Source: Office for National Statistics; Home Office; National Records of Scotland; Scottish Government; Northern Ireland Statistics and Research Agency; Department of Justice, Northern Ireland

Additional Information

Guide to Life Expectancies.

3 Key statistics – labour market and skills

UK/GB/E&W	Country	Region	Old area code	New area code	Employment rate[1] Q3 2013 (%)	Unemployment rate[2] Q3 2013 (%)	Economic inactivity rate[1] Q3 2013 (%)	Median gross weekly earnings[3] April 2012 (£)	Working-age[4] population with no qualifications 2012 (%)
United Kingdom			926	K02000001	71.8	7.6	22.2	505.90	9.9
Great Britain			925	K03000001	71.9	7.6	22.0	508.00	9.7
England and Wales			941	K04000001	..	..	..	508.90	9.6
United Kingdom	England		921	E92000001	71.9	7.6	22.0	512.70	9.5
United Kingdom	Wales		924	W92000004	70.2	7.8	23.7	455.00	11.4
United Kingdom	Scotland		923	S92000003	72.8	7.2	21.4	498.30	10.7
United Kingdom	Northern Ireland		922	N92000002	67.2	7.3	27.4	459.50	17.6
United Kingdom	England	North East	A	E12000001	67.3	10.2	24.9	455.30	11.8
United Kingdom	England	North West	B	E12000002	68.5	8.3	25.2	472.50	11.1
United Kingdom	England	Yorkshire and The Humber	D	E12000003	70.8	8.9	22.1	465.20	11.5
United Kingdom	England	East Midlands	E	E12000004	72.4	7.1	21.9	476.90	9.3
United Kingdom	England	West Midlands	F	E12000005	68.4	9.5	24.2	469.30	13.6
United Kingdom	England	East	G	E12000006	75.7	5.8	19.5	531.00	8.5
United Kingdom	England	London	H	E12000007	70.5	8.7	22.7	613.30	8.4
United Kingdom	England	South East	J	E12000008	76.2	5.9	18.9	555.80	6.9
United Kingdom	England	South West	K	E12000009	74.4	6.4	20.5	476.50	7.0

.. not available

1 Seasonally adjusted data for people aged 16 to 64 from Regional Labour Market Statistics - November 2013.

2 Unemployed as a percentage of all economically active people aged 16 and over. Seasonally adjusted data as published in Regional Labour Market Statistics - November 2013.

3 Residence based data relating to full-time employees on adult rates whose pay for the survey period was not affected by absence.
The 2012 Annual Survey of Hours and Earnings contains further information and tables.

4 People aged 16 to 64 from the Annual Population Survey

Source: Labour Force Survey, Annual Population Survey and Annual Survey of Hours and Earnings, Office for National Statistics; Department of Finance and Personnel, Northern Ireland; Northern Ireland Statistics and Research Agency

Additional Information

Interpreting Labour Market Statistics
Glossary of Labour Market terms
Labour Force Survey
Labour Market Methodology
Monthly data are available from Regional Labour Market Statistics.
Annual Survey of Hours and Earnings
Annual Population Survey

4 Key statistics – education

UK/GB/E&W	Country	Region	Old area code	New area code	Pupils[1,2] achieving 5 or more grades A*-C including English and Mathematics GCSE or equivalent qualifications 2011/12 (%)	Programme for International Student Assessment reading score[3] 2012	Programme for International Student Assessment maths score[3] 2012	Programme for International Student Assessment science score[3] 2012
United Kingdom			926	K02000001	..	499	494	514
Great Britain			925	K03000001	..	..	..	..
England and Wales			941	K04000001	..	..	..	..
United Kingdom	England[4]		921	E92000001	59.4	500	495	516
United Kingdom	Wales		924	W92000004	..	480	468	491
United Kingdom	Scotland		923	S92000003	..	506	498	513
United Kingdom	Northern Ireland		922	N92000002	..	498	487	507
United Kingdom	England	North East	A	E12000001	58.5	..	..	..
United Kingdom	England	North West	B	E12000002	58.9	..	..	..
United Kingdom	England	Yorkshire and The Humber	D	E12000003	57.3	..	..	..
United Kingdom	England	East Midlands	E	E12000004	57.6	..	..	..
United Kingdom	England	West Midlands	F	E12000005	58.8	..	..	..
United Kingdom	England	East	G	E12000006	58.2	..	..	..
United Kingdom	England	London	H	E12000007	62.3	..	..	..
United Kingdom	England	South East	J	E12000008	60.2	..	..	..
United Kingdom	England	South West	K	E12000009	57.5	..	..	..

.. not available

1 Revised (but not final) data published on 24 January 2013, for Local Authority Maintained schools only. More education statistics for England are available on the Department for Education website.

2 Pupils at the end of Key Stage 4 in the 2011/12 academic year. Due to lack of comparability of educational attainment data between countries, only data for England are shown.

3 See Additional Information.

4 GCSE data for England include all pupils from state-funded schools, independent schools, independent special schools, non-maintained special schools, hospital schools and alternative provision including pupil referral units.

Source: Department for Education; Organisation for Economic Co-operation and Development

Additional Information

GCSE and equivalent attainment

Scottish school educational attainment statistics are available on the Scottish Government website.

Wales and Northern Ireland use GCSEs but the way the statistics are compiled varies from that in England.

Statistics for Wales are available on the Welsh Government website.

Statistics for Northern Ireland are available on the Department of Education for Northern Ireland website.

PISA

The OECD Programme for International Student Assessment (PISA) seeks to measure the extent to which students near the end of compulsory education have acquired some of the knowledge and skills that are essential for full participation in modern societies.

Its triennial surveys of key competencies of 15-year-old students are conducted in 65 OECD member and partner countries. In 2012 each participating student spent two hours carrying out pencil-and-paper tasks in reading, mathematics and science. Every PISA survey tests reading, mathematical and scientific literacy in terms of general competencies, that is, how well students can apply the knowledge and skills they have learned at school to real-life challenges. PISA does not test how well a student has mastered a school's specific curriculum.

The mean score for each subject scale was set to 500 among OECD countries in the PISA cycle when the subject was the major domain for the first time. Thus, the reading scale was set to 500 in its first year in 2000. Similarly the mathematics scale was set to 500 in 2003 and the science scale was set to a mean of 500 in 2006. As with any repeated measurement that uses samples, the mean will vary slightly from year to year without necessarily indicating any real change in the global level of skills.

Schools in each country are randomly selected by the international contractor for participation in PISA. At these schools, the test is given to students who are between age 15 years 3 months and age 16 years 2 months at the time of the test, rather than to students in a specific year of school. This average age of 15 was chosen because at this age young people in most OECD countries are nearing the end of compulsory education. PISA covers all students who have completed at least 6 years of formal schooling, regardless of the type of institution in which they are enrolled, whether they are in full-time or part-time education, whether they attend academic or vocational programmes, and whether they attend state-funded or private schools or foreign schools within the country.

The specific sample design and size for each country aimed to maximise sampling efficiency for student-level estimates. In OECD countries, sample sizes ranged from 3,508 students in Iceland to 38,142 students in Mexico. Countries with large samples have often implemented PISA both at national and regional/state levels. In the UK, results are available for each of the four countries of the UK.

5 Key statistics – economy

UK/GB/E&W	Country	Region	Old area code	New area code	Gross value added[1] as a percentage of UK, 2011[2] (%)	Labour productivity, GVA per hour worked[3] 2011 (UK = 100)	Gross disposable household income[4] per head, 2011[2] (£)	Business birth rate[5] 2011 (%)	Business death rate[5] 2011[2] (%)
United Kingdom			926	K02000001	100.0	100.0	16,034	11.2	9.8
Great Britain			925	K03000001	97.7	100.5	..	11.3	9.8
England and Wales			941	K04000001	89.5	..	..	11.3	9.9
United Kingdom	England		921	E92000001	85.8	101.3	16,251	11.4	9.9
United Kingdom	Wales		924	W92000004	3.6	84.6	14,129	9.3	9.5
United Kingdom	Scotland		923	S92000003	8.2	100.0	15,654	10.9	9.1
United Kingdom	Northern Ireland		922	N92000002	2.3	84.0	13,966	6.5	8.6
United Kingdom	England	North East	A	E12000001	3.2	89.6	13,560	11.2	9.9
United Kingdom	England	North West	B	E12000002	9.4	89.7	14,476	11.1	10.7
United Kingdom	England	Yorkshire and The Humber	D	E12000003	6.9	87.9	13,819	10.5	10.0
United Kingdom	England	East Midlands	E	E12000004	6.1	89.2	14,561	10.3	9.8
United Kingdom	England	West Midlands	F	E12000005	7.3	88.8	14,362	10.5	10.0
United Kingdom	England	East	G	E12000006	8.7	97.4	16,608	10.5	9.6
United Kingdom	England	London	H	E12000007	21.9	129.4	20,509	14.6	10.4
United Kingdom	England	South East	J	E12000008	14.7	107.3	18,087	10.8	9.5
United Kingdom	England	South West	K	E12000009	7.7	93.2	16,014	9.6	9.2

.. Not available

1 Estimates of workplace based GVA allocate incomes to the region in which the economic activity takes place. The data are consistent with the workplace based raw (unsmoothed) series published in December 2012, and may differ from those included in previous versions of this table, which were headline estimates. UK figure is less Extra-Regio.
More GVA data are available in Regional Gross Value Added (Income Approach), December 2012.

2 Provisional.

3 See Labour Productivity, Q4 2012.

4 Household income covers the income received by households and non-profit institutions serving households. All household income has been allocated to regions, unlike the figures published previously. See Regional Gross Disposable Household Income (GDHI) 2011 statistical bulletin.

5 Birth and Death rates are expressed as a percentage of active enterprises.

Source: Office for National Statistics

Additional Information

Extra-Regio comprises compensation of employees and gross operating surplus which cannot be assigned to regions. For the UK this consists mainly of offshore oil and gas extraction and the activities of UK embassies and forces overseas.

Regional Accounts Guidance and Methodology.

Regional Productivity Handbook.

Definitions of Active enterprises, Births and Deaths and information on estimation methods are available in the Business Demography 2011 release.

6 Key statistics – housing, transport and environment

UK/GB/E&W	Country	Region	Old area code	New area code	House building: permanent dwellings completed by private enterprise[1] 2011/12 (Thousands)	Annual change in mix adjusted house prices[2] September 2013 (%)	Traffic[3] increase on major roads[4] between 2002 and 2012 (%)	Reduction in total net greenhouse gas emissions[5] between the base year[6] and 2011 (%)	CO_2 emissions per resident[7] 2011 (Tonnes)
United Kingdom			926	K02000001	109.6	3.8	..	..	6.9
Great Britain			925	K03000001	..	..	2.5	..	..
England and Wales			941	K04000001	..	..	2.2	..	..
United Kingdom	England		921	E92000001	89.1	4.2	2.0	-30.9	6.7
United Kingdom	Wales		924	W92000004	4.7	1.4	5.1	-20.6	9.5
United Kingdom	Scotland		923	S92000003	10.1	-1.1	5.8	-30.8	6.8
United Kingdom	Northern Ireland		922	N92000002	5.7	-1.5	..	-17.5	8.4
United Kingdom	England	North East	A	E12000001	3.9	-0.3	5.5	..	8.9
United Kingdom	England	North West	B	E12000002	8.2	0.5	3.0	..	7.0
United Kingdom	England	Yorkshire and The Humber	D	E12000003	8.4	3.0	2.5	..	8.2
United Kingdom	England	East Midlands	E	E12000004	8.6	1.9	4.6	..	7.4
United Kingdom	England	West Midlands	F	E12000005	6.7	2.3	4.7	..	6.7
United Kingdom	England	East	G	E12000006	12.1	2.0	4.3	..	6.6
United Kingdom	England	London	H	E12000007	11.3	9.4	-8.6	..	4.9
United Kingdom	England	South East	J	E12000008	17.3	4.0	-0.6	..	6.3
United Kingdom	England	South West	K	E12000009	12.3	1.3	3.8	..	6.5

.. not available

1 Includes private landlords (persons or companies) and owner-occupiers. Data and further information can be found on the Department for Communities and Local Government website. Northern Ireland private enterprise completions are statistically adjusted to correct, as far as possible, the proven under recording of private sector completions in Northern Ireland.

2 Mix adjusted house prices, taken from House Price Index, September 2013 - released 12 November 2013, allow for differences between houses sold (for example type, number of rooms, location) in different months within a year. The annual rate of change shown is the percentage change between October 2012 and September 2013. Not seasonally adjusted.

3 To calculate the percentage change the volume of traffic is expressed as vehicle kilometres, which is calculated by multiplying the Annual Average Daily Flow by the corresponding length of road. For further information please see the Department for Transport website.

4 Motorways and A roads.

5 Information on the method of calculation can be found on the Greenhouse Gas Inventories for England, Scotland, Wales and Northern Ireland: 1990 - 2011 publication. Additional information for Scottish Greenhouse gases can be found on the Scottish Government website, which include emissions from international aviation and shipping.

6 1995 is used as the Base Year (BY) for emissions of HFCs, PFCs and SF6 in the UK's Climate Change Programme, in accordance with Article 3.8 of the Kyoto Protocol. 1990 is used for other gases. The previous version of this table wrongly gave 1990 in the column heading instead of the base year.

7 The latest data and further information can be found on the Department of Energy and Climate Change website.

Source: Department for Communities and Local Government; Welsh Government; Scottish Government; Department for Social Development, Northern Ireland; Office for National Statistics; Department for Transport; Department for Environment, Food, and Rural Affairs; Department of the Environment, Northern Ireland; Department of Energy and Climate Change

Region and Country Profiles - Directory of online tables

Topic	Type[1]	Last updated	Latest year
Key Statistics			
1 Key statistics – population	NS	Dec-13	2012
2 Key statistics – social indicators	NS	Oct-13	2013
3 Key statistics – labour market and skills	NS	Dec-13	2013
4 Key statistics – education	Mixed	Dec-13	2011/12
5 Key statistics – economy	NS	Jun-13	2011
6 Key statistics – housing, transport and environment	Mixed	Dec-13	2013

Topic	Type[1]	Last updated	Latest year
Population and Migration			
1 Resident population: by sex	NS	Dec-13	2012
2 Subregional – resident population: by selected age groups	NS	Dec-13	2012
3 Migration	NS	Dec-13	2012
4 Subregional – components of population change	NS	Dec-13	2012
5 Subregional – population projections	Mixed	Mar-13	2011
6 Subregional – population density	NS	Dec-13	2012

Topic	Type[1]	Last updated	Latest year
Social Indicators			
1 Crimes committed against households	NS	Feb-12	2010/11
2 Crimes committed against persons	NS	Feb-12	2010/11
3 Recorded crimes: by offence group	NS	Feb-12	2010/11
4 Subregional – selected recorded crimes: by Local Authority	NS	Feb-12	2010/11
5 16- and 17-year-olds participating in post-compulsory education and government-supported training	NS	Feb-12	2009/10
6 Population: by level of highest qualification	NS	Feb-12	2010
7 Age-standardised mortality rates: by cause and sex	NS	Feb-12	2009
8 Subregional – life expectancy at birth and at age 65	NS	Feb-12	2010
9 Cigarette smoking among people aged 16 or over: by sex	NS	Feb-12	2009
10 Alcohol consumption among people aged 16 or over: by sex	NS	Feb-12	2009
11 Tenure of dwellings	Mixed	Feb-12	2010
12 Subregional – mean and median prices of dwellings changing ownership	Non-NS	Feb-12	2009
13 Households by combined economic activity status of household	NS	Feb-12	2011
14 Household wealth: by type	NS	Feb-12	2008
15 Households: by type	NS	Feb-12	2010
16 Subregional: fertility and mortality statistics	NS	Feb-12	2009
17 People in households below poverty thresholds before and after housing costs	NS	Feb-12	2010

Region and Country Profiles - Directory of online tables

Topic	Type[1]	Last updated	Latest year
Economy			
1 Workplace-based gross value added (GVA) at current basic prices	NS	Jun-13	2011
2 Subregional – gross value added (GVA) at current basic prices	NS	Jun-13	2011
3 Labour Productivity	NS	Jun-13	2011
4 Subregional – Productivity	NS	Jun-13	2011
5 Workplace-based gross value added (GVA) per head at current basic prices	NS	Jun-13	2011
6 Workplace based gross value added (GVA): by industry groups at current basic price	NS	Jun-13	2010
7 Gross disposable household income per head	NS	Jun-13	2011
8 Subregional – gross disposable household income per head	NS	Jun-13	2011
9 Subregional – business births and deaths	NS	Jun-13	2011
10 UK regional trade in goods: exports and imports	NS	Jun-13	2011
11 Expenditure on research and development	NS	Jun-13	2011
12 Employment rates	NS	Jun-13	2012
13 Employment: by occupation	NS	Jun-13	2012
14 Workforce jobs	NS	Jun-13	2012
15 Public sector employment	NS	Jun-13	2012
16 Unemployment rates	NS	Jun-13	2012
17 Economic inactivity rates	NS	Jun-13	2012
18 Subregional – labour market	NS	Jun-13	2013

Topic	Type[1]	Last updated	Latest year
Environment			
1 Waste and recycling	NS	Oct-12	2010/11
2 Subregional – household waste and recycling in England	NS	Oct-12	2010/11
3 Subregional – carbon dioxide emissions: by sector	NS	Oct-12	2010
4 New permanent dwellings completed: by tenure	NS	Oct-12	2010/11
5 New dwellings on previously developed land	NS	Oct-12	2010
6 Stock of dwellings: by tenure	Mixed	Oct-12	2011
7 Average distance travelled per person: by mode of transport	NS	Oct-12	2009/10
8 Usual method of travel to work by region of residence	NS	Oct-12	2011
9 Trips to and from school: by main mode of transport and length	NS	Oct-12	2009/10
10 Average daily motor vehicle flows: by type of road	NS	Oct-12	2010
11 Annual rainfall	Non-NS	Oct-12	2011
12 Winter and summer seasonal rainfall	Non-NS	Oct-12	2011
13 Designated areas	Non-NS	Oct-12	2012

1 National Statistics (NS), Non National Statistics (Non NS), or Mixed.

Symbols and conventions

Billions	This term is used to represent a thousand million.
Geography	Where possible Regional Trends uses data for the whole of the UK. When data from the constituent countries of the UK are not comparable, data for Great Britain or the constituent countries are used. Constituent countries can advise where data are available that are equivalent but not directly comparable with those of the other constituent countries.
Provisional and estimated data	Some data for the latest year (and occasionally for earlier years) are provisional or estimated. To keep footnotes to a minimum, these have not been indicated; source departments will be able to advise if revised data are available.
Rounding of figures	In tables where figures have been rounded to the nearest final digit, there may be an apparent discrepancy between the sum of the constituent items and the total as shown.
Seasonal adjustment	Unless otherwise stated, unadjusted data have been used.
Sources	Sources are usually listed as the name by which the source is currently known.
Survey data	Many of the tables, maps and figures in Regional Trends present the results of household surveys that can be subject to large sampling errors. Care should therefore be taken in drawing conclusions about regional differences, and especially with subnational changes over time.
Years	
Reference years	Where a choice of years has to be made, the most recent year or a run of recent years is shown. In some cases a particular reference year may be included, e.g. a past population census years (1991, 2001 etc.) or the mid-points between census years (1996 etc.) Other years may be added if they represent a peak or trough in the series or relate to a specific benchmark or target.
Academic year	For example, September 2006 to July 2007 would be shown as 2006/07.
Financial year	For example, 1 April 2006 to 31 March 2007 would be shown as 2006/07.
Non-calendar years	Data covering more than one year, e.g. 1998, 1999 and 2000would be shown a 1998-2000.
Units	Percentages are shown in italic
Symbols	The following symbols have been used throughout Regional Trends:
	.. not available
	. not applicable
	- negligible (less than half the first digit shown)
	0 nil

Region and Country Profiles Key Statistics Analysis - Notes on Sources, 2013

Coverage: **UK**
Date: **17 October 2013**
Geographical Area: **Region**

Foreword

This document provides notes on the sources used for the analysis in Region and Country Profiles - Key Statistics and Profiles, October 2013. Links to data used and further information are included. All data were published by the Office for National Statistics (ONS) unless stated otherwise, and were correct at the time this analysis was produced.

Population

Population estimates are for 30 June each year. The mid-2012 population estimates are those published on 8 August 2013.

The 2011 rural-urban classification provides estimates of populations that live in types of rural and urban areas in England and Wales. The classification is a revised version of that produced after the 2001 Census, but with additional detail in the urban domain. 2011 Census population estimates for urban and rural areas were obtained via Nomis.

Social Indicators

Life expectancy figures for the English regions reflect mortality among those living in the area in each time period, rather than mortality among those born in each area.

Life expectancy figures for Wales, Scotland and Northern Ireland are for 2008 to 2010. The figures reflect mortality among those living in the area in each time period, rather than mortality among those born in each area. Final estimates for the UK and all constituent countries for 2009 to 2011 will be published in winter 2013.

Life Expectancy at Scotland level provides provisional estimates for 2009 to 2011, rolled forward from the 2011 Census.

Disability estimates are for people (aged 16 to 64) who are disabled according to the definition in the Disability Discrimination Act (DDA disabled) from the Annual Population Survey obtained via Nomis.

Workless households for areas across the UK provides information about households with no employment and the adults and children living in them.

Crime in England and Wales presents statistics from two sources. The Crime Survey for England and Wales (CSEW) provides a measure of people's experience of crime based on responses to a survey of households and does not cover all types of crime, for example fraud or forgery or crimes against commercial property. Recorded crime covers offences reported to and recorded by the police.

Labour Market and Skills

Labour market statistics are seasonally adjusted Labour Force Survey (LFS) headline indicators. Unemployment rates are for all people aged 16 and over. Employment and economic inactivity rates are for all people aged 16 to 64.

Median gross weekly earnings are residence-based estimates from the Annual Survey of Hours and Earnings (ASHE) for full-time employees on adult rates whose pay for the survey pay-period was not affected by absence. Please note that estimates quoted in AHSE Statistical Bulletins are usually on a workplace basis.

Qualifications data are for residents aged 16 to 64 from the Annual Population Survey obtained via Nomis. Please note that these estimates, at national or regional level in England, will not agree with National Statistics published by the Department for Business, Innovation and Skills in the Post 16 Education and Skills Statistical First Release (Table 12).

Economy

Gross value added (GVA) data are workplace based estimates of economic output, based on the incomes of individuals allocated to their place of work.

Labour productivity measures the amount of economic output produced per hour worked and is a key indicator of economic performance.

Gross disposable household income (GDHI) covers the income received by households and non profit-making institutions serving households and is net of tax payments, social security contributions and benefits.

Business Demography covers business births (creation), business deaths (closure) and the stock of active enterprises. The business creation rates are expressed as a percentage of active enterprises.

Housing, Transport and Environment

House building by private enterprise includes private landlords (persons or companies) and owner-occupiers. House building statistics are collated by the Department for Communities and Local Government.

House prices and the annual rate of change are taken from the House Price Index. The house prices are mix-adjusted which allows for differences between houses sold (for example type, number of rooms, location) in different months within a year. The annual rate of change is the percentage change between July 2012 and June 2013.

Major roads are motorways and A roads. Traffic increase data are from the Department for Transport.

Greenhouse gas data are from the Department of Energy & Climate Change. Change is measured from the Kyoto Base Year, which is 1990 or 1995 depending on the gas.

Additional information for Scottish greenhouse gas emissions, including the adjustments necessary to report performance against the Climate Change (Scotland) Act 2009, can be found on The Scottish Government website.

Carbon dioxide (CO_2) emissions are measured according to the point of energy consumption. CO2 emissions data are from the Department of Energy & Climate Change.

Background notes

1. Details of the policy governing the release of new data are available by visiting www.statisticsauthority.gov.uk/assessment/code-of-practice/index.html or from the Media Relations Office email: media.relations@ons.gsi.gov.uk

Copyright

This document is also available on our website at www.ons.gov.uk.

Glossary

Age-standardised mortality rates	A statistical measure to allow more precise comparisons between two or more populations by eliminating the effects in age structure by using a 'standard population'.
Annual Business Inquiry (ABI)	A sample survey of businesses in Great Britain that collects information on employee jobs and output. See the Notes and Definitions for Labour Market and Economy tables.
Annual Population Survey (APS)	A sample survey providing data for local authority districts. It comprises the quarterly Labour Force Survey (LFS), plus data from the annual LLFS (Annual Local Area LFS) boosts for England (2004 and 2005 only), Scotland and Wales.
Areas of Outstanding Natural Beauty	Major areas designated by legislation to protect their landscape importance.
Average dwelling price	Average prices for house purchases registered in the period. See entries for 'Mean' and 'Median', and the Notes and Definitions for Housing tables.
BCS comparator offences	The BCS comparator is a set of offences recorded by the police, which includes recorded theft of and theft from a vehicle, vehicle interference and tampering, domestic burglary, theft or unauthorised taking of a pedal cycle, theft from the person, criminal damage, common assault, wounding and robbery.
Billion	One thousand million.
Birth rate	The number of live births per 1,000 of the mid-year resident population.
British Crime Survey	A sample survey measuring crimes experienced by respondents in England and Wales. Scottish Crime and Victimisation Survey in Scotland and Northern Ireland Crime Survey collect similar information. See the Notes and Definitions for Crime and Justice tables.
Business births	Newly created enterprises. See the Notes and Definitions for Economy tables.
Business deaths	Enterprises that have ceased trading. See the Notes and Definitions for Economy tables.
Cause of death	These correspond to the International Classification of Diseases (10th Revision) codes (ICD10). See the Notes and Definitions for the Population and Migration tables.
Claimant count	A count, derived from administrative sources, of those who are claiming unemployment-related benefits at Jobcentre Plus local offices, primarily Jobseeker's Allowance.
Claimant count proportion	Number of claimants as a proportion of the resident working-age population of the area.
Claimant count rate	Number of claimants in an area as a proportion of the resident working-age population of the area.
Compulsory education	Education is compulsory for all children in the UK between the ages of 5 (4 in Northern Ireland) and 16.
Conception	A pregnancy which leads either to a maternity or an abortion.
CO_2 emissions	Carbon dioxide emissions are measured by 'end user' not 'at source'. This means emissions are distributed according to the point of energy consumption. See the Notes and Definitions for the Environment tables.
Daily traffic flows	These are calculated as annual traffic divided by road length and divided by the number of days in the year.
Death rate	Total deaths registered per 1,000 of the mid-year resident population.
Dependent children	Aged under 16, or aged 16–18 in full-time education and never married.
Dwelling	A self-contained unit of accommodation with all the rooms behind a door, which only that household can use.
Economically active	People who are in employment plus the unemployed.
Economically inactive	People who are neither in employment nor unemployed. This includes those looking after a home, retired or permanently unable to work.
Employees	A household-based measure of people aged 16 or over who regard themselves as paid employees.
Employee jobs	A measure of jobs held by civilians based on employer surveys. The term refers to the number of jobs rather than the number of persons with jobs. For example, a person holding both a full-time job and a part-time job, or someone with two part-time jobs, will be counted twice.
Employment	People aged 16 or over who did some paid work in the reference week (whether as an employee or self-employed); those who had a job that they were temporarily away from (on holiday, for example); those on government-supported training and employment programmes; and those doing unpaid family work.
Employment rate	The proportion of any given population group who are in employment. The main presentation of employment rates is the proportion of the population aged 16 to 64 who are in employment.

Ethnic groups	The classification of ethnic groups is broadly the same as used in the 2001 Census. See the Notes and Definitions for the Population and Migration tables.
Experimental statistics	ONS Statistics that are in the testing phase and are not fully developed. See the Notes and Definitions for the Population and Migration tables.
Extra-regio	Accounts for business activity that cannot be assigned to a specific region. For the UK this consists mainly of offshore oil and gas extraction and activities of UK embassies and forces overseas.
Family Resources Survey	A continuous survey into the living conditions and resources of households. See Notes and Definitions for Income and Lifestyle tables.
Filled jobs	See 'Workforce jobs'.
Full-time employees	In the Annual Survey of Hours and Earnings data this refers to employees who were paid for more than 30 hours per week.
GCSE grades A*–C or equivalent	Equivalent to Level 2 qualifications, see separate entry in Glossary.
General Lifestyle Survey	The new name for the General Household Survey. See Notes and Definitions for Health and Care tables.
Government-supported training	People aged 16 and over participating in one of the Government's employment and training programmes administered by the Learning and Skills Councils in England, the National Council for Education and Training (ELWa) in Wales, local enterprise companies in Scotland, or the Training and Employment Agency in Northern Ireland.
Gross disposable household income (GDHI)	Total household income less certain cost items such as tax payments and social security contributions. In essence, this is the value of the resources that the household sector actually has available to spend.
Grossing	See 'Weighting'
Gross Value Added (GVA)	Regional GVA is a measure of the economic contribution of an area, measured as the sum of incomes earned from the production of goods and services in the region. See the Notes and Definitions for the Economy tables.
Gross weekly earnings	Measured before tax, National Insurance or other deductions. They include overtime pay, bonuses and other additions to basic pay but exclude any payments for earlier periods (for example, back pay), income in kind, tips and gratuities.
GVA per filled job	A measure of labour productivity. See entries for 'Gross Value Added' and 'Filled jobs'.
GVA per head	On a workplace basis this divides the output of those working in a region by the number of people living in the region. This should not be used as a measure of productivity. See 'Gross Value Added' and 'Workplace based GVA'.
GVA per hour worked	A measure of labour productivity that takes account of the variety of hours worked by employees. See 'Gross Value Added'.
Household	Defined as a single person or a group of people living at the same address as their only or main residence and either share one main meal a day or share the living accommodation or both.
Household projections	Household projections are trend-based; they illustrate what would happen if past trends in household formation were to continue into the future. See the Notes and **Definitions for the Population and Migration tables.**
Housing affordability	House price affordability is measured by a ratio of house prices to earnings. This may use mean house prices and mean earnings but the CLG measure compares lower quartile values (See entry below).
Housing completions	Newly built permanent dwellings. A dwelling is regarded as completed when it becomes ready for occupation, whether it is occupied or not. See the Notes and Definitions for the Housing tables.
Index of Multiple Deprivation (IMD)	**A summary measure of relative deprivation at Lower Layer Super Output Area (LSOA) level in England. For more information see:** www.communities.gov.uk/communities/research/indicesdeprivation/
Infant mortality rate	Deaths of infants under one year of age per 1,000 live births.
International migration	A long-term international migrant is defined as someone who changes his or her country of usual residence for a period of at least a year. See the Notes and Definitions for the Population and Migration tables.
Inter-regional migration	Internal population movements based on the movement of NHS doctors' patients between areas within Great Britain. See the Notes and Definitions for the Population and Migration tables.
Jobs density	The number of filled jobs in an area divided by the number of people aged 16 to 64 resident in that area.
Key Stage 4	Covers pupils aged between 14 and 16 (year groups 10 and 11) in England and Wales. Attainment is measured through National Qualification Framework Level 2 qualification.
Labour productivity	GVA per filled job and GVA per hour worked are measures of labour productivity.
Labour Force Survey (LFS)	A quarterly sample survey that provides the main labour market data for the UK.

Life expectancy at birth	This is the average number of years that a person would live if he or she experienced that area's age-specific mortality rates for the specified time period throughout his or her life.
Living Costs and Food Survey	A sample survey replacing the Family Expenditure and National Food Surveys. For more information see: www.statistics.gov.uk/downloads/theme_social/familyspending2010.pdf
Lower Layer Super Output Area (LSOA)	Small areas defined for England and Wales that are designed to be homogeneous and also roughly equal in population size. LSOA's have an average population of 1,500.
Lower quartile	The lower quartile value (eg incomes) is determined by ranking all values in order and identifying the value below which 25 per cent fall.
Maintained schools	Schools funded through local authorities.
Mean, or Average	Is the sum of the values, divided by the number of values.
Median	Statistical term for the value for which half the data are above and half are below. An alternative measure of the average, which is less affected by extreme values than the mean.
Modelled unemployment rates	See 'Unemployment rates'. A statistical model is used to improve the annual APS estimates of unemployment for small areas, by using supplementary information, mainly the numbers of claimants of Jobseeker's Allowance (the claimant count).
National Parks	Major areas designated by legislation to protect their landscape importance.
National Qualifications Framework (NQF) level 2 qualifications	Equivalent to GCSE grades A* to C. See Notes and definitions for Education tables.
National Qualifications Framework (NQF) level 3 qualifications	Equivalent to A levels. See Notes and definitions for Education tables.
National Qualifications Framework (NQF) level 4 and above qualifications	Includes all higher education qualifications. See Notes and definitions for Education tables.
Natural change	The difference between births and deaths. More births than deaths results in the population experiencing natural increase, while more deaths than births in natural decline.
Net migration	The difference between migration into the area and migration out of the area.
Net migration and other changes	This includes changes in population due to internal and international civilian migration and changes in the number of armed forces (both non-UK and UK) and their dependants resident in the UK.
NUTS (Nomenclature of Territorial Statistics) area classification	NUTS is a hierarchical classification of areas that provides a breakdown of the EU's economic territory for regional statistics that are comparable across the European Union. See the **Geography Notes and Definitions at:** www.statistics.gov.uk/downloads/theme_compendia/RegionalSnapshot/rt43-geography-n&f.pdf
Population density	Population per square kilometre.
Population projections	Based on mid-year estimates of the population and a set of demographic trend-based assumptions about the future. See the Notes and Definitions for the Population and Migration tables.
Recorded crime	Statistics compiled from police returns that broadly cover the more serious offences. See the Notes and Definitions for the Crime and Justice tables.
Residence-based GVA	Residence-based GVA allocates the income from employment to individuals' place of residence. See entry for 'GVA' and the Notes and Definitions for the Economy tables.
Resident Population	The estimated resident population of an area includes all people who usually live there, whatever their nationality. Members of UK and non-UK armed forces stationed in the UK are included and UK forces stationed outside the UK are excluded. Students are taken to be resident at their term-time address. See the Notes and Definitions for the Population and Migration tables.
Residual household waste	Household waste that is not re-used, recycled or composted.
Rural/Urban Definition	A classification of LSOA's in England and Wales based on settlement size and relative population density in different areas. (Sometimes erroneously called 'Rural/Urban Classification'.) See www.ons.gov.uk/about-statistics/geography/products/area-classifications/rural-urban-definition-and-la-classification/index.html
Rural/Urban Local Authority Classification	A classification of local authorities in England. See www.ons.gov.uk/about-statistics/geography/products/area-classifications/rural-urban-definition-and-la-classification/index.html
Seasonally adjusted	Data that have been adjusted using a statistical method for removing the seasonal component of a time series.
Service industries	Service Industries include the following sections of the Standard Industrial Classification (SIC) 2003: Wholesale and retail trade, repair of motor vehicles, motorcycles and personal and household goods; Hotels and restaurants; Transport, storage and communications; Financial intermediation; Real estate, renting and business activities; Public administration and defence, compulsory social security; Education; Health and social work; Other community, social and personal service activities.

Standard Industrial Classification (SIC)	The industrial breakdown used for all ONS business surveys has been revised to the Standard Industrial Classification 2007. Some tables still use the Standard Industrial Classification Revised 2003 (SIC2003) . For further information see the Notes and Definitions for the Economy tables.
Standardised Mortality Ratio (SMR)	The standardised mortality ratio (SMR) compares overall mortality in a region with that for the UK. The ratio expresses the actual number of deaths in a region as a percentage of the hypothetical number that would have occurred if the region's population had experienced the sex/age-specific rates of the UK that year.
State pension age	Up to 2009 this was the age at which pensions were normally payable by the state pension scheme: this was 65 for men and 60 for women. From 2010 the pension age for women is being gradually increased to 65 by 2020. The term is falling out of use as data for 2010 become available.
Stock of dwellings	Number of dwellings including vacant dwellings and temporary dwellings occupied as a normal place of residence. Estimates of the stock in England, Wales and Scotland are based on data from the 2001 Census and projected forward yearly.
Total Fertility Rate (TFR)	A measure of the average number of live children that a group of women would bear if they experienced the age-specific fertility rates of the calendar year in question throughout their childbearing lifespan. See the Notes and Definitions for the Population and Migration tables.
Unemployment rates	The proportion of the economically active who are unemployed. The main presentation of unemployment rates is the proportion of the economically active population aged 16 or over who are unemployed.
Weighting	Sample survey data only relates to the units in the sample. Therefore the sample estimates need to be inflated to represent the whole population of interest. Each sample observation is assigned a 'weight' that reflects the population that the sample observation represents. The estimation process that calculates these weights is also referred to as 'weighting' or 'grossing up'.
Workforce jobs	A measure of employee jobs, self-employment jobs, all HM Forces and government-supported trainees.
Working age	Up to 2009 this referred to men aged 16 to 64 and women aged 16 to 59.
Workless households	No adults aged 16 to 64 in the household are in employment.
Workplace-based GVA	Workplace GVA allocates the income from employment to individuals' place of work. See entry for GVA and the Notes and Definitions for the Economy tables.
Work-based learning	Work-based learning for young people (aged 16–24) in England covers Advanced Modern Apprenticeships (AMA), Foundation Modern Apprenticeships (FMA) and 'Entry to Employment'.